# COLONIAL SUSPECTS

FRANCE OVERSEAS: STUDIES IN EMPIRE AND DECOLONIZATION

*Series editors: A. J. B. Johnston, James D. Le Sueur, and Tyler Stovall*

# COLONIAL SUSPECTS

*Suspicion, Imperial Rule, and Colonial Society in Interwar French West Africa*

KATHLEEN KELLER

University of Nebraska Press | Lincoln and London

Portions of an earlier version of chapter 2 originally appeared as "Political Surveillance and Colonial Urban Rule: 'Suspicious' Politics and Urban Space in Dakar, Senegal, 1918–1939," *French Historical Studies* 35, no. 4 (Fall 2012): 727–49. Article © 2012 by the Society for French Historical Studies.

An earlier version of chapter 4 originally appeared as "On the Fringes of the 'Civilizing Mission': 'Suspicious' Frenchmen and Unofficial Discourses of French Colonialism in AOF, 1918–1939," *French Colonial History* 9 (2008): 103–30. Article © 2008 by the French Colonial Historical Society.

Library of Congress Cataloging-in-Publication Data
Names: Keller, Kathleen A., author.
Title: Colonial suspects: suspicion, imperial rule, and colonial society in interwar French West Africa / Kathleen Keller.
Other titles: France overseas.
Description: Lincoln: University of Nebraska Press, 2018. |
Series: France overseas: studies in empire and decolonization
| Based on the author's thesis (doctoral)—Rutgers University, 2007. | Includes bibliographical references and index.
Identifiers: LCCN 2017044995
ISBN 9780803296916 (cloth: alk. paper)
ISBN 9781496206183 (ebook)
ISBN 9781496206190 (mobi)
ISBN 9781496206206 (pdf)
Subjects: LCSH: Intelligence service—Africa, French-speaking West—History—20th century. | Intelligence service—France—Colonies—History. | Police patrol—Africa, French-speaking West—Surveillance operations—History—20th century. | Police patrol—France—Colonies—History. | Dissenters—Africa, French-speaking West—History—20th century. | Dissenters—France—Colonies—History. | Anti-imperialist movements—Africa, French-speaking West—History—20th century. | Anti-imperialist movements—France—Colonies—History. | Africa, French-speaking West—Politics and government—1884–1960.
Classification: LCC JQ3359.5.I6 K45 2018 | DDC 363.2320917541—dc23 LC record available at https://lccn.loc.gov/2017044995

Set in Garamond Premier by Mikala R Kolander.
Designed by N. Putens.

*To my parents, Kathy Keller and Raymond Keller*

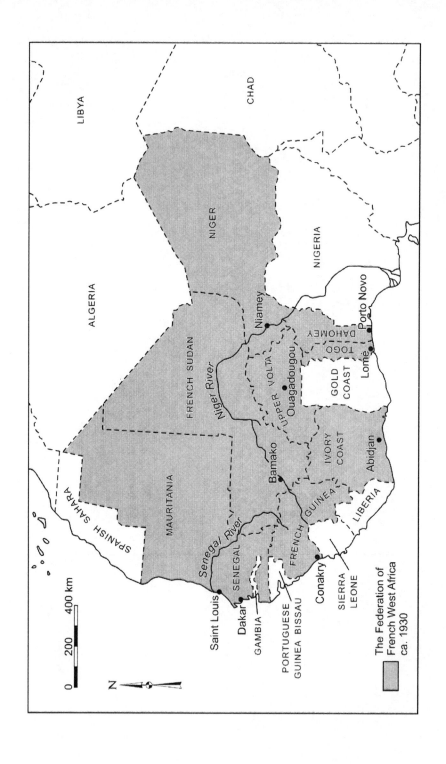

The Federation of French West Africa ca. 1930

# CONTENTS

# ACKNOWLEDGMENTS

It has now been several years since I first sat down with a reel of microfilm in Paris, compelled by the promising title "suspicious persons" in a document catalog. That fortuitous moment began a long journey that ended in this book. Over the years, before and since that day, I have received the support and encouragement of many individuals and institutions who contributed to the completion and publication of this book. It is a great privilege to thank them here.

I received generous financial support from several institutions that allowed for research travel to Paris, Aix-en-Provence, and Dakar. Rutgers University–New Brunswick provided essential support for research in Paris. The Chateaubriand fellowship sponsored by the French Embassy in the United States funded a long stay in Aix-en-Provence. The Social Science Research Council supported several more months of research in France and Dakar. The SSRC also provided support in the form of a book workshop and fellowship. The Dean's Office at Eckerd College and the Provost's Office at Gustavus Adolphus College both provided support for summer travel to finalize a few research questions.

At the University of Notre Dame my love for history and the French language was nurtured and inspired by several wonderful mentors and teachers, including Paul McDowell, Julia Douthwaite, Thomas Kselman, and Doris Bergen. I learned much from them about teaching and scholarship and am grateful to them for encouraging me to pursue my passion for history in graduate school. The Nanovic Center for European Studies at Notre Dame under the leadership of Robert Wegs supported a summer research trip to France that afforded me my first experience in the archives and convinced me that a career in history might be in my future.

Rutgers University–New Brunswick professors shaped me into the historian I am today by pushing me in new intellectual directions. Allen Howard and Barbara Cooper were wonderful guides and teachers as I studied African history; Matt Matsuda and Brent Hayes Edwards provided critical feedback on my scholarship; and Teresa Delcorso gave essential support in writing grants to fund my research. Above all I am grateful for the mentorship of Bonnie Smith, who guided me into the field of French colonial history and also gave me the room to find my own path. Bonnie is quite simply everything I aspire to be as a historian: a consummate professional, a wonderful writer, a patient teacher, a thoughtful mentor, and a generous sponsor of other historians.

Archivists at the Archives Nationales in Paris, especially the microfilm department, provided daily help with inventories and machines. At the ANOM Evelyne Camara and other archivists and staff provided advice, aid with inventories, and access to documents, especially during a brief visit in the summer of 2012.

My fellow graduate students and colleagues in history at Rutgers created a lasting community that continues to sustain me as a scholar. Among my fellow students I am especially grateful to Kris Alexanderson, Joseph Bonica, James Casteel, Brian Connolly, Carmen Gitre, Serguei Glebov, Carla MacDougall, Margaret Smith, and Margaret Sumner. While I was doing research in Paris, Aix-en-Provence, and Dakar, friends and fellow researchers inside and out of the archives helped me in many ways, from showing me the ropes in the archives to cooking dinner together. They provided encouragement and friendship during the research stage of this project. For this I thank Ann Cooper, Raina Croff, Katharine Dunn, Marie Rodet, Jean-Lucien Sanchez, Ibra Sene, and especially Heather Gibson.

I relied on colleagues in French colonial history for help in refining the manuscript and rethinking some important arguments at conference panels and in conversations. For this I offer my thanks to Elizabeth Foster, Emily Marker, and Jennifer Sessions. Andrew Daily generously helped by checking a reference in Paris. I am also very grateful to the many colleagues at Furman, Eckerd, and Gustavus Adolphus who modeled scholarship and teaching while encouraging me to publish my research. A few close friends who happen to also be brilliant historians have listened at length to my ideas and read many drafts of my work. For this I am deeply grateful to my wonderful friends Kristen Block, Gillian Glaes, Louisa Rice, and Rebecca Scales. The two anonymous readers at University of Nebraska Press provided important insights and a number of invaluable corrections to the manuscript.

Finally, and most important, my thanks go to my family. I thank my wonderful husband, Charlie, for his love, support, and patience and for making it possible for me to finish this book. To our son, Oliver, thank you for inspiring me every day with your curiosity and joy. Thanks to the Kellers, DeSolas, and Georges for the care and encouragement that motivated me as I researched and wrote this book in France, Senegal, South Carolina, Florida, and finally Minnesota. Since my first trip abroad to study, in France when I was nineteen years old, my parents, Kathy Keller and Raymond Keller, have been loving, encouraging, and patient even as my own dreams often took me far from them. Thanks, Mom and Dad. This book is for you.

# LIST OF ABBREVIATIONS

AEF   Afrique Equatoriale Française (French Equatorial Africa)

AOF   Afrique Occidentale Française (French West Africa)

APA   Affaires Politiques et Administratives (Bureau of Political and Administrative Affairs)

CAI   Service de contrôle et assistance des indigènes en France (Service of Control and Assistance to Natives in France)

CDNR   Comité de Défense de la Race Nègre (Committee for Defense of the Negro Race)

CGTU   Confédération Générale du Travail Unitaire (General Confederation of United Labor)

ISR   Internationale Syndicale Rouge (International Red Syndicate)

IWE   International Workers of Education (Travailleurs International de l'Enseignement)

LDNR   League for Defense of the Negro Race (Ligue de Défense de la Race Nègre)

PCF   Parti Communiste Français (French Communist Party)

SFIO   Section française de l'Internationale ouvrière (French Section of the Worker's International)

SG   Sûreté Générale (General Security Service)

UIC   Union Intercoloniale (Intercolonial Union)

UNIA   Universal Negro Improvement Association

UTN   Union des Travailleurs Nègres (Union of Negro Workers)

# A NOTE ON TRANSLATIONS

I have translated most simple terms, such as *lieutenant gouverneur* and *gouverneur général* into English, including in the notes. Some terms, such as *renseignements*, Sûreté, and *commissaire*, I have kept in French in order to retain their meaning as much as possible. French terms and organizations have been translated into English, but I have sometimes chosen to use abbreviations reflecting the French terms. The abbreviation AOF, for example, is well known in the literature on French West Africa and more commonly used than FWA.

# COLONIAL SUSPECTS

# Introduction

In the summer of 1937 Baron Paul Von Heinl, holding both Bolivian and Austrian passports, arrived in the Senegalese port of Dakar. His stay in Senegal followed a visit to the British African colony of Gold Coast, where he had met with members of the Nazi Party. In Dakar he claimed to be researching business prospects in the sale of goods such as cameras and hurricane lamps.[1] The passage of such a foreigner to the capital of French West Africa in the late 1930s was not unusual. Dakar was a city that teemed with itinerant Frenchmen and cosmopolitan foreigners seeking opportunity and adventure. A seedy night life featuring "epileptic" dancers, strippers, and lounge singers had emerged to cater to the pleasures of just such a crowd.[2] During his time in Dakar Von Heinl became friendly with a group of Germans that included Count Bielke, an employee of the Maison Peyrissac, one of the oldest Bordeaux-based import-export firms in Senegal.[3] In addition to making business connections, Von Heinl enjoyed a visit to the beach at Les Almadies with Bielke and a few Italians.[4]

Like many visitors to Dakar, Von Heinl might have dined with his foreign friends at the popular Hôtel Métropole, where the head chef, the Vietnamese N'guyen Van Phu, once received a packet of Marxist journals from an anonymous source in Paris. The Métropole did not look lavish from the exterior, but it was the place in Dakar to see and be seen for Europeans seeking to catch wind of local intrigue. N'guyen, as the cook, lived an existence far removed from the lifestyles of the well-heeled patrons who dined at the hotel. He had spent a few grueling years as the cook on commercial steamships based out of Marseilles. Now settled in Dakar with a steady paycheck and guaranteed room and board at one of the poshest addresses in town, he still lived an austere life. He never went out and saved virtually all of his wages.[5]

Just a few years prior to N'guyen's reception of the unexpected journals, Monsieur Peyrissac, owner of the firm where Von Heinl's friend worked, became acquainted with a young Senegalese man named Amadou Sall while spending time back in Bordeaux. Sall had traveled to Paris and to the United States, spoke English, and belonged to the Paris-based group Ligue de Défense de la Race Nègre (League for Defense of the Negro Race). Sall was known to be generally reserved but to share confidences with the aid of a little wine.[6] He also supposedly maintained correspondence with an "extremist" in Niger and somewhat mysteriously sent mail to an address in Brooklyn, New York.[7]

Although from very different strata of Dakar society, tenuous connections link Von Heinl, N'guyen, and Sall. They have something else in common too: they were all considered "suspicious persons" by the police and government general of French West Africa.[8] As a foreigner with two passports who dabbled in Nazi politics and threatened to intervene in the local economy, Von Heinl drew the scrutiny of colonial administrators. N'guyen, a humble cook who kept a scrupulously discreet private life, became known to authorities only when he told them about the arrival of an unexpected package containing Vietnamese-language communist newspapers. Despite his attempt to cooperate with authorities, N'guyen's seeming connection to Marxism alongside stereotypes about Asian communism landed him on a list of suspects under surveillance in 1930. Sall, of course, was an African man who drew the attention of authorities in 1931 as someone who cultivated connections to international organizations considered to be radical, dangerous, and indeed anticolonial.

The surveillance of suspicious persons by the government general was an operation that reached far and wide into the complex society of Afrique Occidentale Française (AOF, French West Africa), a federation of colonies that included Senegal, Mauritania, French Sudan, Niger, Upper Volta, Dahomey, Ivory Coast, Guinea, and, after World War I, Togo as a French mandate. Operating primarily in urban areas, mainly the capital cities of each colony, police inspectors and local administrators conducted investigations of suspects beginning in the era of the First World War. Peaking in the late 1920s and early 1930s, investigations targeted hundreds of Africans, French, and foreigners living in or passing through French West Africa. Suspects were a diverse group of people who appeared to embody various and changing threats to the French in Africa. This book on the surveillance of colonial suspects has been guided by a few simple questions: Who was suspicious, and why? What do suspects and surveillance policies tell us about imperial policy and practice in French West Africa? What do they tell us about colonial society?

Surveillance of suspects was just one aspect of many attempts to police colonial society by French authorities in West Africa. *Surveillance* was a term used frequently to describe a variety of everyday functions of the colonial administration: surveillance of immigration, hygiene, arms, streets, and railroads. These forms of surveillance attempted to monitor and control specific areas of colonial life through administrative checks and bureaucracy. European empires around the world routinely collected and used information on the press, labor, migration, weather, agriculture, geography, disease, religious rituals, and more.[9] The surveillance of suspicious persons, on the other hand, was a very specific form of colonial control that sought to identify and quash potential political dissent and other kinds of behavior that appeared to be in opposition to the goals of the French state.

Recent historical studies have demonstrated the critical importance of surveillance and security apparatuses in building and maintaining modern empires around the world from the nineteenth century onward.[10] In North Africa Martin Thomas has argued that both British and French colonial states in the interwar period were "intelligence states" that depended on the collection of information to function.[11] In French West Africa the

Muslim Affairs Bureau maintained an intensive and constant surveillance over Muslim leaders as of the late nineteenth century.[12] Historians have also acknowledged political surveillance as an important strategy in interwar French West Africa.[13] This book contributes to this growing field of historical scholarship in a couple of ways. It traces the emergence and development of a specific form of surveillance from the perspective of high policy and street-level practice. Furthermore it seeks to move beyond an institutional history to use stories about suspects to provide a glimpse of some of the more transient and marginal elements of colonial society.

### A Culture of Suspicion: Imperial Rule and Colonial Society

Colonial policing has typically been understood as a rational means to secure European colonial property, defend the social and political order, police crime, protect the colonial economy, and prevent rebellion.[14] My investigation into the history of suspicion in AOF reveals that more was at stake. The central argument of this book is that a "culture of suspicion" emerged in French West Africa in the interwar era that came to define the policies and practices of the colonial state and can shed light on certain aspects of colonial society. The culture of suspicion reveals how fears about political dissidence as an existential threat to the French led to attempts to identify suspects who appeared potentially frightening. Policing in AOF reveals an increasingly irrational side to colonial rule in which paranoia, fear, and anxiety dominated decision making.[15] A look into the everyday practice of surveillance also helps elucidate the weakness and vulnerability of the French colonial state even in places where colonial power was at its peak, such as Dakar.[16]

Although at a surface level it may seem that surveillance of political suspects was in direct response to nascent anticolonial nationalist movements, I argue that the identification and surveillance of suspects was more an attempt to manage a rapidly changing colonial landscape in the uncertain years following the First World War. Historians have highlighted postwar efforts to cope with imperial crisis mostly in terms of the political and administrative policy of association or colonial humanism, an attitude that sought to better serve colonial peoples, most clearly embraced by the leftist Popular Front coalition of the late 1930s.[17] While authorities pursued these official policies to cope with dramatic changes, they also, to less public acclaim, instituted other strategies to identify and monitor potential threats in response to rapid demographic and political change. The culture of suspicion can be understood as a response to this era of turmoil that offered a very different solution to the problems facing the interwar French Empire than did policies such as association.

The culture of suspicion exposes an imperial administration that was anxious, fearful, and indeed suspicious, but when we shift the lens to the suspects themselves, it also reveals elements of colonial society who were marginal, dynamic, diverse, and remarkable. Suspects often operated clandestinely as they sought business connections, to share illegal tracts and newspapers, or to engage in eclectic or "disreputable" behavior. As the suspects chose to defy political or social convention through involvement in political parties, extensive travel, or shocking behavior they too shaped the culture of suspicion through their own agency. These stories all emerge in the files of suspicious persons and help create a vivid tableau of colonial encounters. Suspects' lives often tell of transience, marginality, and exception and reveal details and lives that are rarely told in colonial histories. Inscrutability was a key quality of suspicion in interwar French West Africa, and foreigners became the most suspicious of all because authorities could not easily fall back on ready-made stereotypes or assumptions about foreigners' behavior, nor could they easily locate information about their place of birth, family, background, education, or employment. Most surprising, perhaps, the culture of suspicion reveals that French West Africa was becoming a global crossroads of people and ideas. As French, Germans, British, Gambians, Sierra Leoneans, Austrians, Swedes, Vietnamese, Moroccans, and more converged on Dakar with distinct political and personal agendas, authorities grew deeply alarmed. This dynamic and diverse international society, which often became the focus of official inquiries, helped shape the culture of suspicion.

Central to this culture of suspicion was the concept of the suspect. Suspects provide a valuable opportunity to reevaluate the colonial category, an idea that has become indispensable for making sense of colonial rule.

Scholars, especially anthropologists, have shown that categories defined by race, gender, nation, class, and more were central to establishing the hierarchies of power that underpinned the colonial order.[18] Categories such as caste, religion, and tribe served to divide colonial people and establish parameters for creating order and doling out privileges. Colonial categories were constructed and reconstructed by authorities but always remained fragile.[19] In AOF terms such as *French, African, citizen, subject*, and sometimes *tribe* and *religion* served as organizing categories. However, people who lived along the fringes of such fundamental categories, notably *évolués* (French-educated Africans), mixed-race people, African colonial employees, and the Lebanese and Syrian population, all occupied the edges of these groups and straddled boundaries.[20] Suspects too operated on the margins of colonial life and tell us much about those margins as well as the mainstream of colonial society. Yet suspects do not fit into the conventional molds created along race, gender, and class lines. Instead they seemed to occupy an entirely new category, one that was characterized by the ways it disrupted colonial modes of understanding people. This book proposes that the suspect was constructed as a colonial category that can both blur the distinctions between conventional divisions and serve as a new way of understanding how colonial authorities labeled people.

## AOF's Origins and the Interwar Era

The history of the French in West Africa dates to the sixteenth century, when French merchants joined the Portuguese and Dutch in trade for slaves and commercial goods along the coast of Senegal. The French soon established colonial settlements on Gorée Island and at coastal Saint-Louis. In the wake of the 1848 Revolution, African residents of the colonies at Saint-Louis and Gorée gained the right to vote for representatives to the legislature in Paris. By the end of the nineteenth century Saint-Louis and Gorée, along with newer settlements at Dakar and Rufisque, had become full municipal communes and their inhabitants exercised the right to elect representatives to local municipal political institutions and the Chamber of Deputies in Paris. These four cities became known as the four original communes and their people as the *originaires*.[21] Eventually, through their own advocacy, originaires also gained access to both French civil and Muslim courts.[22] The originaires of the four communes maintained their special status into the twentieth century in spite of periods of contestation. The African population in urban areas of AOF came to include évolués and the originaires who had voting rights.

The Federation of French West Africa was established only in 1895, following the scramble for Africa, and the relatively small settlement of Dakar was named the capital in 1902. The new colonial capital underwent a rapid period of buildup that was interrupted with the outbreak of the First World War. The *tirailleurs sénégalais*, an African fighting force created by Gen. Louis Faidherbe when he first began his conquest of the interior of Senegal in the mid-nineteenth century, were now called upon to serve France in Europe's battlefields. Despite the name's reference to Senegal, African men were recruited to serve in the *tirailleurs* from throughout the federation. In the years 1915–16 uprisings in different parts of the federation broke out in opposition to recruitment but also related to general grievances with French rule.[23] In 1918, desperate for more troops, Paris turned for help to Blaise Diagne, who, as the first black African from Senegal elected to the metropolitan Chamber of Deputies, enjoyed considerable prestige among the originaire community. Diagne toured the countryside and offered potential recruits, who were subjects and not citizens, exemption from the hated "native" law code known as the *indigénat* and an expedited path to citizenship.[24] He went on to recruit an unprecedented 70,000 African troops to fight in the French armed forces.[25] Ultimately 200,000 men were mobilized, with 166,000 serving in France, and 30,000 of them sacrificing their lives on the battlefields of Europe.[26] The repercussions of recruitment and wartime service of African troops would reverberate well into the interwar period in French West Africa.

At the end of the war France's empire was larger than ever in terms of territory, having added French mandates over Lebanon and Syria from the dissolution of the Ottoman Empire and parts of Togo and Cameroun from the defunct German Empire.[27] Yet, as in the metropole, where France's victory was mired in anxiety and crisis that continued through the interwar years, the overseas territories confronted problem after problem.[28] Contrary to claims of pacification, French administrators struggled to consolidate their authority while some areas of the empire remained openly resistant to conquest.[29] Revolts in Morocco, Syria, Algeria, and Indochina would soon follow in the 1920s and 1930s.

In the metropole a growing colonial migrant community of Africans, Asians, and Antilleans were becoming more politically active and vocally critical of imperial rule in their home colonies. Some colonial migrants in France were drawn to pan-Africanism, which encouraged African people all over the world to unite, and communism, a movement reinvigorated by the success of the Bolshevik Revolution in Russia. Notably the Vietnamese Nguyen Ai Quoc (Ho Chi Minh) became a founding member of the French Communist Party in 1920. The Sudanese Tiémoko Garan Kouyaté joined the Communist Party and formed his own pan-Africanist and anticolonial organizations. Colonial peoples in France created and joined anticolonial groups such as the Etoile Nord-Africain (North African Star), the Comité pour la Défense de la Race Nègre (Committee for the Defense of the Negro Race), and the Union Intercoloniale (Intercolonial Union).

Just as colonial people were becoming more actively engaged in metropolitan politics, general French interest in empire seemed to wane. The new minister of colonies Albert Sarraut proposed an ambitious plan of economic investment in the colonies, only to see it largely rejected by the legislature.[30] French popular interest had never been strong and failed to gain ground in the interwar era, setting up more challenges for a colonial administration that was already overextended in terms of resources and personnel.[31] With significant colonial contribution to the war effort in terms of labor and military service, politicians and administrators, especially in the metropole, began to feel an obligation to subtly revise the civilizing mission to better justify colonial rule.[32]

One result of this introspection in AOF was the implementation of the formal policy of association, which relied on the use of African elites as partners in colonial rule and was promoted as power sharing. The idea of association, similar to the British policy of indirect rule, dates to at least the early twentieth century, but only became the official policy of the

French government in the early 1920s, when Sarraut became minister and advocated for greater representation for elites throughout the empire.[33] Officially association replaced assimilation, the older idea that French rule should emphasize the spread of French language, culture, and values and thus slowly integrate Africans into the republic.[34] In reality the era of assimilation had always relied on cooperation with African leaders, and by the early twentieth century French authorities had all but given up on assimilation, considering it an impractical if not impossible strategy. Supporters of association advocated for its implementation because they increasingly believed that indigenous institutions could best achieve social stability in traditional societies.[35] Governor-General Martial Merlin helped theorize association in AOF by critiquing prior policies that viewed chiefs as backward guardians of feudalism, superstition, and slavery.[36]

Under association in rural areas French authorities sought to renew relationships with traditional chiefs and reestablish their power through new French institutions.[37] Both Merlin and his successor, Jules Carde, believed that working with chiefs and educating their sons was key to maintaining French power in the rural parts of AOF.[38] Association's plan of reinstating rural chiefs seemed to work well by creating important allies to the French who could govern, but also maintain order and loyalty, an important concern after the uprisings during the First World War. The new role for the rural chiefs also meshed nicely with emerging anthropological ideas about Africans as fundamentally rural, kin-oriented, and responsive to the "natural" and more "authentic" rule of chiefs.[39] Association also served as a financial measure to alleviate the burden on an overstretched administration with limited European personnel in rural areas.[40]

In urban areas Merlin envisioned an expanded role for the évolués in politics and implemented a council of notables and added African évolués to each colony's administrative council. Further integrating évolués into decision making was now described as essential to the famous French "civilizing mission," which was reconfigured to emphasize the spread of democracy.[41] The four communes were declared "communes de plein exercise," confirming the metropolitan-like municipal and electoral institutions that dominated politics there. Cities such as Bamako and Kayes in Sudan,

Porto-Novo in Dahomey, Abidjan in Ivory Coast, and Conakry in Guinea were governed by a commission of both Europeans and évolués.[42]

While association seemed to be a smooth process of integration of compliant chiefs in the countryside, in urban areas it appeared at a moment of deepening political conflict. Originaires and évolués had long been considered important allies to the French. They were trading partners, sometimes fellow Catholics, and even wives and children of the early French colonists.[43] But after the granting of political rights in the nineteenth century, conflicts between the French administration and Africans of the four communes grew. In the 1880s and 1890s the French encountered resistance from the *métis* (mixed-race) community who challenged colonial abuses and attempted to shore up their own influence when faced with an increasingly powerful colonial state along with a more politically aggressive black originaire constituency.[44] The federation responded by trying to consolidate power under the new government general. They interfered in elections, suspended representatives, and otherwise attempted to restrict the voting rights of the originaires.[45] In 1912 Governor-General William Ponty tried to restrict African citizenship in the four communes by transforming this birthright into a naturalization process. Under pressure Ponty ultimately was forced to revise the 1912 decree, but bitterness and opposition remained between the administration and African elites.[46] In the years after the end of World War I originaires and other évolués called for increased African participation in government and veterans voiced dissatisfaction with the results of promises made during recruitment.[47] Association was in some ways an attempt to satisfy these demands for political power but ultimately offered little in terms of widening political participation.[48] The suspicion and enmity between elite African urbanites and the colonial administration would continue into the interwar period in spite of the reforms.

Alongside the adoption of political changes, rapid and significant social transformations accompanied the end of the war. Most important perhaps, demobilized African soldiers began returning en masse to AOF in 1919, causing considerable disorder. Although some French authorities saw the tirailleurs as a group that might serve as a modern vanguard, they soon became aware of the problems associated with demobilization.[49] Concerns ranged from managing the logistics of return to the danger of the spread of influenza in the repatriation camps.[50] Most important, authorities feared the role returning veterans would play in their home communities, given that many now expressed a newfound confidence due to their contribution to the war effort and an awareness of the privileges promised by Diagne.[51] Indeed many tirailleurs who had formerly been slaves or other lowly members of society, forced or lured into recruitment by chiefs, refused to reintegrate into their former positions.[52] Acting brazenly, some tirailleurs extorted villages, committed theft, and otherwise defied colonial and traditional authorities.[53] Many tirailleurs abandoned village life, swelling the populations of cities like Dakar, Saint-Louis, and Bamako.[54] The destabilizing role of the veterans was compounded when French authorities failed to follow through on promises made to the tirailleurs. Few were granted the citizenship promised, and exemption from the indigénat was rarely enforced.[55] Diagne, the great champion of the tirailleurs and advocate of recruitment, warned the government that refusal to fulfill wartime promises could create "agents of revolt."[56]

Political unrest related to workers' demands, high taxes, and other criticisms of colonial rule also surfaced in AOF in the aftermath of the Great War. Railway strikes occurred in 1919 and 1925.[57] In 1920 and 1921 dockworkers and colonial employees in Dakar alarmed officials by striking as well.[58] In a much larger show of political activism, in 1923 in Porto-Novo, the capital of Dahomey, a series of political events occurred in which nationalists railed against high taxes and the government's failure to address grievances. The Dahoméen activists refused to pay taxes and supported a general strike. Although the leaders of the Dahomey protests succeeded in gaining some concessions from the administration, the colony continued to be a political and social battleground throughout the 1920s, with clashes over elections and more strikes in 1929.[59]

AOF was also caught up in larger waves of mobility in the 1920s. Along with African soldiers streaming back into AOF from France or postings in North Africa, foreigners from Europe, the Americas, Asia, and North Africa also passed through the busy port of Dakar. French administrators and businessmen seeking opportunity, along with the first European tourists, joined them.[60] As a result the European population of AOF nearly doubled between 1921 and 1926.[61] Concerted efforts to regulate and slow the arrival of Syrians and Lebanese failed, and six thousand of these migrants settled permanently in the colony by the 1930s.[62] The 1920s also saw the arrival of increased numbers of European women.[63] French women and foreigners generated both anxiety and enthusiasm as authorities and residents wondered how such new additions would alter the French "civilizing mission."[64]

The capital city of Dakar, site of much of this dramatic social turmoil, was undergoing considerable change itself. It was in the interwar era that Dakar emerged as a truly "imperial city."[65] Dakar was a place designed by the French to meet the needs of European governance and life. At the very tip of the peninsula where Dakar sits the French created the Plateau, or "European" quarter, for European residences. It included French-style boulevards, the governor-general's palace, a train station, cafés and hotels lining the central Place Protêt, and the cathedral, which was built between 1910 and 1936.[66] The Medina, or "African" quarter, was built north and west of the city in an attempt to separate Europeans from Africans during the plague outbreak of 1914.[67] Although the creation of the Medina was swift and enforced with violence, it never accomplished a complete segregation of the city.[68] Many originaires refused to move to the Medina, where the population remained low into the late 1920s, even after the French made improvements to public works such as streets, electricity, and drinking water.[69] In between the Medina and the Plateau an area was carved out, known as "Dakar-ville" or "Dakar-propre," which bordered the port and became a commercial center and residential area for merchants.[70] In addition to being a political capital Dakar was also the center for business activity, a naval base, and hub for overseas trade. For the French and other Europeans living or passing through AOF, it was also a social and cultural magnet. Although the population of Dakar was 90 percent African, the city was once described as "the most European city in West Africa."[71] In 1907 half of the entire European population of Senegal was in Dakar.[72] European life continued to revolve around the capital city in the 1920s and 1930s as the city bustled with African politics and commerce, French governance, and an influx of foreigners.

## Government, Police Institutions, and the Law

The government general of AOF seated in Dakar established the administrative setting for investigations and surveillance of suspects. The governor-general too was based in Dakar, where he wielded power, in theory, over the entire federation of French West Africa from a majestic palace. He reported to the Colonial Ministry in Paris and was in frequent communication with the minister but had considerable autonomy within the federation to promulgate orders (*arrêtés*) by decree. He handed out directions to the lieutenant governors, collected and circulated information from the ministry, and received information from the various lieutenant governors, the police, Political Affairs Bureau, and other administrators.

Each colony of the federation was headed by a lieutenant governor who reported to the governor-general. Colonies of the federation were further divided into territorial administrative units known as *cercles* (circles). Each circle was headed by a European circle commander who supervised African *canton* (municipalities within circles) chiefs and village chiefs.[73]

The different police services of the government general and the colonies of the group took on the primary role of investigating suspects, conducting surveillance, and generating the reports and correspondence that was ultimately compiled by the government general. The Sûreté Générale (SG, General Security Service) was the main police service of AOF. The SG was a division of the government general within the Affaires Politiques et Administratives (APA, Bureau of Political and Administrative Affairs). Most frequently police inspectors in the SG conducted investigations, but circle commanders, lieutenant governors, employees of the city of Dakar, and the Colonial Ministry in Paris all communicated information about suspects that ended up in the governor-general's office. The *commissaires* in municipalities such as Dakar, Saint-Louis, and Rufisque investigated crime but also served the SG. Police institutions functioned with few employees. For example, in 1924 Dakar's police had one commissaire central, two lower commissaires, three secretaries, and three inspectors.[74]

Just as AOF's authoritarian government differed significantly from the government of the Third Republic that ruled metropolitan France, colonial law diverged considerably from metropolitan law. The difference in the law had important consequences for suspects because activities that were legal in France—subscribing to a radical newspaper or belonging to a union—were outlawed in AOF. Laws on the press in AOF also varied from French metropolitan laws. In 1921 and 1922 laws were promulgated limiting access to the foreign press. In 1928, after the proliferation of anticolonial groups and publications in the metropole, an expansion of the 1921 law forbade the distribution of "anti-French materials" as well.[75] Even Marcel de Coppet, the Popular Front governor-general, further restricted freedom of the press.[76] In a similar fashion, unions, vibrant and politically powerful in France, were mostly illegal in AOF. In 1920 the right to syndicalism was extended only to workers with French civil status. In 1937, under the Popular Front, the laws on unions were extended to include other Africans considered évolués. In other words, access to union membership remained limited.[77] Although there was a Senegalese Socialist Party as of 1925, they were careful not to be too radical.[78] Communism, like syndicalism, was legal and thriving in the metropole but was essentially forbidden in AOF until the era of the Popular Front, when a small communist cell was permitted with only French members.[79] These differences related to the press, unions, and political parties meant investigations into suspects could have far greater consequences in French West Africa than in metropolitan France. Being caught exchanging illegal newspapers or belonging to a pan-Africanist group could lead to arrest or, for foreigners, expulsion.

*Sources*

The critical primary documents used in this book come from the archive of the government general, especially from the divisions of police (SG) and the political affairs bureau (APA). These records include files labeled "Suspects," "Suspicious persons," "surveillance of foreigners" or "surveillance of foreigners and suspects," and "suspected propagandists" as well as files designated "communism," "pan-Africanism," "Garveyism," and "propagandists" and lists of suspicious journals and associations. I estimate the total number of suspect files examined from 1914 to 1939 in this project at around four hundred. However, as I do not rely on quantitative analysis, I hesitate to put an exact number on the total number of suspects. For example, government correspondence sometimes includes a list of "suspected communists" with several names, but provides no other information on them. Although surely these people were considered suspects, I have not included them in my analysis (or total numbers) unless documents offered information beyond rudimentary name and address. Also, because this study relies on the archive of the government general, it is very possible that there were many more suspicious persons kept under surveillance in locations such as Conakry, Abidjan, Bamako, or Ouagadougou in Burkina Faso, where documents remain and were not accessed for this study. However, many suspects from colonies outside of Senegal were signaled to the governor-general. Therefore, although it is likely that many suspects were not reported to the government general, the archives of the government general provide evidence from all the colonies of the federation and arguably include the most important suspects.

Police documents on suspects are valuable but complicated sources. They provide an opportunity for teasing out the greatest fears and smaller preoccupations of the colonial administration. The documents are also especially helpful in discerning how surveillance, and therefore colonial power, operated on an everyday basis. However, such files are difficult and delicate to use as sources about the suspects. Most suspects were not famous people, and it is rare to find traces of their lives in other sources, making it challenging to cross-reference or build on their stories. When possible I have turned to the press, memoirs, and secondary sources to round out their stories. Police documents recount the lives of suspects from the perspective of colonial authorities and likely contain exaggerations, misunderstandings, and even falsehoods. Yet although they must be used with great caution, police archival evidence provides narratives of marginal people, revealing traces of encounters that are both political and personal in nature. In fact police documents offer a rare opportunity to peek into intimate or peculiar details of lives that are impossible to find in other sources. N'guyen Van Phu's scrupulously quiet private life is described in his file, while Baron Paul Von Heinl's landlady is pumped for information. Amadou Sall was suspected to be part of a group of Africans who participated in a "native exhibit" at the Colonial Exposition of 1931.[80] Sources on "suspicious persons" provide rich details that more typical administrative sources and few memoirs and newspapers ever could. Vignettes from suspects' lives tell stories of adventures across the desert, pamphlets burned in a hotel room, a bottle of champagne shared with a prostitute and the postmaster, a café where sailors could clandestinely exchange newspapers, and the endless arrivals and departures of steamships. Although the documents pose challenges, these challenges are worth facing for the rich rewards in telling narratives about suspicious persons.

### Organization of the Book

The first two chapters approach the history of surveillance from the point of view of the colonial administration. Chapter 1 narrates the emergence of the surveillance of suspects as part of a particular political strategy developing out of the First World War and into the interwar period. This chapter highlights the global and local forces that shaped surveillance policies and situates them in the context of the emerging policy of association. Chapter 2 examines the practice of surveillance of suspicious persons through an analysis of techniques such as shadowing, postal control, port police, informants, denunciations, home searches, and gossip. The chapter also reveals the differences between urban and rural strategies of investigation and surveillance.

The subsequent three chapters examine the lives of the suspects themselves to tease out a new history of colonial society from the margins alongside a history of the colonial state. Organizing such stories has proven complicated. French authorities perceived of and treated suspects differently based on their race, gender, nationality, occupation, and political affiliation. Sometimes they categorized suspects as groups, creating "Pan-Africanism" and "Communism" files, for example. Police inspectors made sure to note when a suspect was an originaire. But more often than not the archival record suggests that they lumped suspects together with little regard to such differences. In fact it is precisely this messy mixture of race, origin, and background among suspects that makes them stand out as a peculiar concern of the colonial administration. Yet in order to make sense of the suspects' lives for this book I have chosen to impose order on this unruly group by dividing them into three chapters that correlate primarily to their legal status in AOF. Foreign suspects, the subjects of chapter 3, were the largest group of suspects under surveillance. Hailing from Europe, British Africa, Asia, South America, and the United States, their lives demonstrate incredible variety. However, as people who originated from outside AOF or metropolitan France they had one important thing in common in terms of the law: they could be swiftly and relatively easily expelled from the colonies for breaking a law. The chapter also includes French colonial subjects from other colonies, such as Vietnam and Algeria, who were not technically foreigners according to the law but who were so clearly viewed through a lens of foreignness by officials as to be considered foreigners. Chapter 4, on metropolitan Frenchmen living or traveling in AOF, recounts the stories of an eminently privileged category of people who could legally enter the colony as freely as they could travel in any French territory and who could also profit from informal and sometimes close relationships with colonial authorities. Chapter 5 focuses on the surveillance of political networks created by African suspects from AOF and colonial efforts to repress them. Africans from AOF could be citizens or subjects depending on their place of birth or sometimes service in the armed forces. Citizens and subjects had quite different relationships with the law, as citizens had access to French law and subjects were ruled under the indigénat and customary law. Nevertheless AOF Africans were not foreigners and could not be expelled. Black Africans who held citizenship still did not enjoy the immense advantages that whites from metropolitan France did. Indeed my chapter divisions sometimes create some rather odd groupings. Surely the Gambian labor activist Edward Francis Small, discussed mostly in chapter 3, had more in common with Arthur Beccaria, a Senegalese pan-Africanist and a subject of chapter 5. Both were African men making connections in AOF to further political causes that advocated for the rights of black people oppressed by colonialism; both men were probably viewed through a similar lens by the French administration. However, as a foreigner Small was easily and perfunctorily expelled for a minor infraction, while Beccaria, a citizen and longtime resident of Dakar, was threatened in other ways but could not be expelled. White men like Von Heinl made strong connections with the European community perhaps as much as some French suspects did. However, white Frenchmen were not viewed with the same suspicion that plagued foreigners and had entirely different rights in front of the law. Furthermore the division of suspects into chapters that are not based entirely on race is intentional. In my quest, as outlined above, to demonstrate that suspects formed a new colonial category that was not grounded fundamentally on racial difference, I have purposely chosen to divide them according to legal status rather than focus on the ways race or ethnicity might have divided them in the eyes of colonial administrators.

By 1937, when Von Heinl, N'guyen, and Sall had all been investigated as suspects, the administration had become deeply invested in identifying and keeping watch over suspicious persons and had investigated hundreds of suspects. The people who came under scrutiny were from around the globe. Some were engaged in political activity, some were social misfits, and others remained a complete mystery. In order to understand how and why such practices operated, we must look to the origins of these policies in the years after the First World War.

# 1

## "A Vigilant Surveillance"

### Creating Suspicion in Interwar French West Africa

In 1921 Governor-General Martial Merlin received seemingly ominous news from the Colonial Ministry about a conspiracy that threatened to spark a communist revolution. According to Paris, "communist agencies and directive committees gave instructions to their diverse groupings in order to prepare, in Asia, a vast Islamic movement, which will be a prelude to the worldwide [*universelle*] revolution and will have repercussions in the Muslim countries of northern Africa." Although Asia was meant to be the origin of the movement and no threat to sub-Saharan Africa was mentioned, Merlin took the report seriously, alerting the lieutenant governors of the colonies of this news and requesting they "send . . . a confidential summary . . . of the state of native opinion by telegraph . . . and exercise a very vigilant surveillance as much over the Muslim and fetishist milieux as over the more or less Europeanized groups." He asked to be sent "the tracts, brochures, prints, and in general, all instruments of revolutionary or tendentious propaganda circulating in the colony." Merlin's actions came as a swift response to the ministry's communication. Nevertheless he also admitted that no threat of revolt seemed to exist in his domain in Africa. He wrote, "Although no disturbing symptom has yet to be signaled in West Africa, we must collect all indications relevant to the propaganda that the communists could undertake either directly, or by intermediary of affiliated association, in order to create in the black countries a movement that is favorable to their cause." He emphasized, "I must add, in ending, that our natives, be they citizens of the four communes or those who maintained their original statute, have until now, only been preoccupied with commercial affairs, local politics and Muslim proselytism and it does not seem likely that they will turn towards a Pan-Africanism or communism which does not resonate with any idea or feeling amongst them." Nevertheless he also referred to a "danger of contamination" that was "pressing" and recalled that AOF was especially at risk in areas served by ports where "elements of all kinds mix and cross one another, where news brought by ships can be easily and rapidly put into circulation, amplified and distorted by those wishing to cause disorder."[1] Merlin's admission of the lack of a real threat is overshadowed by the urgency with which he agreed to attempt to contain the situation. His response and actions reflect the colonial administration's increased emphasis on the surveillance of radical propaganda in the interwar era in spite of little evidence that such propaganda existed or would be welcomed by the population of AOF.

In the interwar era AOF's authorities identified suspects, conducted investigations, and placed people under surveillance. But what were the origins and the reasoning behind such a policy? Martin Thomas has shown that interwar colonial intelligence gathering in North Africa responded to a thriving nationalist movement in Algeria and armed rebellions in Morocco and Syria.[2] Yet in AOF, as Merlin reminds us, very little evidence of nationalist or revolutionary activity existed. In this chapter I argue that the strategy of political surveillance, which was critical to creating the culture of suspicion, emerged through the convergence of a variety of forces, including precedents established in AOF during the First World War, a global red scare, the fears of the Colonial Ministry in Paris, and the choices made by officials in Dakar. Surveillance was deeply influenced by fear and paranoia, not rational decision making. It also emerged as part of a set of responses to the imperial crisis the French seemed to face in the aftermath of the Great War. I trace precedents to and the emergence and development of surveillance as a political strategy enmeshed in a web of various influences from Paris to Hanoi, to other parts of the empire, and finally Dakar.

## The Origins of Colonial Policing in French West Africa

Unlike the British in India, with their reference to the Mughals, or the French in Syria and Lebanon, who relied on Ottoman institutions, the French did not use prior models for the earliest creation of police services in Senegal.[3] As early as the nineteenth century, when French settlements along the coast of Senegal were growing, municipal policing institutions were imported from the metropole to protect European property and the increasingly diverse population of Europeans, Africans, and mixed-race people.[4] The earliest goals of policing were broad and included the prevention of crime, the maintenance of order, cleanliness of streets, and the pursuit of criminals, but also other kinds of regulation such as the inspection of hotels and cafés and the "surveillance of the fabrication of bread."[5] In 1825 Buignoz, a court official, called for the creation of a Commissaire de Police in and around Saint-Louis in addition to a judicial police bureau already in place because of the growth of the population and businesses. Buignoz identified a host of motivations, such as "the white population in Saint-Louis is growing. It contains artisans and workers whose pasts are not always known. This population must begin to come under some kind of surveillance." His concerns extended to the mulatto population "born on the land and who can easily support the climate"; the growing black population, "very numerous and inclined towards stealing"; and "foreign negroes [who] come to the city often, certain to find Muslim hospitality" and "other negro thieves who return, long ago chased from the city."[6] Although Buignoz here references mostly concerns about crime, his brief description of the various elements of the population in need of surveillance, French, Africans—especially Muslims—and foreigners, previews the major groups that would become objects of political surveillance into the mid-twentieth century.

Policies of surveillance of the populations of Senegal and later AOF in the mid- to late nineteenth century lacked uniformity and developed slowly over time as the colonies were established. Three distinct threads of surveillance activities can be detected in this period, however. First, in the mid-nineteenth century authorities identified the *marabouts*, Muslim leaders in Senegal and Mauritania, as potential opponents who could inspire their devoted followers to oppose colonialism. Second, as early as the 1890s they targeted the Lebanese and Syrians, whom they considered intruders in the economy and potential carriers of disease. Third, shortly after the federation was established, governors-general Ernest Roume and William Ponty attempted to impose a general surveillance over the politics and economy of the "native" population.

As French authorities sought to secure territory and establish rule in rural Senegal and Mauritania in the late nineteenth and early twentieth century they created a Muslim Affairs Bureau to monitor Muslims and investigate various questions related to the practice of Islam.[7] The Bureau collected information on Muslims, including well-known figures who were monitored with the use of bureaucratic forms known as *fiches de renseignements* (information forms).[8] By World War I Muslim Affairs was conducting surveillance over Islamic schools, courts, and the pilgrimage to Mecca.[9] Perhaps most important, going back to the 1880s the Muslim Affairs Bureau conducted surveillance over marabouts. As they attempted to control these powerful leaders, French authorities also tried to co-opt them.[10] The legendary Amadu Bamba Mbacké, leader of the Mouride Sufi brotherhood, for example, was exiled three times beginning in 1895 because French authorities considered his presence in the Senegal peanut basin to be destabilizing. Bamba's "fanatical" followers were former warriors and slaves who frequently came into conflict with newly appointed chiefs over issues such as taxation.[11] In 1912 Bamba was permitted to return to his homeland after having publicly acknowledged that the French were allowing Muslims to practice their religion in peace. David Robinson describes the complicated relationship between Bamba and the French as he transitioned from agitator to accommodator. Even after Bamba encouraged his followers to serve in the French Army during the First World War he remained under strict surveillance that essentially restricted him to his home.[12] As with suspect individuals in the interwar era, Muslim leaders were considered potentially powerful political agitators. Unlike most interwar political suspects, however, the marabouts were also understood to be important allies who could help the French impose political and economic control over rural areas. Surveillance of Islam that began in the nineteenth century continued throughout the colonial period. Sometimes the police investigated Muslims suspected of pan-Africanism, but the Muslim Affairs Bureau also continued to conduct surveillance over marabouts, Muslim propaganda, and other questions related to Muslim life.[13]

French authorities also made a concerted effort to monitor foreign populations, especially the Lebanese and Syrians, who were consistently targeted for special surveillance beginning in the 1890s.[14] The Lebanese and Syrians were despised by the French administration as outsiders and itinerant merchants who could undercut French traders. Surveillance of the Syrians (as they were often known) related primarily to scrutiny of their health and business practices. A regular "sanitary" surveillance was conducted over the Syrians. When an epidemic broke out in 1900, the governor-general asked the different communities of Senegal to send him a report on Syrians living within their domain, including specific comments on the "sanitary state" of each individual. The Circle of Tivouane responded in a typical report, "There are still only four Syrians at this port, three men and one woman. Their sanitary state is excellent."[15] As early as 1908 the European Chamber of Commerce in Dakar complained in a letter to the government general that Lebanese and Syrians were dominating trade with fraudulent practices and demanded protection.[16] Unlike Muslims who had only their leaders placed under surveillance, the entire Lebanese and Syrian community was subject to monitoring and scrutiny by French officials.

In terms of the rest of the population, it was the task of administrators to collect information of a political nature. In 1902 Governor-General Roume sent instructions to his lieutenant governors requesting "a monthly report on the political, administrative and economic situation of the colony, accompanied by the most interesting excerpts from reports from the administrative chiefs and the Chief administrators of the circles."[17] By 1914 French authorities were attempting to firm up control of the outer regions of AOF and the administration was desperately trying to collect information about the territories they now claimed to rule. Gathering a variety of information by the circle commanders was considered essential to bolstering their authority. In 1914 Governor-General Ponty sent out a scathing circular to the lieutenant governors lamenting that "certain administrators" were ignorant of their own *cercles*, especially in economic matters. He reminded them that they needed to keep two journals, logging such information as the "history and origins of the circle, its composition, its borders, its political, administration and judicial organization." In addition they would keep a daily journal that would log new information as well as "a note placed next to each item of information [that] will reveal the origin, name, and quality of profession of the individual who reported it and whether the information is more or less reliable."[18] Vigilance toward the collection of information was considered a solution to correcting the "ignorance" of administrators. Later, in the interwar era, authorities would attempt to streamline both police institutions and the collection of specific political information.

### World War I Surveillance Policies

During the First World War foreigners absorbed the focus of authorities' fears, and once again the Syrians and Lebanese took a central role in surveillance policies. Now instead of health status, authorities inquired about the Syrians' loyalty to France. Fear that these subjects of the Ottoman Empire might place their allegiance with the enemy led to restrictions over their movement, including the requirement that they seek permission before traveling.[19] They also continued to be criticized for their business practices. Commissaire Abbal remarked in 1916 that Syrians were undercutting indigenous shops with their prices because of "all kinds of privations they are able to impose on themselves." He noted that prices were already cheaper at Syrian shops than in either indigenous or European-owned stores. Abbal complained too about the continued arrival of Syrian migrants, writing, "The police can but signal once again the daily arrival of Syrians without resources, but who are welcomed by their compatriots with the greatest eagerness."[20] In 1918 Interim Governor-General Gabriel Angoulvant, in a letter to the Ministry of Colonies, went on a particularly vitriolic tirade against the Syrians, whom he considered war profiteers. He claimed, "In Senegal, especially in Dakar their fortune has been remarkable, many of them have luxury cars, indeed even automobiles. Those who knew them before the war when they miserably scraped by in little shops can now see their sumptuous establishments."[21] Lumped together by nationality, culture, and (before and during World War I) their status as Ottoman subjects, Syrians and Lebanese were suspicious based on their group identity and not as individuals.

It was during the First World War that the government general and officials from the colony of Senegal also began to systematically keep track of other foreigners, especially enemy nationals. Bernard, delegate of the government of Senegal in Dakar and key proponent of surveillance of foreigners during World War I, told the governor-general, "The current circumstances require us to redouble the surveillance of foreigners and especially individuals of suspect nationality."[22] Bernard had developed a plan to utilize immigration services, put in place to identify foreigners in 1911, to monitor the actions of foreigners in the colony. When a boat arrived in the port of Dakar the commissaire of immigration and a doctor or other "sanitary agent" would meet each passenger on board before departures and arrivals.[23] In 1916 the lieutenant governor of Senegal advocated "the establishment of a discreet but tight surveillance of all the foreigners who descend in Dakar."[24] This policy points to a larger shift in French thinking about surveillance of populations. Instead of the previous model of relying solely on administrators' summaries of the political and economic situation, lists of foreigners residing in the colonies, or simple immigration control, the actions of foreigners would become a specific focus of surveillance, both as a group and as individuals.

During the First World War various institutions participated in the surveillance of foreigners. Bernard asked the municipal police of Dakar to take charge of the task of surveillance of foreigners and "assure that the policing of these individuals be carried out with the greatest vigilance and discernment."[25] The Service of Civil Affairs undertook the task of centralizing intelligence collected by the municipal police, the armed forces, and the metropole. They also investigated suspects, including "Syrians and other Ottoman subjects, their travel and migrations, measures against hostile Ottoman subjects, the expulsion of suspects, surveillance of neutral ships and surveillance of suspicious businesses."[26] Civil Affairs took on myriad responsibilities during wartime, including "passports, policing of military arms and ammunition, contraband of arms, trade with the enemy, correspondence with invaded regions, deserters and disobedient soldiers of allied nations, diverse regulations relating to wartime, identity cards for foreigners, measures concerning individuals from Alsace-Lorraine, instructions relative to the repression of the spreading of false information, and offenses committed by the press."[27]

In fact the Civil Affairs Service and the navy were so overwhelmed with attempts to police the foreign population and the port during the war that a "special inspector" from the metropole was brought in to help, Noël Paoli. He held the rank of inspector fifth class of the Police Spéciale and, by his own admission, was "one of the youngest" in France.[28] The Police Spéciale ran intelligence operations in metropolitan France and was charged with the collection of information that was of interest to national security. Civil Affairs brought in Paoli, who was, theoretically, under their jurisdiction, although his role was broadly defined to include aid to the police and the navy as well. In fact Jules Carde, then the director of Civil Affairs, claimed to have dispatched Paoli from the metropole specifically because the commander of the navy "expressed the wish for help." Paoli's specific task was "surveillance and intelligence," and his duties were supposed to be restricted to those "normally included in the functions of a Special Police Inspector." For example, he was not to be stamping passports, but he would also not be permitted to function as "an agent of the Sûreté," that is, a regular policeman.[29]

Paoli introduced an important new element into AOF's policing strategy. He approached his task by seeking out specific foreign individuals and conducting comprehensive investigations on them, finalizing each inquiry with a detailed written report. His method contrasted significantly with the use of lists of foreigners and rudimentary comments regarding their health and loyalty to France that dominated prior to his arrival. Paoli also created a system of classification to streamline information. These methods would lay the groundwork for the creation of the Sûreté Générale in 1922, and his reports appear to have established a precedent for investigations of suspects into the interwar era.

Paoli's investigations into the lives of individual suspects occurred in urban areas of Senegal such as Dakar and Saint-Louis, but surveillance of foreigners in rural areas and small cities continued to rely on list making and the general knowledge of administrators. In 1918 an administrator in the circle of Niani Ouli, Senegal, provided an information sheet on the three foreigners in his domain, including details on their origins, travel, and prior employment. He wished to see them all expelled from the colony.[30] His colleague in Rufisque sent in a report the same month on thirty-eight Syrians, listing under "sentiments" for France either "very good," "good," "doubtful," "bad," or "very bad."[31] The initiative of the administrator clearly played a significant role in whether or not an individual foreigner was scrutinized in detail. Although the practice of individual investigations was developed by Paoli in this period, some of those investigations remained limited in scope, and they continued to exist alongside more basic forms of surveillance.

Paoli's integration was not smooth, however, suggesting his new style initially caused disruption. He responded angrily when he was accused in 1918 of conducting an illegal search, claiming that he had been accompanied by an officer of the judicial police and that the search had been approved by the commander of defense. In fact, he claimed, various branches of AOF's administration as well as the judicial police were preventing him from doing his job. In April 1918 Paoli reported to the governor-general, "I have not been able to carry out my duties as 'police spéciale' without every move I make being immediately offset by the involvement of the Commissaire of the Navigation Police or the municipal police." According to Paoli, it was a personal, not an organizational, problem. He claimed, "My posting to the Government General was taken badly by certain people who wanted me to be subject to their service as well as others who saw me as an adversary."[32] Bureaucratic confusion, ill will, or both, created problems for Paoli. For example, the municipal police requested information on a certain Grivot family from the Ministry of the Interior in Paris. They sent the information back to the commissaire of police in Dakar, but the information never reached the government general nor, to his consternation, Paoli and his one-man division of the Special Police.[33] The delegate of Senegal in Dakar was accused of trying to usurp Paoli's authority when Paoli accused Félicie Abeille, nicknamed "Magdy," of "defeatist remarks." The delegate of Senegal, after learning about the allegations against Magdy, called Paoli before the central commissaire, apparently not trusting Paoli's police work.[34] The commissaire of the navigation police also became involved when, according to Paoli, he "could not find anything better to do than intervene and criticize my procedures."[35] The public prosecutor, however, came to Paoli's defense, claiming that his work was "indispensable" to the judicial police and that "the two polices, *la police spéciale de la Sûreté* and the judicial police must likewise help each other in all ways."[36] Paoli's failure to easily integrate into the administration of the government general appeared to precipitate his repatriation to the metropole in January 1919, when his duties were taken over by a gendarme named Lahargouette.[37] Paoli's story of administrative power struggles and misunderstandings exposes the unwieldy institutions that governed surveillance prior to 1918. The question of jurisdiction over specific domains created confusion and conflict among the police, the navy, Civil Affairs, and Special Inspector Paoli. Although a police reorganization in 1922 would seek to remedy these problems, poor communication of information continued to plague policing institutions.

### Interwar Empire Shapes the Suspect

During the war official fears gravitated toward enemy nationals who could potentially sabotage the French war effort. But even before the war ended, concerns about new forms of dissent emerged to trouble French officials and ultimately transform the definition of suspicion into the interwar era. As the tirailleurs returned to AOF from the metropole it became clear that they would insist on the rights and rewards promised in return for their service.[38] Soon colonial authorities would begin to imagine the possibility that these soldiers who had served in Europe were not just demanding that promises be kept, but they, along with African students and workers who had traveled to France, were agents of revolutionary propaganda. However, it was not the government general of AOF that would instigate this transformation in conceptualizing suspicion from an essentially foreign threat to one from within, but the ministry in Paris. Thomas has described "the tendency among French security agencies to read colonial dissent through the prism of metropolitan preoccupations."[39] In the case of French West Africa the development of interwar surveillance policies involved the preoccupations of both the metropole and the empire as a whole.

Almost as soon as the war ended, radical ideologies seemed to proliferate rapidly and widely. Revolutionary movements struck fear in the heart of imperial metropoles in Paris, London, Amsterdam, and Washington DC.[40] Colonial critics were inspired by various sources, from Wilson's doctrine of self-determination to the literary scene in Paris, which awarded the Goncourt Prize to the Martinican René Maran for his novel *Batouala*, an unabashed criticism of the colonial administration in central Africa. Pan-Africanist thought took on growing significance with the emergence of black political and cultural scenes in Paris, New York, and London.[41] This movement gained high-profile attention when W. E. B. DuBois convened a pan-African conference in Paris in 1919 to coincide with the peace conference. Pan-Islam, a transnational force declared by an Ottoman sultan in the nineteenth century, also generated fears that Muslims of the French Empire would place their allegiance outside of France.[42]

Perhaps more important than these anticolonial doctrines, French authorities feared the emerging influence of communism. The success of the Bolshevik Revolution in 1917 and the founding of the Parti Communiste Français (PCF, French Communist Party) in 1920 made the threat of communist revolution appear pressing. In metropolitan France politicians, ministers, and the police united to thwart communist agitators among immigrants and colonials.[43] In the interwar era Algeria, Lebanon, and Syria all witnessed the creation of their own communist parties.[44] The United States, Greece, Italy, and Japan all sought to suppress communism at home as well.[45]

In response to this international climate the Colonial Ministry in Paris assumed a decisive new direction in colonial thinking under the leadership of Albert Sarraut, who held the post of colonial minister from 1920 to 1924. Sarraut is best known for his plan for *mise en valeur*, or economic development, in the colonies, a vision that reimagined the civilizing mission along the lines of technological advancement in order to bring economic benefits to France and vital infrastructure to the colonies.[46] Sarraut also oversaw the implementation of the political policy of association in which French authorities established new forms of power sharing with African elites by co-opting traditional rural leaders and creating increased representative opportunities for some urban Africans.[47] Sarraut had an additional agenda, which was to fight communism in the French Empire.[48] Although not touted as loudly in public rhetoric as association or mise en valeur, this new strategy, characterized by paranoia and a rising anxiety about the loyalty of colonial subjects, was an essential part of Sarraut's new colonial approach, which made overtures toward technological progress and humanism but also sought new ways to exert control over colonial populations. In fact Thomas argues that the entire economic policy of mise en valeur was largely driven by the hope that productive economies would head off the appeal of communism among colonial populations.[49]

The ministry under Sarraut and metropolitan police institutions united to monitor and attempt to prevent political radicalism among colonial and foreign populations in France. In 1923 the ministry created the Service de contrôle et assistance des indigènes en France (CAI, Service of Control and Assistance to Natives in France) to conduct surveillance over Indochinese, African, Caribbean, and Malagasy groups in the metropole.[50] As a former resident-general of Indochina, Sarraut was especially concerned that Vietnamese communities in the metropole would be exposed to subversive ideologies and transport them back to the colony.[51] In the early 1920s the Prefecture of Police scrutinized Russians for communist agitation and Italians for fascist activity.[52] Soon the attention of the Paris police became suspicious of Algerians who were monitored for a range of reasons, including nationalism and high unemployment. In 1923, when a homeless Algerian man murdered two French women one afternoon in the middle of a busy neighborhood, public outrage led to action. The Paris Prefecture of Police created a North African brigade to collect statistical information, monitor, and "aid" Algerians in France.[53] The North African brigade required Algerians to register with them, monitored their neighborhoods and cafés, aggressively pursued them as criminals, and sometimes forcibly repatriated them.[54] With the CAI, the North African brigade, and Sarraut's overall leadership of the ministry, the metropole was increasing surveillance of colonial people in a variety of ways in the early 1920s, just as the government general of AOF was implementing its own surveillance plans.

While new surveillance policies in France may well have influenced policies in AOF, another ministerial effort to monitor colonial dissidence almost certainly convinced administrators in Dakar to ramp up the surveillance of politics. Sarraut began a vigorous collection, centralization, and diffusion of information on "revolutionary propaganda" around the French Empire as well as in other parts of the world. Beginning in 1922 the Colonial Ministry sent monthly reports to the governors-general of each French overseas territory on global revolutionary activity. Governors-general within the colonies participated in this project by collecting and transmitting information to Paris, where it was organized, summarized, and expedited throughout the empire.[55] AOF's governor-general in turn requested that the lieutenant governors inform him of "all communications relating to communist, Garveyist, and German propaganda."[56]

The ministerial reports covered revolutionary activity in France, the French colonies, and around the world. The first dispatch sent in 1922 described interactions between the PCF and Vietnamese in France, including Ho Chi Minh. It addressed the founding of the Union Intercoloniale (UIC, Intercolonial Union), a group led by the Malagasy communist Samuel Stéfany and Ho, which sought to transcend the racial divisions among colonial people in the metropole.[57] Officials in the governor-general's office likely noticed the mention in the report of the Union's newspaper, Le Paria (Pariah), which published "a letter and an article devoted to Louis Hunkanrin, the Dahoméen teacher, victim of 'tyranny.'"[58] This May 1922 report described a broad range of propaganda activities, including by the Swiss League of Defense of the Rights of Man, Marcus Garvey's Universal Negro Improvement Association in the United States, and the activities of German spies in British India, where agents were said to be providing subsidies to Gandhi.[59] In August 1924 two and a half pages of a report were devoted to describing the activity of the Confédération Générale du Travail Unitaire (CGTU, General Confederation of United Labor) before moving on to the specific topic of "the Communist Party and the colonies."[60] According to the ministry's report, the PCF was especially interested in recruiting colonial people living in the metropole into their ranks.[61] These reports set a template to create a global summary on radical propaganda and appeared to ratchet up paranoia as revolutionary activists emerged in France, the empire, and around the world.

The ministry's reports focused considerable attention on the role of Moscow in spreading communist propaganda abroad. The ministry warned of a special Soviet propaganda distribution being organized with the aim of reaching the French colonies.[62] The Fifth Congress of the Communist International had apparently allotted "a subsidy of 3 million [gold rubles] to the colonial section" for a program that included colonial propaganda efforts and "organizing bands of rebels, fomenting revolts, encouraging rebelliousness."[63] They were also said to be buying arms and publishing and distributing tracts all over the world with a special center in Dahomey.[64] In 1925 the ministry specifically alerted the governor-general in Dakar of two Bolshevist groups: "the International Committee for the liberation of natives in the colonies" and the "World Combat Union in favor of the equality of the races, the goal of which is to obtain aid and assistance for Muslims wishing to shake the yoke of the European powers." The groups appeared threatening because "they are all the more likely to recruit adherents because they do not use communist propaganda."[65] Although communist propaganda and activism had yet to surface in French West Africa, the ministry warned of what appeared to be a massive effort to bring it to the colonies.

Reference to radical activity in AOF occurred only sporadically in propaganda reports throughout the 1920s. On the other hand, in June 1922 the ministry described the trials of communist propagandists in Tunisia and the dissolution of a communist cell in Algeria.[66] The same report noted that as Gandhi's ideas were gaining support in French India there was now potential "terrain prepared for a national-Bolshevist action."[67] It also detailed communism in Angola, the Dutch East Indies, Mexico, and China but did not mention any revolutionary activity in AOF.[68] In 1924 a report included comments on communism in Egypt, British India, and the Dutch East Indies and "revolutionary movements in southern China" and "the Soviets and China."[69] Throughout 1924 and 1925 a section detailing "revolutionary action in the colonies" routinely listed Tunisia, Algeria, Madagascar, and Indochina, but only rarely AOF.

A few incidents hinted that propagandists were making inroads into AOF. By August 1922 the ministry was aware that a group of Sierra Leoneans had attempted to create a Garveyist group in AOF, although "no French subject was a member of the suspect group."[70] In 1923 the incidents of political activity in Dahomey were mentioned in the report and for being published in the *Paria*.[71] The PCF was also actively trying to spread propaganda in AOF. In November 1925 it was noted that the Communist Party in France received 40 francs from Senegal. The ministry's report commented, "Despite the small amount of the gift, the intention was appreciated." The report claimed that the PCF was very interested in Senegal: "They are protesting against the measures that have been taken in the colony against blacks and whites suspected of Bolshevist ideas."[72] However, the ministry admitted this was not a significant threat: "In West Africa, and particularly in Dahomey and Senegal only the youth could be tempted to lend an ear to Councils coming from outside, and besides, would never imagine the adoption of Bolshevist doctrines."[73] Both the ministry in Paris and the government general in Dakar seemed aware that few Africans in AOF were interested in revolutionary doctrines.

In the metropole itself the ministry identified blacks from around the empire who were engaged in radical politics. As of late 1924 the Senegalese Lamine Senghor, who came to France as a soldier in 1919, had joined the UIC and began to regularly appear on the radical political scene and show up in reports on propaganda activities.[74] Senghor had joined the list of revolutionary colonials in the metropole alongside Bloncourt, a Guadeloupian involved with the Section française de l'Internationale ouvrière (SFIO, French Section of the Worker's International) and various anti-imperial groups; Camille Saint-Jacques, a French-born Haitian, who was a dedicated communist and anti-imperialist; a Guadeloupian communist named Joseph Gothon-Lunion; and the Vietnamese Nguyen The Truyen, a member of the UIC who later fought for independence for Indochina.[75]

Although Senghor was an important leader of radicalism, few fellow AOF Africans from within the growing community in Paris were engaged in radical politics. World War I had introduced a significant number of French West Africans to Europe through the army. While most of the tirailleurs were demobilized and returned to AOF, some remained and were joined by workers and students.[76] Among metropolitan blacks at that time their political sentiments likely lay with the legacy of Diagne and the possibility that working within the French system could bring Africans into the fold of French citizenship.[77] Nevertheless in 1926 ministerial reports began to include a section devoted to the activities of the "colonie noire" alongside the "colonie indochinoise" of Paris.[78] Of course the "black colony" included all blacks in Paris involved in revolutionary organizations, including those from Afrique Equatoriale Française (AEF, French Equatorial Africa, the other French federation in Africa) and the Caribbean as well as AOF. In June 1926, for example, Senghor was cited for having made a trip to Le Havre on behalf of his new group, the Committee for Defense of the Negro Race (CDNR, Comité de Défense de la Race Nègre).[79] Also in 1926 the Sudanese agitator Tiémoko Garan Kouyaté, who would become notorious among metropolitan and colonial officials for his extensive political activity, made his first appearance in reports. Oddly enough, in one of the earliest mentions of Kouyaté, at a meeting of the CDNR, he was reported to have "declared that the Association create dance halls so that the adherents have some distraction and inexpensive restaurants where they can consume healthy food"—a far more modest demand than his radical politics in later years.[80] However, such a comment included in a report sent to all parts of the empire is suggestive of the minute detail often included in propaganda reports that typically reached forty pages or more. Kouyaté and Senghor were the most important of the small number of AOF Africans surveilled for radical politics in the metropole.

The year 1927 was a critical turning point for anticolonial radicalism in the French Empire. Security services in Tunisia repressed a communist network there. The Vietnamese Nationalist Party was formed in the midst of growing anticolonial sentiment. Also in 1927 the League against Imperialism and Colonial Oppression brought together anticolonial activists from all over the world along with their European allies in two important meetings in Brussels and Amsterdam.[81] Most important for the history of AOF, the CDNR was reborn as the Ligue de Défense de la Race Nègre (LDNR, League for Defense of the Negro Race) under the leadership of Senghor and Kouyaté. The LDNR escalated its activities, and its growing role in Paris became clear in the "black colony" section late 1920s propaganda reports. In June 1928 a report devoted four and a half pages to describing the activities of the "black colony, especially the undertakings of Kouyaté."[82] In 1929 "Kouyaté made it known that the party planned to organize a communist cell in Dakar."[83]

The activities of Senghor and Kouyaté aside, in comparison especially with Indochina, where in 1926 Nguyen Ai Quoc was said to be spreading "Bolshevik propaganda," revolutionary activity in AOF seemed almost nonexistent. In 1930 a report on Indochina described the posting of communist signs, the distribution of tracts, and sabotage of the railways and strikes in Tonkin and Annam on the first of May. In Thai-Bin the French resident was forced to face a crowd of three hundred protestors who brandished the hammer and sickle while one of the leaders encouraged them to attack the French leader. One report described "a thousand natives, armed with sticks [who] attempted to occupy the village of Benthay."[84] These and other "grave" incidents around Indochina are in striking contrast to the minor nonviolent activities of joining groups and sharing newspapers that characterized "revolutionary" activity in AOF.

Nevertheless these reports on revolutionary propaganda by the ministry almost certainly had an effect on the governors-general who received, read, marked up, and sometimes forwarded excerpts to the lieutenant governors. In an October 1924 report authorities in Dakar marked the phrases "The *Paria* of October printed 3,000 copies. 2,000 are reserved for the colonies" and a description of how the *Paria* would be delivered under the guise of packages of books.[85] In December 1924 an excerpt from a propaganda report was typed up in Dakar describing a letter from Senghor asking African veterans of the tirailleurs sénégalais to join the Union Intercoloniale. Senghor had promised to "undertake an examination of the question of pensions of the former Senegalese tirailleurs who are mutilated or disabled and their widows and orphans."[86] This excerpt also included the ministerial reports' comments on "the Bolsheviks and the blacks" and "of Bolshevism and Islam."[87] Having done so occasionally in the past, the government general began to send out excerpts of propaganda reports to lieutenant governors on a regular basis in 1931, concentrating on the section describing black groups in Paris.[88]

Propaganda reports suggest that part of the stimulus behind increased political surveillance in AOF came not only from within the colony but from the ministry in Paris and from news of revolutionary activity around the world, especially in the French colony of Indochina, where authorities witnessed violent and large uprisings. The ministerial reports, closely read and shared by the governor-general's office, reveal the influence of the ministry in pushing the governor-general of AOF to focus intently on the surveillance of international revolutionary propaganda. As governors-general in Dakar digested propaganda reports on a monthly basis they were inundated with news about communism, pan-Africanism, and anticolonial movements around the world. Yet although such activity rarely seemed to implicate AOF, authorities became fearful that their colony was ripe for the incubation of such activity. Well before any evidence existed that communist or other emancipatory doctrines were spreading in AOF, authorities, such as Merlin, instituted policies of surveillance largely based on knowledge about propaganda activities outside AOF.

## Dakar Shapes Suspicion

As the First World War ended authorities in Dakar identified a host of problems that their police services faced. They embarked on the creation of the Service de Sûreté Générale, a new institution that organized and centralized police surveillance in the 1920s. The experience of poorly coordinated and haphazard surveillance during World War I along with concerns about migration and the economy led authorities to reform police institutions in the interests of national security. It seems that the lesson learned from the problems of Paoli's tenure and wartime difficulties was that in order to be operational, the *police spéciale* needed a department of its own and the police structure as a whole needed reform. In 1918 an unsigned report to the governor-general proposed a new institution expanding the surveillance used during wartime to create a general policing body for AOF. The report claimed, "[The goal] of this new instrument of high surveillance . . . is to centralize under . . . [the governor-general] . . . all information received from the metropole as well as all that can be collected in Dakar or in the other colonies of the Federation on all matters related to national defense and the general security of the colonies and territories placed under your direction."[89]

The proposed new police service was designed especially to respond to problems perceived to arise from increased immigration.[90] The growth of the port of Dakar had long been linked to fears about foreigners. Accordingly the proposal lamented that an economic boom had brought "a veritable influx of people, in consideration of whom we must recognize measures of surveillance and the necessary precautions." This document also criticized the "excessive kindness to numerous foreigners, who, under [the] guise of Francophile sentiments or their status as a citizen of a neutral country have moved into our territory either as business representatives or by managing to slip into the personnel of a French company." In order to ensure "economic interests and national security," the flood of "undesirables into the country" would no longer be tolerated. At the time the greatest threat was identified as "Syrians and other Ottoman subjects who invade from day to day without any control, hiding the nature of their true origins." Syrians and Lebanese were again widely criticized for what was described as their failure to aid in the war effort as well as their large stake in the French economy. The author of the report castigates the governor-general: "If your hospitality must be great and welcoming, that does not imply that we do not have the right, nor the duty to inform ourselves on those that we receive under your leadership." The report claimed the "ever-increasing number of foreigners who pass through the port, either in transit or to reach the Southern colonies," made for "an urgent need to create a very severe control in regard to them immediately as well as in the future." The new police service would increase surveillance of ships, including neutral vessels stopping in Dakar's port, claiming the crews of these ships "most often are composed of extremely undesirable elements."[91] These fears about foreigners, especially Syrians and Lebanese, echo the motives behind policing tactics undertaken during the war.

The new police institution streamlined and reorganized policing services. It would not replace all of the police services, but it would transform the existing institutions, such as the municipal police and navigation police to better work together.[92] The new police organization was to mainly centralize information. It would include five administrative sections: a direction and administrative service, an "active" section of general information (Renseignements Généraux), a criminal records office, a scientific laboratory, and archives of the police. The general information section, the only active section of the new organization, would be charged with surveillance. The new police service's goals were to "seek and centralize information of [a] political, administrative, and judicial nature relevant to the internal and external security of the colonies of the group. It is charged with special surveillance of foreigners, the floating population, immigration and emigration, the press and bill-posting, contraband of arms and ammunition, peddling."[93] The general surveillance carried out by the Renseignements Généraux would also work to gather information for the benefit of the judicial police as well as collect political information. The new police service meant that from 1922 onward an organization existed in AOF that was specifically charged with the collection of political information.

The creation of the nonactive sections of police archives and records reveals an increase in the bureaucratization of the administration and the collection and centralization of information from both metropole and colony as a new organizational strategy. In addition the privileging of specific and detailed kinds of information on individuals meant that a growing invasiveness also characterized surveillance practices. An increased sophistication in the collection of information occurred as information would henceforth be gathered by a new professional police service and centralized in a bureaucracy. As of 1918 surveillance in AOF had become a priority in policing.

Between the initial proposal in 1918 and the creation of the Sûreté Générale under the leadership of Governor-General Merlin in 1922 a subtle shift in administrative priorities occurred. The 1918 proposal was created with the general aim of bolstering security through the collection and centralization of information, but concerns about foreigners, especially Lebanese and Syrians and other "undesirable" migrants, were at the root of motivations behind the new institution. The *arrêté* creating the Sûreté of 1922 showed apprehension about foreigners and migration, but the institution as a whole took on a broader scope, emphasizing the role of the organization to "research and surveil all actions of a nature to trouble or compromise the security of the political regime or to harm the sovereignty of France."[94] This was more definitively an institution charged with political surveillance than the one first envisioned in 1918. The shadow of wartime experiences dominated the earliest impetus for the organization, but the rise of international radicalism seemed to loom on the horizon once the new police organization officially came into being.

Although Merlin presided over the creation of the police services as well as the earliest stages of association, it would be under the tenure of Governor-General Jules Carde, who took on the leadership role in 1923, that the new police service was finalized and association fully implemented. Carde, raised in Algeria, had served in several colonial posts in French Africa (Ivory Coast, Equatorial Africa, and Cameroon) before becoming governor-general.[95] Carde and his cohort of leaders in in AOF—including Joost Van Vollenhoven and Gabriel Angoulvant—embraced the well-known interwar policies of mise en valeur and association.[96] As an advocate of association, Carde worked to encourage education for the chiefly elite and established institutions such as a limited electoral college to create more opportunities for the évolués to share their concerns with the government general and governments of each colony.[97] The legacy of association was mixed, but Carde saw himself as a humanist leading Africans toward economic and "moral progress."[98] In terms of mise en valeur, the economic goals of the era, Carde worked to develop the African labor force through health care initiatives and the mobilization of forced labor, but not ultimately technological advancement.[99]

Carde was also an adamant believer in the use of police institutions to repress dissident activity. In 1925 he called for an increase in surveillance. He cited information coming from the metropole and "diverse sources." He wrote to his lieutenant governors, "I urge you, to exercise in the most urgent manner, a discreet, but vigilant surveillance in all European and indigenous milieux, in such a way as to observe the slightest indications of propaganda in action or in gestation." He insisted his administrators adhere to a high level of vigilance. "This surveillance should be directed indiscriminately towards all suspect individuals or those who are simply susceptible . . . to favorably accept revolutionary doctrines, no matter their social class, whether they are in business, in industry, the Administration or the Army."[100]

His insistence was no longer on the bureaucratic necessity to gather information but to cast a net of surveillance as widely as possible. He wrote, "No information should be considered insignificant, no lead abandoned until the minutest investigations [are] completed." Carde's urgent circular warned that dangers that might have once seemed far away were now imminent. He then linked the international threat directly to AOF writing, "Senegalese participated in the latest meetings of the colonial section of the communist party, tracts are being prepared, the *Paria* will be distributed in thousands of copies. We must organize an effective defense against the flood which threatens to be unleashed on the coast of West Africa."[101] Carde had a tendency to see radicalism in any political opposition, once referring to the assimilated republican activist Hunkanrin as "the Bolshevik of Dahomey."[102] His urgency and devotion to the identification of suspects are reflected in the hundreds of files collected on suspects by the government general in the mid-to late 1920s. When he moved on to his position as governor-general of Algeria, he brought his preoccupation with surveillance of politics with him. In 1934 he attempted to create a surveillance system in Algeria to police the habits of radio listeners for foreign programs spreading anticolonial doctrines.[103]

Police surveillance would be transformed again in the 1930s as French West Africa's government general coped with the crisis of the Great Depression. On the one hand, the economic disaster seemed to preclude much possibility of political dissidence. Catherine Coquery-Vidrovitch describes a "pauperization of the countryside" as a result of the economic crisis in which attempting to survive overtook any impulse toward revolt.[104] On the other hand, discontent among urbanites only seemed likely to grow as workers suffered and city populations grew. Laborers who relied on the cash crop economy were hit hard. Rising prices on imports from France also meant problems for urban workers, and wages dropped precipitously.[105] Economic turmoil in the countryside meant the migration of rural people to cities in search of opportunities, draining rural areas of workers and expanding the ranks of the unemployed in cities.[106] AOF's overall population barely increased in the early 1930s, but cities such as Dakar and Abidjan saw their numbers grow by 71 percent between 1931 and 1936.[107] Concerns about political threats would now be combined with the troublesome currents of economic distress.

The Great Depression coincided with another revision of the police services, which was undertaken by Governor-General Jules Brévié. In 1931 the General Security Service became the Central Service of Security and General Information (Service Central de Sûreté et de Renseignements Généraux) and was led by a director of the Sûreté, which was placed under the Direction of Political and Administrative Affairs of the Government General. The *arrêté* (order) officially creating the new service reveals it to be an umbrella organization for all policing activity in AOF (save for the *gendarmerie*, which remained under military control), including judicial, municipal, railroad policing, immigration, emigration, control of foreigners, control of the press, investigations for families, passports, the anthropometric service (physical criminology), and the scientific police.[108] Now, under the new service, police agents would work together instead of under separate agencies. Brévié described the tasks of the new institution: "All information of interest to public order and political security collected in the circles by agents of the Police and Security, with the exception of information of a purely judicial character, will be simultaneously communicated twice, once to the Lieutenant Governor of the colony and the other, if sufficiently interesting, to the Governor General."[109]

The name of the new organization, Central Service of Security and General Information, indicates that the collection of information (*renseignements*) was one of its main goals. However, unlike the Sûreté Générale of 1922, no provisions were made for an individual *service de renseignements*. Instead all police agents were to take part in the collection of intelligence, to the detriment of a special police. This lack of distinction appears to have initially led to some confusion and eventually another departmental reorganization. In 1932 the central commissaire of Dakar wrote in his annual report on the organization and functioning of the Sûreté, "The Section of the Judicial Police and Renseignements . . . has among its duties judicial matters as well as, in principal, the *renseignements généraux*."[110] By the 1937 annual report, however, the Renseignements Généraux was listed as a separate entity with its own commissaire, while the judicial police was directed "in principal" by the Commissaire Central.[111]

The reorganization was not merely an attempt to streamline unwieldy administrative branches. In fact it was another attempt at improving the political police. Brévié makes clear in a circular about the new service that it was actually motivated by a need for greater and more efficient political policing. He claims the police underwent a reorganization because of "the troubling development of extremist propaganda in all domains, aided by the current economic crisis, the large influx of foreigners of all races and nationalities, some of them questionable, the large increase in the number of natives emigrating to France and abroad, and finally the development of criminality, facilitated by new roads and other means of travel."[112] Here Brévié lays out the fears that would characterize political police surveillance in AOF until the Second World War: extremist propaganda, foreigners, educated and well-traveled Africans, and criminals.

Unlike in 1922, the government general explicitly spelled out the political threats at the root of the reorganization. In a letter to the lieutenant governors, Brévié cited his specific concern over the activities of the Internationale Syndicale Rouge (ISR International Red Syndicate) of Moscow.

He noted that at the Fifth Congress of the ISR it was stated, "Partisans of the ISR among black workers must work toward the important task of winning over the majority of the masses of black workers to the ISR." Brévié cited at length the instructions of the ISR and their goals, including organizing black workers into revolutionary unions. The ISR, he wrote, hoped to "create factory committees and revolutionary delegates elected by the workers," with the ultimate goal of encouraging strikes and allegiance among blacks to the ISR. The ISR also recorded the abuse of blacks by imperialists, especially through "the creation of <u>black armies</u>, [therefore] <u>it is advisable to create agitation</u> and a systematic propaganda in order to interest them in the battle against imperialism." Brévié took the threat of the ISR seriously, writing to the lieutenant governors, "I insist once again, and very strongly, on the <u>urgent necessity</u>, in the current circumstances to intensify our vigilance, for all administrators in all circles to work towards the organization and re-organization of the Services de Sûreté et Renseignements in order to communicate to the Government General the maximum information."[113] Although the newly organized Service de Sûreté grouped together a variety of policing activities, including order police and judicial police, its creation was explained to both the Colonial Ministry and the lieutenant governors as having the purpose of stemming propaganda and revolt.

It is not surprising that the Service de Sûreté et Renseignements Généraux was created under the leadership of Jules Brévié. He has been described as an "ethnographer-administrator" with great interest in his career in "native" affairs.[114] But during his tenure as an administrator in Sudan and Niger Brévié prioritized surveillance of the local populations. In 1922, as the commissaire of the Territory of Niger, Brévié showed considerable concern for political surveillance, after having been warned by the ministry of revolutionary activity in other parts of the empire. He claimed that one might assume the people of landlocked Niger would not be very receptive to propaganda given that coastal people "hate us sometimes much more than those of the interior." However, he described the "more uncultivated peoples of the hinterland" as "impulsive and spontaneous," who, "although in no way Bolshevized," "could suddenly revolt, pushed by some disruptive agents." In addition to "Bolshevist agents," the threat of Arab Islam was also of concern to Brévié, who wrote, "One is led to believe that our African hinterland must be particularly watched [because] the borders of the Sahara are incessantly traveled by marabouts coming from Mecca who have crossed through Egypt, Tripoli and Egyptian Soudan where [there exists] a parallel propaganda in favor of pan Islamism and an anti-European action of local nationalist elements."[115]

In 1923 Lieutenant Governor Brévié wrote to his circle commanders of the importance of "a police organized and functioning in a permanent manner . . . above all at the end of the war in order to follow the movement of anti-European opinion developed by diverse politico-religious organizations among the populations of North Africa." He listed as the prime threats Bolshevist communism, Muslim nationalism, and Garveyism. He warned the circle commanders to avoid the false security of the "absence of means of communication and the primitive mentality of our charges." Despite the remote locations of most populations, he did not discount the possibility that "trouble makers" could slip into the population and "exploit local reasons for discontent." In fact, he claimed, "despite its distance from the coast, the colony of Niger is, in its situation, particularly threatened by propaganda from the exterior. First of all, the route to holy sites used by most pilgrims in West Africa crosses Niger from the West to the East. . . . Everywhere along this route our pilgrims come in contact with populations strongly influenced by bolshevist and neo-Muslim campaigns; it is therefore indispensable to keep them under tight surveillance once they have returned to our territory after a more or less long stay in Mecca."[116] Here again Brévié signals his two main fears: Bolshevism and Arab Islam.

His comments on the threat of pan-Islamism are typical of French colonial attitudes toward Islam. Beginning around 1912, with the work of the administrator-scholar Paul Marty, French authorities had developed a particular notion of "black Islam"—an Islam they imagined to be strongly influenced by pre-Islamic animist traditions, but not purely Islamic like the orthodox Islam of Arabs and Moors.[117] Brévié's rhetoric echoes not only stereotypes about Islam but also a strong tendency on the part of administrators in the interwar period to perceive international threats to French colonial authorities as coming from the Middle East, North Africa, Europe, and the United States.[118]

Evidence suggests that surveillance of suspicious activity was in fact more likely a personal preoccupation of Brévié and that Niger was no different from other colonies in its exposure to radical ideas. Brévié's concern with surveillance appears to have been extraordinary, as evidenced by his treatise on the subject in a sixteen-page circular sent to his colleagues in 1923. Most lieutenant governors did not advise their subordinates on surveillance until the 1931 reorganization specifically required them to do so. When one of his successors, Lieutenant Governor Théophile-Antoine-Pascal Tellier, dealt with reorganizing surveillance in 1931, he also wrote a circular to the circle commanders, but of only four pages. Tellier did mention in his circular that due to its geography Niger was vulnerable to the spread of ideas via nomadic peoples, but he never mentioned specific threats that targeted Niger.[119] Brévié went on to become governor-general, and his concerns with political radicalism accompanied him.

Under Brévié's tenure as governor-general (1930–36), fears seemed to proliferate and calls to expand surveillance were repeated. In 1934 he wrote to the lieutenant governors reminding them of his orders in 1932 to "organize in each district a permanent information service, of sound constitution."[120] By 1934, however, his tours of the colonies showed that "Renseignements" organizations were not "yield[ing] satisfactory results": "Almost everywhere, it seems to me, a very serious effort needs to be undertaken or carried through. The current circumstances require an intensification of vigilance, and local administrators who allow themselves to be surprised by events, for having neglected to finalize the 'listening' networks and the surveillance aimed to inform on all fluctuations in native thinking will bear a serious responsibility."[121] New targets of potential threats were identified for monitoring by such institutions. A 1934 circular warned, "The seasonal migratory currents which move through the Federation are the preferred vector agents of new ideas and merit serious attention."[122]

Although the governor-general and the Service of General Sûreté oversaw policing activity overall, under the reorganization of 1931 each individual colony was entitled to have its own Sûreté. Local administrators adapted the apparatus of the Sûreté Générale to meet their local needs. In fact many of the colonies other than Senegal struggled to conform to policing regulations, especially surveillance, due to a lack of funding and personnel and the vast territories they were meant to administer. Although the governor-general often demanded an ever-increasing and tighter surveillance, lieutenant governors and the circle commanders were often left to their own devices as to how to make surveillance operations work best in their circle. Regional geographic or social conditions, or at least French perceptions of them, meant administrators adapted to local conditions in order to collect information better. In a 1932 circular to the circle commanders of Niger, Lieutenant Governor Tellier wrote, "The geographic situation of your territories puts you in frequent contact with nomads from the desert regions. It should be clear that there is a great advantage for the military commander responsible for the police of your area to be made aware of all news that is peddled in your circle."[123] In Niger authorities focused on the movement of information through traveling groups, while a place like Dakar concentrated on individuals arriving at the port.

The governors of Mauritania perceived many but different problems. In 1932 the lieutenant governor wrote that the "hinterlands, inhabited by nomads of the Maure race," were a refuge for criminals and ex-convicts. This "out of control" territory was the source of "calls to dissidence," and the "task of the Sûreté Générale is entirely linked to questions of indigenous politics." However, another region of Mauritania, the Chemama on the right bank of the Senegal River, was "in all ways analogous to the territories of the left bank which belongs to the colony of Senegal: same land, same population, and same evolution." The key concern there was "extremist propaganda" as there were many sailors, some of whom had been to France and were involved in "advanced workers organizations.'" The lieutenant governor claimed the budget of Mauritania was too small to deal with these two different sets of problems and asked if the colony of Senegal could take over the job of *sûreté* in the Chemama. The governor-general denied his request.[124]

The era of the Popular Front (1936–38), a leftist coalition in metropolitan

France, did not significantly change institutions of colonial surveillance.[125] At times the Popular Front has been touted for its overtures toward greater freedom and openness in the colonies, but the government did not last long enough nor were reforms extensive enough to eliminate surveillance policies.[126] In fact surveillance remained an important aspect of rule in the Popular Front. At the helm of the Popular Front's government in AOF was Marcel de Coppet, who most often is described by historians as a liberal and reformer.[127] De Coppet was an experienced colonial administrator who had a "reputation for liberalism and socialism."[128] As an administrator and employee of the colonial government, de Coppet supported colonial rule but "condemned . . . the injustices, violence and abuses of colonialism."[129] He is best known for working to decrease the abuses of forced labor, although his intentions were clearly better than the results achieved.[130]

De Coppet's record as a lieutenant governor and governor-general suggests that while he opposed colonial abuses, the use of political surveillance was always compatible with his socialist and liberal views. Surveillance was, in fact, a nonviolent solution that likely appealed to him. When he was lieutenant governor of Dahomey de Coppet adopted new methods to try to improve the function of the security service in his domain. He complained that the goals of "general surveillance of [the] European and indigenous milieu, the investigation and arrest of trouble makers are not being met because the functionaries of the Service de Sûreté and the circle administrators are too scattered to work together effectively when they are not unfortunately thwarted."[131] Dahomey was a trouble spot for authorities, being that it was also the site of considerable agitation, including the strikes and protests of 1923 and a growing bourgeois nationalist movement. De Coppet clearly believed this political dissidence could be calmed with recourse to police institutions that would collect and coordinate information. He wrote, "The increased evolution of certain indigenous groups, their accessibility to the influences of militant European milieus and the extreme sensitiveness of Lower-Dahomey and the resulting political complexity, make it more and more necessary to have an efficient section of the Security Service in closer collaboration than ever with the circle administrators."[132]

In 1935 de Coppet was at the center of a political crisis that stemmed from the general economic depression and from the political activity of a group called Young Dahoméens influenced by similar movements in Gold Coast and Nigeria.[133] Brévié expressed confidence that de Coppet could handle the current situation as he was ready to use "fear and immediate repressive action," including the stationing of troops in the vicinity if needed.[134] De Coppet's prioritization of surveillance to keep control over the "evolution" of indigenous people, their politics, and their exposure to European ideas, as well as his willingness to resort to violent means for the collection of taxes, contrasts with images of de Coppet as the gentle colonizer who claimed that Dahoméens simply wanted the same rights as the Senegalese in the four communes.[135] This incident involving de Coppet is striking not only because it shows a different side of his personality as a governor, but also because it reveals how a situation considered imminently grave was dealt with by a lieutenant governor. His response to the threat of the young Dahoméens was to ratchet up surveillance, call in outside assistance, but eventually turn to violence if necessary.[136]

With regard to politics, the Popular Front in AOF also showed itself to be restrictive. Prior to this era any interest in communism on the part of a European or African was sufficient grounds for suspicion and surveillance. The regime of the leftist coalition changed this slightly by permitting unions for the first time and limited participation in communist organizations. Under the Popular Front trade unions were formed and strikes broke out in a variety of professions, from tugboat workers to cooks and domestics.[137] A communist cell was formed by a group of Europeans, with the accord of Louis Ponzio, administrator of the district of Dakar. Ponzio recommended that only *électeurs*, or African *originaires* with citizenship, be admitted into the cell. The group agreed "to spread serious propaganda [only] among disciplined and disinterested *électeurs*," while also claiming to be committed to improving the situation of Africans.[138] Limiting access to the Communist Party even under the Popular Front reveals that communism remained unacceptable when spread among the educated but subject population and that the Popular Front's political policy left previous political regulations largely unaltered. The Popular

Front created important political reforms in French North Africa, where political prisoners were released, nationalism was revived, and "an explosion in worker militancy and trade union activism" occurred.[139] But in AOF incremental rather than dramatic changes occurred. The policy of surveillance of suspects was not substantially modified under the new regime.

## Summary

In a 1937 report on policing in Dakar, the central commissaire detailed the problems involved in juggling the many duties of the commissariat. His main complaints related to mundane issues of everyday urban control. Daily traffic, for example, annoyed him, as "the public in Dakar does not go out without a car." However, regarding the issue of subversive propaganda the commissaire wrote, "There are no facts to suggest that the mass of Senegalese, those of Dakar in particular, are subjected to political influences susceptible to provoke disaffection with France and the republican regime throughout the year 1937." Moreover those elements of subversive propaganda that did exist were not revolutionary ideas but "take on a character of religious nationalism."[140] Indeed these comments by the police echo almost exactly Merlin's comments from 1921. They suggest that the need for surveillance of the population in order to collect intelligence on threatening forms of propaganda was related to a fantasy of high administrators more than to a legitimate threat within the population.

The police services of AOF seeking suspected propagandists or other political "suspects" created their policies at several levels. They responded to what they perceived as local problems, such as the growth of the port and the arrival of foreigners during and after the First World War. Individual administrators and colonial officials, including Paoli, Merlin, Carde, Brévié, and de Coppet, all shaped institutions of surveillance by imposing specific methods and particular goals on policing institutions.

However, AOF was not only subject to the decisions of local administrators. A rapidly changing international climate that stoked fears about communism and anticolonialism also deeply shaped colonial policies of surveillance, shifting from a wartime emphasis on enemy nationals to international radical politics in the interwar era. AOF was a government that was deeply embedded in an imperial system that stretched from a center in Paris to the Caribbean, Africa, Asia, and around the world. The changing currents in global and imperial politics were processed by the Colonial Ministry in Paris, setting off an agenda of increasing surveillance and control even in those colonies not yet touched by the wave of anticolonial radicalism. As news about radicalism in the French Empire as well as India, China, and the United States reached Dakar, officials acted. While local conditions in Dakar were critical to shaping the new policing institutions and policies, revolutionary activity in Paris and Vietnam also contributed to building the culture of suspicion.

There is no direct link between the political changes caused by association and the development of the new Sûreté, which was charged with surveillance as of 1923. In fact the policies developed independently, with different root causes. Yet it is important to consider how and why the two policies emerged at the same time. Both association and increased police surveillance were in part official responses to the growing demands of an elite African population that lived in AOF's cities, especially Dakar and Saint-Louis. As I explained in the introduction, friction between the originaires and the administration flared up in the immediate postwar era as returning veterans joined them in demanding expanded rights for Africans. Merlin himself expressed fears about the évolués, saying, "Favoring the intellectual development and the material progress of the natives also renders them more vulnerable to the self-interested calls and fallacious promises of professional agitators."[141] Here Merlin identifies the area where association and increased political surveillance intersected. In the minds of colonial officials the "intellectual development" and "material progress" of Africans made the urban aspects of power sharing inevitable, but they also appeared to make urban elites more susceptible to anticolonial doctrines. The narrow success of assimilation policies had created a class of Africans who deserved a stake in government, an idea that was widely agreed on in metropole and colony, but elite Africans also seemed to be politically volatile. Therefore we might understand both association and police surveillance as they developed in the early 1920s as distantly rooted in assimilation policies that created an African elite. Indeed Africans who spoke French, exercised citizenship rights, and participated actively in colonial society might have been seen as important allies to the French, but the long history of conflict now made them appear to be dangerous foes. The advent of global radicalism in terms of communism and pan-Africanism seemed to be a likely avenue for their frustrations with the French government. To a degree, association sought to assuage the elites by granting new forms of power sharing. Yet authorities, perhaps knowing these paltry concessions would not be enough, also began a discreet program of political surveillance to identify and monitor potential dissidents among them. Rural chiefs were expected to maintain control through traditional means, but modern police services would provide an opportunity to stem the potential political activism of elites in cities. Ultimately, just as French authorities were creating new avenues for political engagement for elite urban Africans through association, they were also creating a new policing institution to keep watch over the political activities of these same elites.

The anxiety over the potential of dissidents invading their shores suggests that administrators had serious doubts about their ability to maintain French sovereignty and repress rebellion. As fears increased about the possibility of AOF being infiltrated by propagandists, so too did the way potential threats were defined—as pan-Islamism, Garveyism, communism, and workers' activism. Authorities were themselves aware that such doctrines had little appeal to the populations of AOF. Nevertheless officials decided that vigilant surveillance was needed to prevent the propagation of such ideas. Historians have acknowledged that paranoia shaped institutions of colonial surveillance, but it seems that in the case of French West Africa, it was perhaps the most significant factor driving authorities to conduct political investigations.[142]

Once colonial authorities constructed the profile of a suspect as an international political agitator, suspects were identified and investigations and surveillance of suspects were conducted by police. But how was the plan for surveillance put into action? What can the practice of surveillance tell us about how power functioned in French West Africa? These questions are taken up in the next chapter.

# 2

# "Proceed with a Discreet Surveillance"

## *The Investigation and Surveillance of Suspects*

The opening image of Julien Duvivier's 1937 film *Pépé le Moko* is a map of the city of Algiers. As the scene unfolds, a police inspector laments the challenges of policing the Casbah, or "native quarter" of the city. He describes the problems posed by the geographic tangle of the city, "in its reaches, torturous dark alleys, alleys like traps . . . alleys that cross, overlap, lace, and unlace in a jumble of labyrinths." Furthermore, he claims, the size and diversity of the population thwart policing efforts. The inspector asserts, "There are forty thousand people where there should be ten. Forty thousand come from everywhere, those from before the conquest, those of barbaric past and their descendants, simple, traditional, and for us mysterious: Kabyles, Chinese, Gypsies, Heimatlos, Slavs, Maltese, Blacks, Sicilians, Spaniards, and women of every country, every shape."[1] *Pépé le Moko* goes on to follow the clumsy efforts of the French and Algerian police to hunt a European criminal mastermind played by Jean Gabin who is hiding in this seemingly impenetrable part of the city. As the opening of the film indicates, the inscrutability of urban spaces and populations in colonial North Africa plays a prominent role in the conflict at the heart of the film between police and criminal.

Though the setting is different and the story nonfiction, the theme of a police bewildered by urban people and spaces still resonates in the surveillance of suspects in interwar French West Africa. Rhetoric explored in chapter 1 related to the development of surveillance policies reflects a confident administration, determined to leave "no lead abandoned until the minutest investigations were completed."[2] Yet, as authorities developed and enacted practical strategies to gather information, conduct surveillance, and share evidence with each other, they struggled to impose the vigilant and ubiquitous surveillance over AOF's spaces and population they initially envisioned. In this chapter I examine the day-to-day practice of surveillance and investigations by colonial officials in French West Africa, especially in urban areas.[3] The actions of police inspectors, postal workers, rural administrators, informants, and French officials throughout the empire provide a valuable opportunity to observe the colonial state at work. My analysis of surveillance practices moves beyond the ideology and high-level policy of the government general and Colonial Ministry to consider the quotidian dynamics of the deployment of power in AOF. For example, the everyday practice of discreet surveillance suggests the influence of republican policing strategies imported from the metropole. But the various methods used to identify and investigate surveillance also suggest that investigations of suspects were often haphazard, opportunistic, and unsystematic. The surveillance of politics in interwar AOF, while repressive, ultimately operated in ways that diverged significantly from the broad plans outlined at the highest levels, often revealing colonial police and administrators to be as frustrated with policing as the fictional inspectors hunting down Pépé le Moko.

## Identifying Suspects

In 1921 Governor-General Merlin proposed a broad surveillance when he declared that lieutenant governors should "exercise a very vigilant surveillance as much over the Muslim and fetishist milieux as over the more or less Europeanized groups."[4] However, the majority of investigations and surveillance ultimately took place in urban areas over Europeans and "Europeanized" Africans. The main reason for this was that the profile of a suspect as imagined by authorities quickly began to match particular urban types, especially Africans perceived by authorities to be elites. Fears about Africans who traveled to France, served in the French Army, or showed interest in the new pro-black political groups coming out of the metropole meant elite urban Africans became prime suspects.[5] For example, in 1927, when the LDNR, headed by Kouyaté, began to make contacts in Dakar, a police inspector reported, "A constant surveillance is being exercised over the literate milieux of Dakar and the least incident will be reported with great urgency."[6] In 1931 Governor-General Brévié directly connected concerns over the arrival of radical printed materials to "the important increase of the number of natives from French West Africa emigrating to France or abroad."[7] Foreigners and white metropolitan French men and women, as potential agents of Western political radicalism, were also potential suspects, and they too were most likely to be found in cities. As a transit point for soldiers, students, sailors, and outsiders the capital city of Dakar especially came to be understood as the epicenter of suspect activity. Encouraged by the Colonial Ministry to seek out political radicalism through a vast surveillance, the government general and police of French West Africa ultimately mostly identified people who coincided with urban populations: African "elites," foreigners, and French.

Merlin's order to conduct surveillance of the population suggests that colonial authorities would use policing methods to identify suspects. In reality, however, most of the information that identified suspects for the Sûreté came from other parts of the French Empire and not through active police work at all. French colonial authorities from Paris and around the empire informed each other constantly about the potential travel of known suspicious persons or about the possibility that individuals arriving in AOF or neighboring colonies might engage in political activity. The Colonial Ministry in Paris played a key role in the identification of suspects, especially by dispatching information gathered by the CAI, which surveilled colonial subjects in the metropole. The ministry informed the governor-general in Dakar frequently about the activities of Kouyaté, whom they feared would one day return to AOF and sow revolutionary ideas. Suspects signaled by authorities abroad were subject to surveillance in AOF, but many of the people described in correspondence to the government general never even came to AOF. For example, in 1928 the ministry sent out a notice that a Chinese man named Li Fat had been expelled from French Oceania for running a clandestine gambling operation, presumably in case he try to visit another French colony, but he never set foot in West Africa.[8] Kouyaté also never returned to AOF.

Of course the government general also informed their colleagues in the metropole and other parts of the empire about the departure of potential suspects from AOF. In 1923 the director of APA reported that the "Portuguese mulatto" Joachim Joseph Garcia, who was "mixed up in a suspicious milieu in Porto-Novo [Dahomey]," had departed by ship for France. In the same letter he noted that in June Kodjo Goyave Quenum would be heading for Le Havre, and he recommended a "discreet surveillance" for this Dahoméen, who, while in France, claimed to be a prince and became involved in metropolitan pro-black movements.[9]

One important way French authorities could identify suspects on their own was through the bureaucratic checks at ports where foreigners, metropolitan agitators, and cosmopolitan Africans were all destined to pass. Ships and ports were critical sites to identify potential activists making their way to the colonies.[10] Administrators in AOF relied on authorities aboard ships to collect information on passengers before they even arrived in local ports. In 1919, when the liner the *Plata* arrived in Dakar, the captain turned in a Swiss passenger named Arthur Geissbuhler, who had "surreptitiously embarked in Marseilles and did not emerge from the coal holds until two days after the departure of the ship." Gendarme Lahourgouette investigated Geissbuhler and found his papers and visa in order. The only subsequent hint of suspicion was that Geissbuhler appeared to be "well educated even though he says, and his papers prove it, that he is a simple apprentice cheese-maker."[11] Gossip was collected on board a ship traveling from Bordeaux to Dakar about the Argentinean Ernest Sona. He apparently tried to "monopolize the attention of a passenger in first class, Gomis, a functionary in Dakar's Public Works department, and to convince him that France alone should bear the responsibility for the last war."[12] Yet for all the help police received from ship captains and other eavesdroppers, information gathered aboard ships was not always effective in providing surveillance over suspects. Sona disembarked from the ship and disappeared into the city before police could be notified. Ponzio wrote to the director of the Sûreté Générale, "Having been warned too late of the facts that I report to you, I could not have this foreigner followed and I do not know what relations he has in the city."[13]

The special port police, headed by an inspector of police with a staff of two brigadiers and two writers, took charge of regulating emigration and immigration, collecting deposits, and confirming the validity of letters of guarantee in 1922.[14] But the port police did more than stamp passports and collect money. A 1922 report congratulated the port police on the success of their mission, claiming, "The regulations on emigration and immigration were strictly applied. It is permissible to affirm that the regulatory exercises at the port of Dakar over Frenchmen, foreigners and natives of the group [AOF] who enter or depart from the territory of the colony do not permit the possibility for fraud to pass unnoticed. Individuals, who by their suspicious looks, their origins or the genre of their occupations attract attention on the occasion of their debarkation or embarkation in the port of Dakar, become the object of intelligence reports."[15] In March 1930 an Italian named Antonio DiPietrantonio was caught up in the bureaucracy of the port. When he arrived in Dakar accompanied by his French cousin Armand Sbicca, DiPietrantonio lacked sufficient funds for the required foreigners' deposit. French authorities advised him to seek a solution to his financial problem with the Italian consulate in Dakar, but he "seemed annoyed and declared having difficulties with the Italian authorities following a certain arms trafficking that he was involved in during his stay in French Somalia."[16] At this point DiPietrantonio was labeled a suspect, and further investigation revealed that he had been involved in selling arms to "rebellious natives" in Somalia.[17] As the port police verified every individual who arrived in or departed from Dakar, they occupied a central position in identifying suspects, especially considering that suspicion due to fears about international propaganda became closely linked to foreigners and Africans who traveled abroad. Ultimately checks at the port yielded mixed results in identifying suspects. While a suspect such as Sona might slip through the cracks at the port, others such as DiPietrantonio fell into authorities' laps through simple questioning.

French officials also used simple techniques, like reading the international press, to identify suspects. This strategy alerted administrators to Bertil Hult, a Swedish sportsman who made a motorcycle trip between Stockholm and Cape Town, then used information gathered during his trip to write an article critical of the French Foreign Legion.[18] The subsequent investigation of Hult amounted to reading news about him and requesting information from French consulates. The Swiss Zimmerman's file follows a similar pattern. In 1934 Zimmerman wrote an article titled "The Whip and the Rope" about forced labor abuses in AOF and published it in his own Ivory Coast journal, *La Défense*. Both Hult and Zimmerman actively sought to distribute their articles in AOF as well as in Europe.[19] But because Hult and Zimmerman remained in Europe (outside of France) the investigations fizzled out.

Spontaneous denunciations to the police also provided leads for authorities to identify suspects.[20] In 1931 Madame Suzor, a planter in Vol Doriba, Guinea, reported her employee Gabriel Chal. Suzor said of Chal, "According to his own declarations he was charged, when he lived in Morocco, with the posting of signs and the distribution of communist tracts: three of his comrades of the communist party would soon join him."[21] The German Rosie Graefenberg, a journalist who traveled in AOF in 1929, was already under police surveillance when she was denounced by Charles Gerthenvich, a fellow German. Principal Inspector of Police Gaston Lenaers reported that Gerthenvich, who was originally from Munster but was living in Dakar, "presented himself to the service to, he said, make some important revelations regarding espionage." Gerthenvich "claimed [to Graefenberg] to be an ex-officer of the German Navy" and told authorities that she "shared confidences with him," revealing that Graefenberg was engaged in planning a plot to use a large amount of money "to push the Moorish Chiefs to an uprising against France."[22] Gerthenvich's claims were never substantiated or pursued as Graefenberg had already left the country. Nevertheless such allegations were taken seriously.

Administrators often identified people they met in the course of carrying out their duties as suspicious and subsequently conducted investigations. Subjective opinions and personal perceptions played an important role in designating an individual suspicious, often without any additional evidence. When Joseph Arthur from Gold Coast came to Tiendougou in Guinea in 1921 he was considered especially dubious because of his clothing. The local administrator noted, "His appearance was suspicious, very well-dressed in a light gray suit, wearing a gold monocle."[23] Arthur's attire indicated that he was an educated, foreign African, and therefore potentially a troublemaker. Other individuals were flagged whose appearance or dress deviated from expectations for certain national or ethnic types. In 1925 the appearance and actions of a Moroccan named Larbi Diouri brought him to the attention of authorities. Diouri had become "well-known among the Moroccan element of Dakar. He landed in the colony about six months ago coming from Casablanca. He only stayed about eight days in Dakar during which he stayed at the home of his compatriot Driss Guenone, customs forwarding agent, living at 75 rue Vincens."[24] When, a month later, Diouri was in Saint-Louis a detailed report described him as "always dressed in European clothes, wearing a fez, looks like an Egyptian type or young Moroccan. Brags among his entourage to have spent time in Egypt and to have been received by Marshal LYAUTEY. His style at first seduced the small Moroccan community of Saint Louis which is composed above all of old traders; after staying here for several months, he already no longer interests anyone among his fellow Muslims."[25] Diouri's appearance was considered unusual and made him stand out as suspicious, but little other information indicated a political purpose to his travel. In 1930 the consul of Tripoli sent concerned messages to Dakar, alerting them to the travel plans of the Austrian Joseph Riesinger. The consul described Riesinger's speech as "German with a strong Austrian accent. . . . [He] uses vulgar and provincial expressions." The consul characterized Riesinger's "social milieu" as "very low" and commented on his own "instinctive distrust" of the man.[26] The subsequent investigation and surveillance of Riesinger revealed prior exploits in various French African colonies and unusual travel, but it was the consular official's uneasiness about Riesinger's class status that initially singled out the man as suspicious.[27] For foreign Africans like Arthur and Diouri, suspicion was indicated by a cosmopolitan and sophisticated dress. For a European like Riesinger it was lower class speech that suggested he was out of place.

If the rhetoric of governors-general is to be believed, political policing was meant to be a vast and pervasive operation, but suspects were mostly identified in ways that were convenient and frequently haphazard. The port provided the most complete and simple venue for vetting identity and questioning potential suspects. Otherwise authorities relied on instinct, gossip, and luck and, above all, followed up on information sent from other agencies around the empire.

### Collecting Information

Once suspects were identified, police relied on a variety of methods to collect information on them. Typically authorities began by making inquiries to other branches of the imperial government if the person hailed from another colony or the metropole. But when the suspect was local, authorities were not above relying on gossip and opinion and sometimes resorted to directly asking acquaintances of the suspect for information.[28] In 1922 the Senegalese Idrissa Faye, who had served in the army during the war, requested reenlistment in the army for three years as a radio employee in Paris. His military record already described him as suspect. Faye's former boss at the Compagnie Française de l'AOF (French Company of AOF) responded to a request for information by saying, "I myself fired Idrissa Faye who was satisfactory as an employee, but whom I surprised several times in the middle of giving revolutionary speeches and exciting the employees and native workers to revolt against the whites."[29] When Paul Von Heinl, the Austrian businessman, visited Dakar in 1937, police asked for information about him among locals who might have had contact with him. The landlady at Von Heinl's lodgings was questioned but "could offer no information on her guest, other than that he goes out frequently equipped with 'nice cameras.'"[30] Such direct interventions were ultimately less common likely because they were not as discreet as other methods.

Ports, where it was more difficult for suspects to remain hidden from authorities because they were required to present their papers, frequently became sites of surveillance where information could be collected. Consider the story of Mohammed Saad Eddine Djibaoui, a Syrian who admitted to involvement with the revolutionary Moroccan leader Abd el-Krim. French authorities in both AOF and Morocco were never quite sure of Djibaoui's exact whereabouts or the purpose of his extensive travel. He was at times interrogated by authorities, but occasions for questioning him presented themselves only when he was arriving at or departing from a port. In October 1923 Djibaoui "arrived at Fez coming from Casablanca, Marseille and Port Said. He expressed his intention to go to the Rif, but thwarted, he went to Taourirt." In 1924, "on 18 January we find him in Marseille. In April, he is in Tunisia where the English Vice Consul stamps his passport." Djibaoui's file shows twenty-seven visas obtained between July 1923 and November 1924. The Moroccan authorities wrote, "We also followed him from July 1923 to November 1924 from Egypt to Dakar and across North Africa without knowing anything of his occupations or resources."[31] Confounded by his extensive travel, authorities could occasionally catch up with this suspect only when he crossed borders and was required to present a passport or apply for a visa.

Colonial authorities also recruited informants among the African and possibly European population. The use of informants was not unique to AOF, but they were used widely and predominantly in metropolitan surveillance and in North Africa.[32] Information collected from informants is sometimes only hinted at in final police reports. For example, in late July 1931 Police Inspector Gaston Braud reported the following in Dakar: "A few Europeans sitting at the terrace of the Metropole for lunch were talking about the 'red day' of August 1. One of them commented that he had spoken that morning with a black who informed him of the presence of a 'certain revolutionary English journalist' . . . and declared that posters would even be put up on the walls of Dakar for the occasion."[33] The "English journalist" in question was the Gambian labor leader Edward Francis Small, who had been agitating for the causes of communism and organized labor in Senegal. This critical piece of information may have been provided by an eavesdropping diner who spontaneously shared it, but more likely by an official informant. In other cases, the role of informants is clearer. Fofana

Coulibaly, a Guinean former teacher who worked as an accountant for the Direction of the Artillery, was denounced through information that came from an "authorized source." This source claimed Coulibaly was "in continued relations with Mr. Small, Francis, Edward," the communist and labor leader, and a "known militant."[34] The denotation "authorized" suggests that the source of the information was a paid political agent. A recruited informant was apparently also used to trail Arthur Beccaria, head of the Dakar section of the League for Defense of the Negro Race. In 1927 a policeman wrote, "A correspondent who was watching [*surveillait*] Beccaria told me that the above named just received some journals called 'la Voix des Nègres' a clearly communist publication. . . . I asked my correspondent to ask Beccaria for a packet for distribution."[35] African informants were considered a potentially rich resource, allowing for the collection of intimate information about suspects, and likely contributed extensively to surveillance reports.[36]

The postal control served to both identify suspects and collect information on them beginning in the First World War. For, example, the Swiss Henri Lier, working in trade in Porto-Novo, had sent correspondence betraying "anti-French sentiments" that was intercepted by the Ministry of War and was subsequently placed under surveillance until he could be expelled from AOF.[37] In 1917, when the Uruguayan Samuel Sempol tried to send mail to Montevideo through the captain of a commercial ship, his letter was discovered by a police agent. His interlocutors had German-sounding names and he was suspected of developing business relationships with them.[38]

Although postal controls were specifically described as wartime necessities, the mail continued to be monitored into the interwar period, especially in searches for forbidden newspapers. In December 1933 it was reported that information had been leaked of "the presence at the Central post office [in Dakar] of an Inspector of Police of the district who verifies the content of packets of newspapers."[39] The same report revealed that the newspaper *Journal des Peuples Opprimés* (Journal of Oppressed Peoples) no longer used the postal service to send packages but relied on couriers aboard ships.[40] Foreign or suspicious newspapers were forbidden, and the mail provided a unique opportunity to prevent their arrival in the colonies. Kouyaté's mail from the metropole was systematically controlled, and many of his letters are copied in police files.[41] In the case of two Gabonese men living in Dakar involved with the publication of the journal *L'Echo Gabonais* (Gabonese Echo) in the early 1920s, a rigorous surveillance of all their correspondence was conducted.[42]

Registered mail and return addresses could also provide clues to suspicious mail in lieu of direct postal controls. For example, Armand Angrand, an originaire of Gorée Island, by profession a "publicist and municipal councilor," who had links with other political radicals, including the French publisher Jean Daramy D'Oxoby, was already on the radar of the French police in 1922.[43] The lieutenant governor of Senegal had asked the delegate of the colony of Senegal in Dakar to "proceed with a discreet investigation on Mr. Armand Angrand who, based on printed materials addressed to him, appeared to be in relations with the UNIA [Universal Negro Improvement Association] in New York."[44] These suspicions were confirmed when a postman delivered a registered letter from Marcus Garvey, leader of the UNIA, to his address on rue Carnot in Dakar. While Angrand's fellow Garveyist in Dakar, the Sierra Leonean Bob Williams, wisely refused to accept a similar package, Angrand "accepted as if he was waiting eagerly" for the arrival of the package, which contained issues of the forbidden paper the *Negro World*.[45] Subsequently Angrand's home was searched and copies of the *Negro World* as well as other propaganda tracts from Garvey were discovered along with evidence that Angrand was trying to create a political group called the Comité de l'action Sénégalaise (Senegalese Action Committee).[46] Much like immigration checks at the port, the postal control allowed for a direct and bureaucratic form of surveillance.

In conducting investigations, French colonial police sometimes turned to more invasive methods, most notably home searches, which required warrants. In 1918, when Noël Paoli first instituted the practices of the special police, he conducted a search of the home of the Portuguese Bento José Dos Santos, a ship chandler living on rue Caillé in Dakar. Paoli acquired a warrant from the naval commander in Dakar because Dos Santos "spoke indiscreetly concerning the defense of the port of Dakar during a recent voyage to Tenerife and Las Palmas; he also, otherwise, criticized the piloting service of Dakar and transported letters from this port to the port of the Canaries." The search conducted on the home of Dos Santos was, however "fruitless, no object or document of interest to the National Defense was found in possession of Dos Santos."[47]

A few years later home searches were used in breaking up a Garveyist group in Dakar. Although as early as 1920 the government general and the Ministry of Colonies began receiving information from the Belgian Congo that a Sierra Leonean named Wilson was spreading "anti-European propaganda" as an affiliate of Marcus Garvey's Black Star Limited shipping company, action was not taken on the issue until 1922.[48] It was not surveillance that led the police to conclusive evidence on Wilson, but a denunciation from a man named Gibbs, the proconsul of England. Gibbs claimed he got into a fight with Wilson and sent to the police "a cigarette case which he claimed he picked up off the ground where the quarrel took place and he found in the said case a receipt for a letter bearing the number 552 and the postmark of Rufisque addressed to the 'Universal Negro Improvement Association New York America' directed by Marcus Garvey, the well-known agitator."[49] Authorities likely knew the incident of the cigarette case was a charade and Gibbs's information a denunciation. But it was sufficient evidence to allow them to conduct a search. Following up on this "serious lead," Inspector Pourroy suggested obtaining a search warrant from the prosecutor to conduct searches in Rufisque and Dakar "to seize at Wilson's domicile all papers dealing with the actions of these individuals."[50] The registered letter sent from Rufisque to Garvey was actually sent by John Farmer, who, it was soon learned, was sharing a room with Wilson in Rufisque. Pourroy carried out a search of the men's home and discovered a variety of incriminating documents, including photographs, copies of the *Negro World*, posters announcing a speech by Garvey, and meeting minutes titled "UNIA Propaganda Dakar May 5, 1922."[51] A similar search occurred at Wilson's primary residence in Dakar, where Farmer was interviewed and denied any connection with Garvey.[52] In this case colonial authorities were careful to closely adhere to the law, even if it meant following up on a bit of planted evidence. Their attention to the letter of the law is suggestive of the importance it played in systematizing and codifying investigations of suspects.

Although police insisted on legalizing their searches with warrants, they were also willing to circumvent and manipulate the law. In 1930 authorities in Bamako received information that Moudou Kouyaté, brother of Tiémoko Garan Kouyaté, and one of his coworkers at the post office were to receive a package containing copies of *La Race Nègre* (Negro Race), the paper of the LDNR. In spite of consistent surveillance, no evidence of the arrival of the package was uncovered. Inspector Jean Barreyre took advantage of a simultaneous investigation of some burglaries at the post office to acquire a warrant to search the homes of the men, even though they were not suspects in the burglary case. The search turned up photos and letters of Kouyaté as well as copies of *La Race Nègre*.[53] In this case authorities adhered to the law but did not hesitate to use a patently false excuse to obtain a warrant.

When the police followed the letter and spirit of the law for their searches, they were often confounded and unable to penetrate private residences. The case of the Egyptian Aziz Atta Kahhal illustrates this. In 1931 the circle commander in Baol wrote to the governor of Senegal about a visit Kahhal paid to Diourbel.[54] Kahhal, upon arriving in Diourbel, "immediately went to the former home of CHEICK ANTA M'BACKE (villa de Paris).... He conferred for a long time with Serigne TAKO, son of Cheick ANTA, received at the villa de Paris diverse Mourides who had come to greet him, notably, the ex-secretary of Cheick ANTA, named Amadou DAO and diverse somewhat suspicious persons."[55] Kahhal's apparently close relationship with important Muslim leaders seemed alarming to authorities. However, they could but observe from the exterior because, "during this foreigner's time in Diourbel, the entryway of the villa was guarded by two Mourides who forbade entry to visitors not offering guarantees of absolute discretion. On the day of the 29th an informer who arrived to visit the foreigner was refused entry, being unknown to the Mouride doormen." The sheer number of Mourides who visited this "foreign MUSLIM" indicated that Kahhal was involved in something suspicious and important. The circle commander at Baol commented that "Kahhal's connections to certain advanced persons and subversive ideas are worth knowing and appear fairly suspicious, especially considering the Soviets are becoming more and more active." Kahhal's case reveals much about how French surveillance operations functioned. First, while there was little hesitation in labeling someone a suspect, there was fear of offending Muslim leaders. The circle commander tried to infiltrate the group with an informant, and yet the investigation remained outside the home as the informant was denied entry and no cause for a warrant was found. Kahhal had been "summoned to the Commissariat of Police where he showed a passport in order established in Cairo and stamped by the police in Dakar."[56] This direct intervention of summoning Kahhal before authorities failed when no legal excuse could be used to expel him from the colony. Attempts to find a way inside of Kahhal's tightly guarded residence or to deport him failed. French officials often aggressively pursued suspicious activity, but frequently such efforts failed.

## Discretion, Shadowing, and Republican Values

In picturing the surveillance of suspects perhaps the first image that leaps to mind is that of an undercover police agent shadowing a suspect through dim allies or observing from behind a newspaper at a dubious café or bar. French authorities used such methods to collect information, and indeed clandestine surveillance provides an opportunity to consider not only how surveillance operations functioned but also the values that underlay policing methods. Shadowing, a discreet form of surveillance, was pioneered by the French metropolitan police and was used to collect information on suspects in AOF. While it may seem like a staple of police work, it was actually an innovative strategy with a unique history that was known as "a special French technique which surprised German policemen during the Occupation."[57]

The origins of shadowing and other methods of discreet political policing are intimately tied into the politics of republicanism in metropolitan France dating to the late nineteenth century. At the inception of the Third Republic in 1870 some republican leaders intended to maintain the interventionist and aggressive secret police that had been used under the reign of Louis-Napoleon, arguing that such forceful policing was necessary to preserve the republic. Other republicans feared that an "attack police" that would disrupt meetings and destroy tracts would sully their reputation. These republicans ultimately prevailed in advocating for a noninterventionist "police based on sheer observation" that could protect the republic from those who wished to destroy it.[58] Such methods better represented the values of a republic that sought to distance itself from practices that tainted the authoritarian regimes of the past. The metropolitan political police force, called first the Special Police then, in 1937, the General Information Service (Renseignements Généraux), emerged along these lines and maintained distant observation as its preferred method of political policing through the interwar era. They formed "research squads" that investigated anarchists, communists, and other "social movements." Their methods included "direct surveillance," such as the collection of information from the press, interception of mail, and shadowing of suspects.[59] This observational political police developed for the protection of the republic became the model used by French colonial authorities to conduct surveillance in French West Africa's cities.

Discreet and observational surveillance was an important part of AOF's strategy to collect information about suspects. In 1925 Governor-General Carde called for "a discreet, but vigilant surveillance."[60] In Angrand's file the Political Affairs Bureau was asked to "proceed with a discreet investigation."[61] During the investigation of Small, a senior police official, H. Dirat, specifically instructed Inspector Braud to avoid direct confrontation, writing, "Let us limit ourselves, for the moment, to a tight surveillance. At the least incident arrest and expel him."[62] The investigation of Boubakar Awe, who "professes advanced ideas," was described as "very discreet."[63] *Vigilant*, *tight*, and *daily* were also part of the lexicon of surveillance operations, but no term was as important or as often mentioned as *discreet*.

Discretion not only characterized the overall philosophy of AOF's policing; it surfaced in practice as well. Shadowing was used to collect information about European and African suspects who frequented Europeanized areas of Dakar and other cities. When the German Graefenberg passed through Dakar, police most likely shadowed her to uncover the following: "She spent the morning in the city. She spoke with several people. She seemed above all interested in the foreigners who live in AOF and sought to inform herself notably on the number of Russian subjects inhabiting the colony." The police inspector filing this report could not find out much more, however, and Graefenberg left Dakar at noon aboard the *Brazza*.[64] Shadowing was meant to be the epitome of a discreet surveillance, but it was not always effective. One agent reporting on Graefenberg claimed, "I have the feeling that the surveillance failed to remain discreet, as from the beginning Madame Graefenberg gave the impression that her movements were not passing unobserved."[65] Shadowing was likely combined with the use of informants in the in-depth investigation of Small when he visited Dakar. A November 1930 report stated, "He only spent one night in Dakar at the home of his compatriot Samuel Darboa . . . residing at 38 bis rue Félix Faure," an address in the Plateau. He was likely observed at the train station when he "boarded the train as far as Kaolack."[66] When he returned to Dakar by boat from Zinguinchor, Senegal, in June 1931, police indicated that a "surveillance on Small and his companion was organized."[67] This surveillance allowed authorities to observe that "numerous natives, whose political sympathies appear to be won over by the communist party, visited him frequently."[68] Small was also observed with the Guinean Fofana Coulibaly going "to the restaurant owned by his compatriot Auguste WILLIAMS on the route de Médina one evening."[69] When the Frenchman Pierre Magard visited Saint-Louis in 1930, his movements were apparently shadowed. Magard's acquaintances, transactions, and meals were all noted with interest by police agents. On July 11, 1930, it was observed that "M. Magard left his hotel at 15:30 and telephoned from the Hotel des Postes to Dakar. He could not be understood in this telephone conversation except for the following words 'Give me only the number.' Next he went to the government office and to the Aéropostale Company. At 18:00 M. Magard drank a bottle of champagne in his room in the company of M. Scala, director of the PTT [post office] and a prostitute."[70]

The link between a surveillance practice such as shadowing and republican political policing is especially relevant to the history of AOF because the contradictions between republican values and authoritarian methods in metropole and colony have been at the heart of historical debates about AOF under the Third Republic. Alice Conklin's pioneering work on AOF's administration demonstrates that republican politics indeed influenced colonial policy in a way that went beyond window dressing.[71] But other works have questioned what appears to be Conklin's guiding presumption that republican values dominated in the metropole while the colonies were ruled mostly by authoritarianism. Mary Dewhurst Lewis has questioned the republican values of the metropole, showing that the rhetoric of universalism that supposedly characterized Third Republic France was actually quite limited, especially when it came to immigrants' rights.[72] Gary Wilder proposes seeing metropole and empire in a combined "imperial nation-state" where elements of both republicanism and authoritarianism existed throughout. He argues that "there were universalist and particularist dimensions of republican and colonial poles of the imperial nation-state, each of which contained emancipatory and oppressive dimensions."[73]

I propose that the use of republican-style policing methods in interwar cities in AOF reveals a new way of approaching the role of republicanism in AOF. Surveillance and investigations of suspects were meant to repress political dissent, curb exposure to radical politics, and forbid distribution of foreign and some metropolitan press. Therefore they provide ample evidence of the repressive side of imperial policy. Yet the surveillance strategies and methods embodying discretion and observation also reflect the republican values that helped shape republican policing dating to the origins of the Third Republic. One possible explanation for the use of republican policing methods is that police inspectors who came from the metropole to work in AOF found them convenient and familiar. However, they also seem to fit particularly well in the time and place where they were used. Discreet policing operated primarily in urban areas where the French were most committed to republican politics, specifically the four communes. Given the rising tensions between the elite African populations of cities and the French administration in the early interwar years, a discreet surveillance that not only embraced republican values but, more important, obscured police activity from the public would have been desirable. Authorities could avoid further antagonizing the African évolué populations while still attempting to monitor and repress their political activity. Consultative councils created under association were supposed to respond to African political demands. But colonial authorities still feared that the most assimilated among Africans would rebel against them by turning to radical politics. Ultimately, although political freedoms for African urbanites appeared to be growing in the interwar era, urban spaces were discreetly becoming environments increasingly subject to colonial repression. If, as Wilder claims, both impulses existed simultaneously in different poles of the empire, here it appears that the contradictions of empire allow for a single institution to contain both values at once. Republican-style surveillance methods therefore became useful tools of repression in interwar French West African cities.

### Limits of Urban Police Surveillance

As mentioned, the profile of a suspect was that of an urbanite, and cities, especially Dakar, became prime sites for surveillance. Dakar's space, organized by grid-like streets and public space such as train stations, cafés, and squares, helped facilitate surveillance techniques such as shadowing. Nevertheless much of the geography of the city still remained outside the purview of investigators. The early administrative rhetoric imagined a ubiquitous and thorough surveillance, but almost all surveillance of political suspects took place in areas designated for European housing, government, and business: the Plateau and Dakar-Propre. The French administration had great political and economic stakes in the European areas, which might account for the concentration of surveillance activities in these parts of the city. However, what is striking is that the Plateau and Dakar-Propre were so privileged that the Medina was almost completely neglected by police operations. In fact the Medina did not even have a commissariat of police as late as 1930.[74] At that time Dakar's police reported, "The creation of a commissariat of Police in the Medina is urgent. For more than a year an inspector was detached there permanently, but this measure is insufficient to respond to the needs of a population growing all the time."[75] Indeed the request for a commissariat likely reflected policing needs that went beyond the desire for political-style surveillance. There are a variety of possible explanations for the focus of surveillance primarily on the Plateau and Dakar-Propre. In colonial understanding and rhetoric of urban areas, the Plateau was always central, while the Medina was marginalized. The Plateau was considered the true city, while the Medina was "semi-urban," rural, or the "African quarter."[76] Local maps up through 1957 did not even include the Medina's streets, which were numbered, not named.[77] Another possible reason for the intense focus of surveillance in the Plateau is that it was the only place possible to use metropolitan techniques. Thomas writes that colonial agents "found it easier to gather useful intelligence about the literate, urban indigenous elites close to the centers of imperial power" than about other people.[78] While it might be tempting to view the European areas as the ultimate sites of colonial power, given the apparent limits on police activity in other parts of Dakar, they could instead be viewed as the only places where authorities *had* the means to deploy power and conduct true surveillance operations. As historians of colonialism have shown, the reach of the colonial state was never all-powerful but highly fragmented.[79] Many territories remained untouched or failed to be transformed by colonialism.[80] Frederick Cooper, drawing a distinction from Michel Foucault's description of "capillary" power, argues that colonial power was "arterial in most colonial contexts—strong near the nodal points of colonial authority, less able to impose its discursive grid elsewhere."[81] The practice of urban surveillance reveals how even in a place like Dakar, a key node of colonial power, colonial authority could still prove to be weak, disjointed, and highly concentrated in a very limited space.

Furthermore suspects could sometimes entirely evade police observation even in the most saturated sites of colonial urban power. In 1936 the Lebanese journalist Mohamed El Houmani stopped briefly at the port of Dakar while in transit to Sierra Leone. Authorities had been advised in advance that he was suspicious and kept watch over El Houmani when he arrived but had no other clue as to what they should expect. Aboard the SS *Canada*, El Houmani "received . . . around 11 a.m. about a hundred Libano-Syrian visitors who arrived at the quay in small groups." One group had traveled to Dakar especially for the occasion. Unfortunately for those who welcomed him, "Houmani did not have a visa for AOF and was not authorized to disembark in Dakar, which disappointed his partisans who had the intention of honoring him with an enthusiastic reception." Although the lack of a visa prevented El Houmani from spending several days in Dakar, something for which he "expressed regret," he was apparently allowed to leave the ship for a short time to attend a lunch in his honor with about twenty people, including several Lebanese merchants of Dakar. To the dismay of authorities, at the lunch "no speech was made. During the meal El Houmani was not very talkative and made no allusion to the goal of his trip to AOF." Authorities remained clueless as to El Houmani's importance. They could only comment, "After his departure, certain of his compatriots let it be known that the French authorities in Lebanon refused El Houmani access to the French colonies of AOF." Two weeks later a telegram from the minister of colonies informed the governor-general that El Houmani "is a former teacher dismissed for particular morals-stop-Became a nationalist and anti-French publicist and made numerous voyages abroad."[82] El Houmani's suspicious activity was played out in the most public of spaces—the port of Dakar—where he received around a hundred visitors, including those who had traveled to the city specifically for the chance to see him. Yet authorities remained ignorant to his goals. El Houmani's case suggests that authorities were not only frequently baffled by space, but that surveillance could be entirely ineffective as a means to collect intelligence even in places where French power was at its height.

### Rural Surveillance

The strategies used in cities could not be employed in rural areas, where colonial administrators were few and far between and distant and discreet observation was usually impossible. A contrast with rural surveillance techniques, which relied on direct inquiries, reinforces how starkly urban and rural surveillance practices diverged.[83] In the countryside the colonial state relied on traditional authorities to conduct political surveillance for them. Brévié wrote detailed instructions in 1934 on how to cultivate rural informants. He argued that once the chiefs realized "the circle commander is, for them, a strong source of counsel and support, as well as a vigilant censor, the chiefs will no longer hesitate to come to him spontaneously and warn him of difficulties or dangers that could occur in the district." Of course authorities counted on chiefs to supply all kinds of information on revenue, agriculture, customs, and more that was useful to the colonial administration, but political intelligence was also of great importance. Brévié also recommended using religious leaders as sources of information. He suggested trying to "play off the natural antagonism between the sedentary marabout . . . and the wandering marabout" in order to prevent the spread of "witchcraft and charlatanism." "Thus," he infers, "we will avoid the danger of leaving unguarded foreign elements tempted to exploit local causes of discontent in order to fanaticize credulous minds and lead them to rise up against our administration."[84] In rural areas political surveillance was to be conducted by the same traditional authorities invested with power to rule under association and possibly by marabouts friendly to the administration.

A 1935 directive from the captain of the gendarmerie to his officers reveals how rural investigations operated. Instead of queries to other authorities and surveillance, as would occur in a city, "the commander of the circle [rural district] brigade would discreetly make an inquiry into the person in question." If the person was "widely or honorably known (such as an adjunct to the mayor, a municipal councilor, French businessman or native notable) there is no reason to bother him." However, if the person was unknown, "the chief of the brigade should summon the person to his office on some sort of pretext of a <u>military order</u> for French citizens and subjects and a <u>control of foreigners</u> for the others."[85] In rural areas surveillance was supposed to be discreet but out of necessity often involved direct intervention with the suspect, unlike urban surveillance.

Another look at the case of Joseph Arthur of Gold Coast illustrates the way rural surveillance depended on traditional sources of knowledge and direct questioning. Arthur, first identified by his unusual appearance, was ultimately considered a suspect because he had links to a "society subsidized by blacks from America and the African Coast" and the masons of Freetown, Sierra Leone.[86] While Senegalese authorities were on the lookout for him, Arthur showed up in Tiendougou, Sudan, in July 1921. When he came to have his passport stamped, a local administrator used the opportunity to question Arthur, who claimed that the purpose of his visit was to learn more about the local trade in fabrics. After this interview the administrator wrote, "No longer being able to monitor his movements and actions, I went to see Father Luezié to ask him if he knew someone who could give me information."[87] Authorities relied on direct questioning of the suspect in this case, then turned to a Catholic priest for more information.

When Small was traveling in the countryside, visiting places such as Kaffrine, Senegal, authorities lost track of him. A report by the political bureau to the governor-general claimed, "It has not been possible to find a trace of him for several days, despite the fact that a special surveillance was prescribed for him in the regions of Diourbel and Kaolack. It is supposed that he returned to Bathurst or maybe Soudan."[88] Vast rural spaces meant discreet and observational surveillance was often impossible.

Furthermore rural surveillance often turned up little of interest. When Louveau, the circle commander of Baol who claimed to have discreetly collected information on Awe, described the investigation, he admitted that in spite of his Awe's interest in politics, "his influence is null and he knows few people. Besides, the spread of advanced doctrines harmful to our colonization leaves little to fear in the region of M'Bake-touba, center of Mouridism, where the great majority of inhabitants are devoted to Serigne Mamadou Moustapha, natural enemy of communism." He ended his letter saying, "Currently in Baol everything is absolutely calm."[89]

Rural political surveillance was not nearly as common as urban surveillance when it came to seeking out radical politics, mostly because radical political doctrines were associated with urban areas. When it did occur, it tended to rely on social networks and direct confrontation, unlike urban surveillance, which relied on bureaucracy and the geography of urban space. Mahmood Mamdani's concept of a "bifurcated" colonial state in which "urban power spoke the language of civil society and civil rights, rural power of community and culture" mirrors the circumstances in AOF, where distant observational surveillance reigned in urban areas and direct confrontation occurred more often in rural spaces. Outside of colonial cities, Mamdani claims, "custom came to be the language of force."[90] As in Mamdani's model, when political surveillance did occur in rural areas of AOF it took the form of direct confrontation, although not necessarily force.

## Organizing Information

Thomas claims that intelligence work in North Africa was "more office work and record keeping than cloak and dagger."[91] Such was the case in AOF as well, as organizing and sharing information seemingly took up more time than actually collecting information. Bureaucratic forms, or *fiches de renseignements*, were devised to guide agents in the collection of information well as to standardize and systemize that knowledge.[92] In 1930 a form was created to be used in files of communist suspects. This "model for individual information" designed "to serve in the political and administrative surveillance of the following [individual]" asked for the name, birth date, parents, nationality, race, home address, and "if possible" fingerprints and a photograph.[93] A second page demanded a detailed list of information on "family situation," "individual resources: revenues, income, pensions, inheritances, property, real estate, personal fortune," and "political opinions: nature, manifestations (words and actions), newspapers, party, sect or association." Under the heading "Morality-Conduct" the document advised that the suspect be investigated in terms of his "integrity, assiduity at work, habits of unsuitable intemperance, (polygamist, gambler, special morals), company, dignity, correctness, character (violent, quarrelsomeness, excessive or taciturn, sneaky) Debts, complaints nature and of whom, motives, acts of integrity and courage, language, etc."[94] Such recommendations reflect the way political investigations also frequently took on broad moral dimensions.

These forms were meant to aid in the organization of information on suspects. However, the long list on this 1930 document designed for investigating communist suspects was clearly an ideal and not a reality. The brief nature of most files suggests agents were unable to follow through on the collection of the extensive moral and political information desired. Countless examples of one-page files or stories of suspects who disappeared without a trace show that the goals of surveillance were rarely met in a basic way, let alone in the intense and detailed way suggested by the form. This is in contrast to what has been described as the meticulous organization of materials by French metropolitan political police. Jean-Marc Berlière writes that the police archives are most interesting for their "fine demonstration of how the police machinery worked. As soon as a name was quoted, a file was opened, in which from then on all the notes concerning it were kept . . . by the means of a simple but methodical accumulation."[95]

In 1930 the government general organized this system by creating lists of suspicious organizations, and "individuals having more or less direct relations with revolutionary organizations" were drawn up.[96] The list of local "organisms" in Dakar included the League for Defense of the Negro Race, the International Workers of Education, the Association of Veteran Senegalese Soldiers, Café Waiters Society, the Senegalese Action Committee, and others, mostly workers' groups.[97] Creating lists of groups and suspects did not seem to influence surveillance practices by, for example, increasing information on suspects. However, organization and filing even of repetitive paperwork seemed to give a sense that knowledge was being ordered.

*Sharing Information*

While collection of information lagged, different offices made concerted efforts to share the information they did manage to obtain. More than any other topic, perhaps, circulars and reports on surveillance discussed the sharing of information. It was believed that the key to manipulating and exploiting information was to disperse it to as many authorized branches of the administration as possible. Voluminous amounts of correspondence copying reports on suspects are a testament to this method. As a consequence authorities seem to spend much more time communicating the same reports repeatedly rather than collecting new information. For example, in 1935 instructions on the "research and surveillance of suspects from a national point of view" focused on improving collaboration between the gendarmerie and the Sûreté Générale and describing who would be approved for access to lists of suspicious persons, while taking the establishment and accuracy of such lists for granted.[98]

Administrative headaches related to the sharing of information dated to at least the First World War. Here is just one example. At the start of the war, the Spaniard Felipe Codina was suspected of having commercial connections with Germans. Codina's businesses in Tivouane and Diourbel in Senegal had consistently employed foreigners, including Swiss and Germans, and was, according to rumor, "completely anti-French." Supposedly Codina himself celebrated German battle victories.[99] Authorities determined that one man could clarify all the issues and debunk gossip surrounding Codina: a businessman named Laigneau in Rufisque.[100] By the time administrators in Rufisque were contacted a month later, it was discovered that Laigneau was being treated in a hospital in Dakar. Although police were ordered to visit Laigneau in the hospital to find out what he knew, it seems they never did. As late as May 1917 Codina requested and received a passport to travel to France, as Dakar had not been informed that "this Spanish subject was suspect" and Codina's passport was not marked "suspect," as was conventional at the time.[101] The minister of colonies reprimanded the Colony of Senegal for its "negligence" and demanded a "report determining responsibility."[102] Codina's case, with its masses of repetitive paperwork and lack of communication between appropriate officials, suggests the failure of the system due to a lack of coordination, especially in the earliest attempts at surveillance across regions and different bureaucracies. In the interwar era, as surveillance expanded significantly and now included French and African suspects, communication between branches increased significantly, but misunderstanding and confusion persisted.

*Interpreting Information*

Information was shared between different branches of the bureaucracy that ruled AOF, but a clear system for dealing with information was never developed. Berlière points out that metropolitan institutions were plagued with the same lack of methodology. Files were put together "without any discrimination as to the quality and truth of the information."[103] This was more or less true in AOF until after the Second World War, when a system based on the alphabet was developed that judged the quality and reliability of the information.[104]

When it came to communism, authorities showed little ability to discern between a legitimate threat and one entirely imagined. The communist paranoia that sometimes gripped French officials prevented them from seeing the complexity of political movements, especially those indigenous to Africa. For example, the bourgeois nationalist newspaper *La Voix du Dahomey* was regularly described as communist.[105] Pierre Johnson, one of the leaders of the bourgeois nationalist movement in Dahomey and codirector of the *Voix*, was said to be "at the head of a group of malcontents trying to push public opinion to obey a watchword that is very certainly communist."[106] Thomas concurs that "time and again, the intelligence community in French North Africa and Syria exaggerated Communist capacity to manipulate indigenous nationalism and popular attachment to Islam."[107] This provides an important caution against taking police reports at face value but also suggests a more complex side to African political movements, which to the French could be distorted and understood as purely communist or anticolonial but which functioned in reality as complex entities with shifting allegiances. The tendency of colonial authorities to oversimplify the political movements in question suggests the role paranoia (particularly over the threat of communism) continued to play, not only in creating the need for surveillance but in the interpretation of its results.

Although in many cases French officials did not seem to spend much time determining whether or not an individual suspect was actually a veritable threat, they were not above determining that someone who appeared suspicious was truly harmless. For example, in 1931 officials reported that a tirailleur named Fassa Marra, stationed in Cahors, France, had "bragged to his parents about joining a communist cell" there. An investigation, however, determined that Marra had dictated his letter to a civilian who must have added the incriminating words. The local police in Cahors reported that Marra was not a member of the local communist cell.[108] The same could be said for the case of Audrée Delmas, a wealthy and eccentric Frenchwoman who traveled in rural parts of AOF. Delmas's voyage was followed with rapt attention by colonial authorities, but the chief of the Sûreté eventually concluded, "Considered at first as a suspect, Mme. Delmas was recognized as manic, neurotic, hysterical."[109] Paranoia and simplification ruled investigations, but police occasionally were clear-eyed enough to exonerate suspects.

## Staffing the Police

Who were the men creating the files on suspicious persons, and what can a look at their lives tell us about how investigations were conducted? Documents in the archive of the government general do not document details of the day-to-day operations of investigations. We can only imagine how cases were assigned, inquiries undertaken, and decisions made to pursue or abandon a lead. Frustratingly, many files lead to a dead end with no resolution to a story about a potentially interesting suspect. Some records are signed simply by the director of the Sûreté, leaving unclear the role of ordinary police and inspectors in investigating cases. The most important omission is the lack of mention of African police agents. We know Africans worked as agents for the Sûreté, especially through mentions of former agents, but it is unclear how they participated in political policing.[110] In North Africa Muslim agents of the Sûreté were hired in increasing numbers in the 1920s.[111] Around 1940 the Sûreté in Dakar began keeping track of African agents alongside European personnel files, but before then it is difficult to come by specific sources on the names or specific roles of individual African police serving in political intelligence roles.[112] Informants are not mentioned by name, of course, and the role of African police agents is rarely stated in the files of the SG and APA.

On the other hand, French police inspectors directed investigations and frequently signed reports that were sent to the governor-general's office.[113] Personnel records provide a look into the lives of the Frenchmen who served as colonial police inspectors.[114] They were employed by the Colonial Ministry but were not technically administrators in the colonial service. Instead they were policemen (*policiers*) who had served in different policing roles in metropolitan France prior to serving in AOF. For example, Abel Tournois had been a special inspector at the Prefect of Police in Paris since 1913. In 1922 he took up duties as inspector of police in AOF until 1937, at which point he was reintegrated into the Paris judicial police.[115] Each police official was deployed (*détaché*) from his home prefect for a specific period, usually three years, and then reintegrated when his time was over. The appointment to AOF could then be renewed for another three years, or he could return to his original post or retire.[116] Many police inspectors renewed their contracts multiple times and often retired after the last reintegration. Charles Moiret retired and soon after died in 1940 at the age of forty-four due to chronic malaria, liver problems, and other ailments he suffered during his overseas service.[117]

No clear specialization emerges among the inspectors in their police service before heading overseas. Dorothé Morère was a *sergent de ville*, while Moiret was an *inspector de police mobile*.[118] The training and experience of the police inspectors was limited to their role as policemen. Unlike administrators who might have studied at the École Coloniale, personnel files of police give no evidence that they trained in areas relevant to understanding the societies they were policing or colonial administration in general. They did, however, sometimes engage in continuing education related to police work. Moiret did a training course in photography at the Judicial Identity Service in Paris.[119] Prior education was also not very extensive, listed as "primary" in almost all cases of police inspectors.[120] Inspector Gaston Braud was an exception; he completed secondary education through the baccalaureate.[121]

The lack of higher education among police is in contrast to a small sample of administrator files. Louis Ponzio, administrator of the District of Dakar and the surrounding area, who was often involved in investigations, spoke Italian, was "very fluent" in the Sudanese language of Bambara, and studied classics at the university level.[122] Maurice Beurnier, chief administrator first class and delegate of the general secretary, spoke some "elementary English" and had a *licence* in letters.[123] Ferdinand Rougier, lieutenant governor of French Sudan, spoke German and had a law degree.[124]

Along with their education, the careers of inspectors before entering the French police services also indicate modest backgrounds. Among prior employments are farmer, cook, and railroad employee.[125] Braud was the exception, as his career before entering the police was as an accountant for the bank Crédit Lyonnais.[126] Not surprisingly, under the category of "fortune" on personnel forms for each policeman the section was either left blank or answered "none."[127] A few other common threads emerge in the backgrounds of the colonial police inspectors. Most of the men studied here were married, although three were divorced (one of whom remarried twice).[128] Military service was also a common denominator; Braud, Moiret, Morère, Tournois, and two others, Ernest Larra and Paul Verges, had several years of military service, most of them in the First World War.[129] Their average age of entry into the colonial service was the late twenties.

Although their political affiliation might seem relevant, in the personnel files their "politics" were described only in the following terms: "the family does not concern itself with politics" or "no politics" or, in Morère's case, "correct."[130] Inspector Gaston Lenaers, who was born in Belgium but naturalized French, was the only policeman whose politics were specified; he was a "Republican."[131] It is difficult to discern the significance of this information (or lack of information). Because the men were hired for their skills as police officers, including their ability to investigate crime, it seems likely that politics played only a small role in the decision to transfer them to the colonies.

Other evidence indicates that police self-selected for deployment to West Africa for personal, not political reasons. In 1922 Moiret and Morère both personally solicited employment as police inspectors in AOF.[132] Braud, after having served for eight years in Dakar, chose to resume his post in Paris, only to request a return to AOF in 1940.[133] While some police seemed to believe that a stint in the colonies would have positive career consequences, in reality it seemed to have had the opposite effect. Once returned to their original unit of administrative service, some police, as in Braud's case, found that the promotions they earned while serving in the colonies were not recognized. Braud lamented these circumstances in 1940, writing to colonial authorities in Vichy, "My period of deployment having finished in October 1939 I was re-integrated in my original administrative unit [Prefecture of Police] on Nov. 27, 1939, with my previous title of Special Inspector without them taking into account the authoritative functions I regularly exercised for more than eight years because it was for 'another community and in another hierarchy' according to the terms of the response

I was given."[134] Instead of providing advancement, colonial service could impede a police career.

A closer look into the lives of two police inspectors can provide deeper insight into their motives to serve in the colonies. Jean Pourroy, born in 1868 in Orcières in the Hautes-Alpes, first joined the police service in AOF in 1905, serving as a *commissaire de police* in Conakry.[135] Pourroy's brother was employed on the railroad in Conakry, but if his presence partially drew Pourroy to West Africa, it was certainly not the only attraction.[136] Far from Paris, money problems followed Pourroy. In 1908 the Société Crédit de la Place Clichy wrote the Colonial Ministry claiming that Pourroy owed them 236 francs.[137] Pourroy denied the debt or any knowledge of the *société*.[138] Also in 1908 a Monsieur L. Gandillon claimed a debt from Pourroy and asked the ministry for his address.[139] In 1914 Pourroy's ex-wife, Jeanne Vareschal, wrote to the minister of colonies asking for help in collecting money he owed her for support of their daughter. Pourroy claimed the girl was old enough to live without her father's support. After the daughter's fiancé left for the front, Vareschal described how she "begged M. Pourroy through several urgent letters to please continue the payments until the end of the war."[140] No follow-up to her request appears in the file. It appears likely that Pourroy sought escape from financial and personal problems in a colonial career.

Gaston Braud, born in 1902 in Vesoul in the Haute Saône, had worked at the Prefecture of Police in Paris since 1927 before engaging in the colonial police in Dakar in 1930.[141] Divorced, with no children, Braud had twenty months of experience in North Africa after the completion of his military service and was looking to expand his experience in the French Empire when he requested to be deployed to French West Africa in 1928.[142] His apparently eager request not fulfilled, he asked in 1930 about employment in Indochina before being accepted by police in AOF.[143] His requests for an overseas position suggest a possible desire for adventure. Like Pourroy, however, Braud may have been trying to escape his divorce. In 1931 the minister of the interior wrote to the minister of colonies, "Mme Braud claims to be searching for her husband" and requested his address in AOF.[144] Braud responded in March with a post office box to be communicated to his former spouse.[145]

Braud attempted to use the colonies as an escape route one last time. As mentioned earlier, in 1940 he had recently retired but requested to resume his post in Dakar. He claimed that he had lost some of the authority he enjoyed in AOF, which was certainly true. Lest we assume this humiliation combined with colonial nostalgia might have been the main motivation for his desire to return, Lefevbre, director of the Sûreté Générale in Dakar, described his surprise that Braud wanted to return. He wrote of how Braud in his last year in Dakar suffered from a "physical state that was highly influenced by his low morale." Lefevbre concluded, "Certainly since his return to France many events have occurred which could modify his point of view."[146] Lefevbre inferred that escape from the German occupation was Braud's true motive.

AOF's metropolitan policemen seemed to have few overt political motives in their work pursuing suspects. Because the governors-general, lieutenant governors, and other high-level administrators shaped surveillance and investigative policies, they probably played little role in the decisions described in chapter 1. However, their backgrounds suggest that AOF's police, like other Europeans who chose colonial careers, were mostly motivated by personal concerns, including career advancement, escaping the past, and possibly finding adventure.[147] In fact, as we shall see when we look at French suspects under surveillance in chapter 4, some of the police had motives very similar to those suspects who also sought escape and reinvention in the colonies.

## Summary

Scholars have described colonial governments as beset by competing interests, failing strategy, and lack of coordination. Such states were never as strong and interventionist as colonial authorities would have liked to believe.[148] Historians of colonial policing in places such as India and North Africa have also demonstrated the failure of webs of surveillance to operate as planned.[149] The Muslim Affairs Bureau in AOF, despite having ambitious goals of collecting information and maintaining surveillance over Islam, never achieved its goals due to inefficiency and lack of funds and personnel.[150] In AOF investigative practices suggest that the vigilant surveillance envisioned by officials did not function as effectively as they hoped. Authorities tried to develop a methodology for use of tools like the port, postal control, and informants to identify suspects and collect information. But officials also relied on a variety of ad hoc, random, and opportunistic techniques in an attempt to stifle dissident politics. Authorities wrote up numerous forms, reports, lists, and correspondence regarding surveillance. When lacking quality sources, they would occasionally turn to rumor, gossip, and opinion to gather information. Far from being a methodically and rationally designed undertaking, colonial agents and employees resorted to trusting intuition, as they judged a person suspicious based on stereotypes of behavior or appearance as often as on an individual's actions. Most often AOF's police and political affairs bureau relied on information obtained from other authorities—the Paris Ministry, British African colonial authorities, and other French colonial officials. Sometimes suspects existed to authorities only as a paper trail, when government officials from other parts of the French Empire warned AOF of the arrival of suspicious persons, many of whom never appeared. Colonial police trailed suspects around AOF's urban spaces, observed them in public places, monitored mail, searched homes, and engaged agents and denunciators to collect information.

By modeling colonial police methods on a metropolitan policing strategy that advocated discretion, authorities demonstrated the influence of French metropolitan rhetoric and tactics. Discreet surveillance shows how easily colonial officials combined republican and repressive impulses as they tried to maintain a veneer of republicanism while also trying to repress dissent.

But these same surveillance methods, particularly shadowing suspects around the city, only worked in the geography of a built environment that was conducive to French methods. The legibility of a grid-like space and public areas such as train stations, cafés, and squares in the European neighborhoods of Dakar meant police could operate clandestinely while collecting information. However, focusing efforts on particular locations, like the Plateau and Dakar-Propre, while virtually abandoning surveillance efforts in places like the Medina shows how essential particular kinds of urban space and understandings of the urban environment were to shaping surveillance practices. As with the fictional case of *Pépé le Moko* some urban spaces remained outside the official grasp of the colonial state. Of course sometimes investigations were successful and authorities were able to break up political networks, a result that will become clear in chapter 5. However, urban spaces that seemed baffling or unknowable could foil surveillance plans, as could people who evaded police or kept hidden whatever information authorities sought. Simultaneously rural areas, although also considered potentially dangerous sites of radical ideas, adopted very different surveillance practices. Using direct, interventionist practices in rural areas that relied on a few administrators and traditional authorities coincided with established patterns of rule in such places. Furthermore rural spaces made discreet surveillance virtually impossible.

French colonial police from the metropole brought their methods with them, but probably not their political motives. Their history and the way they carried out investigations and surveillance show the messy everyday deployment of colonial power. *Policiers* were conducting surveillance, but their personal stories suggest that, like suspects, they too sometimes hoped to find escape and adventure. It is to the stories of the suspects that I now turn.

# 3

# Enemies, Charlatans, and Propagandists

*Foreigners under Surveillance in AOF*

In 1927 the Austrian Joseph Riesinger traveled through Niger and French Sudan while on an expedition from Oran, Algeria, to Lagos, Nigeria. Riesinger's mission, he claimed, was to win a prize from the International Club in New York, which was offering $100,000 to the first person to visit twenty-seven nations and cover eighty thousand kilometers in six months "without resources."[1] The adventurer was accompanied by his pregnant wife, and together the pair left a rather poor impression on French authorities, who noted that the couple absconded with a goat in Algeria and a rented canoe in Niger.[2] Upon arriving in Gao, Sudan, just prior to the birth of their child, French administrators urged the Riesingers to take a boat to Bamako and then a train to Dakar. Riesinger ignored this advice, and his wife gave birth in Gao, where she and the baby were attended to by an African doctor of the Assistance Medical Indigène and local women provided a layette for the child. The lieutenant governor of Sudan said with disdain that the family, who were also fed and lodged by the "natives" of Gao, showed a "frustrating lack of consideration."[3] In spite of Mrs. Riesinger's reportedly ill health the family continued on toward Tillabéry, Niger—almost in the opposite direction from Dakar—by canoe and then to nearby Niamey in Niger. When, in 1930, the Riesingers were set to arrive once again in AOF, Riesinger was labeled "suspect" and the lieutenant governor of Niger lamented his return, wondering "what new misadventures Riesinger will face" on this next voyage.[4] When French authorities ratcheted up surveillance and security efforts following World War I due to fears of radical propaganda, they likely did not imagine suspects such as Joseph Riesinger, who was considered anti-French but was not suspected of links to any political organization. While some foreign suspects were indeed political radicals, many others were merely shady characters, swindlers, or bothersome wandering voyagers. The wide-ranging profile of the foreign suspect that emerged in the interwar years suggests that much more than a fear of political radicalism was at stake in the identification and surveillance of foreign suspects.

In interwar France a preoccupation with the mystery and danger of foreigners can be found on both an official level and within popular culture. Parisian authorities were virtually obsessed with the fear that foreigners would disrupt domestic politics in the 1920s.[5] French intelligence reports are filled with "endless chatter on spies," including stories of Italian, Russian, and German agents involved in intrigues around the world.[6] The spy novel took over from the genre of war memoir to spin tales of heroism and action and naturally plunged readers into a milieu of foreign intrigue.[7] Popular films helped foster images of foreigners in colonial Africa as dangerous or shady interlopers. The 1934 film *Le Grand Jeu* featured Pierre, a Frenchman, as the main character who, while serving in the Foreign Legion in Morocco, befriends a Russian with a "murky past."[8] In the 1935 British film *Sanders of the River*, set in colonial Nigeria, the villains are portrayed as Italian merchants who intervene in an otherwise positive relationship between the British and "native" rulers.[9] Whether in metropole or colony, shady foreign interlopers seemed to trouble both real and fictional French.

Concern and fascination with foreigners were phenomena not unique to AOF but part of broader patterns of interwar concerns about international intrigue. Yet, as this chapter shows, foreigners also played a particular and critical role in the development of AOF's culture of suspicion. In the interwar era foreigners made up the largest group, about one third of all suspects under surveillance. But their numbers in the colony, while growing in the 1920s, certainly did not constitute such a significant percentage of the population.[10] Foreigners emerged as the prime suspects partly because radical and dangerous politics were so often linked to foreign places: the Soviet Union, the United States, and Vietnam. But the intense and unwavering interest in foreign suspects on the part of French authorities in AOF suggests that French police understood foreignness as a critical element of suspicious behavior that threatened to destabilize colonial society as well as politics. While in theory the surveillance and control of foreigners was about monitoring a *legal* category of people for *political* activities, in reality foreign suspects in AOF were also scrutinized for a wide variety of socially disruptive behavior. All foreigners, as outsiders, were initially somewhat suspicious to French authorities, but when they blurred clear categories or engaged in political or social behavior outside the bounds of expectations they were considered particularly suspect and worthy of deeper scrutiny. Such people confounded authorities by crossing borders, engaging in morally or politically suspicious behavior, and generally calling into question the organizing principles of colonial society. The culture of suspicion that gripped colonial authorities pushed them to seek suspects who might be radical propagandists but also to investigate misfits, charlatans, and troublemakers. Surveillance of suspicious foreigners, I argue, was partly an attempt to assert authority over a group of people who appeared to threaten the social organization of colonialism.

## Defining Foreignness

Like other colonial categories, the legal definition of foreignness had to be created. That definition is worth considering in some depth because notions of foreignness conjured powerful meanings to authorities in AOF. In France the idea of foreigners came into being only during the French Revolution, when the concept of citizenship emerged, defined by nationality.[11] Gerard Noiriel points out that the notion of immigration in France did not even exist until 1870.[12] What is striking is the near lack of distinction between foreigners and immigrants in records on surveillance in AOF's archives. Although permanent residents had specific legal obligations that visitors did not, from the perspective of the French police long-term residents were always foreigners. Foreignness, especially among the largest population of foreigners—the Lebanese and Syrians—always evoked anxiety and suspicion even as some foreigners became a familiar group in the colonies.

Under French law, the Federation of French West Africa was considered primary over the individual colonies within the group. Therefore Mauritanians in Senegal were not considered foreign. However, Gambians, whose entire territory was located within Senegal's border but who lived under British sovereignty, were foreigners. Moroccans, who come from a French protectorate, were legally considered foreigners although they were *protégés français*, whereas Syrians and Lebanese in the interwar era were nationals of a French mandate.[13] Individuals from other French colonies were not considered French nationals and yet could not legally be treated as foreigners. But in terms of being cast as suspicious, these colonial subjects were typically treated as foreign. As I mentioned in the introduction, this chapter shares the spirit of the French administration's understanding of foreigners to mean all individuals not hailing from metropolitan France or a colony of the Federation of French West Africa.

### Regulation of Foreigners

In the early twentieth century the mayor of Dakar lamented the increasing immigration of European, Asian, and African foreigners to the colony and his inability to regulate their entry or "to assure an effective daily surveillance of all those who live there, especially in Dakar where they are as diverse as they are numerous and of all origins."[14] A series of laws was enacted to attempt to regulate and limit their entry into the colony. A 1906 law required all foreigners in the colony of Senegal to register with the mayor within one month of their arrival.[15] In Dahomey the same law was adopted in 1907 in order to limit "foreign natives" from Togo and Nigeria who were not "generally from the most healthy [*saine*] part of the population."[16] This group of unwanted foreigners was described as including "more or less authentic businessmen, bandits fleeing justice in their countries, [and] Muslim agitators expelled from foreign colonies."[17] In 1911 officials sought to use regulations to control the arrival of

Syrians who were described by the governor-general as a risk to business, the economy, and even "public health and order." The law also required each foreigner to provide "documents proving his identity and morality," a medical certificate, and a deposit for a return ticket. The explicit goal of the law was to avoid the entry of "individuals who, having abandoned their home country, find themselves homeless, having no means of existence and exiling themselves to adventure."[18]

The interwar era brought a host of new protocols governing the entry of foreigners. As of 1921 every foreigner arriving in Senegal had to declare his or her nationality, identity, and place of lodging for the visit. Foreigners planning an extended stay were required to apply for an identity card that doubled as a residency permit.[19] Obtaining the so-called foreigner's identity card was no easy task. The administrator charged with distributing cards was to "do a serious investigation of the morality, the usual behavior, and the means of existence of the foreigner."[20] However, an initial rejection for an identity card simply resulted in a "mitigated expulsion," which meant that on a return visit the person could reapply.[21] In 1922 the law was extended to include "natives indigenous to foreign African colonies," suggesting Europeans and Lebanese and Syrians were initially the main targets of the law.[22]

Although in theory these laws added a new layer of regulation to the entry and activity of foreigners in AOF, Andrew Arsan describes the new laws as "skeletal controls" and points out that they failed to prevent the entry of criminals and did not allow any possibility of preselection of migrants through a visa system.[23] The foreigners' card was meant to be the main level of regulation of foreigners, but it functioned only after the foreigner had arrived in the colony. AOF's administrators tried repeatedly to manage the entry of foreigners but were continually thwarted in their efforts by the Colonial Ministry as "hundreds of thousands of migrants . . . disembarked in AOF each year."[24] The ministry insisted on protection for Lebanese and Syrians because of a long-standing special relationship between France and the Eastern Mediterranean shaped by Orientalist romantic notions and a religious connection to the Catholic Maronite community.[25] As a result colonial administrators in Dakar were unable to effectively regulate immigration to the colony, especially in the interwar era.

Clandestine immigration was possible as well. In many cases authorities failed to identify every individual who disembarked from an arriving ship, and if a foreigner arrived by land there would likely be no inspection at all. Foreigners who never registered their names nor applied for the foreigner's card could slip away undetected. According to one Senegalese official, in 1923 foreigners only had to declare their identity, apply for the identity card, and pay a deposit on their return trip once they had moved into a residence. The administrator complained that requiring foreigners to present themselves to pay the return trip deposit, something they often neglected to do, led to the significant cost of paying for the return trip of indigent foreigners.[26] Arsan suggests that the foreigner's deposit was not even meant to be a deterrent to the arrival of foreigners, but was more likely an "essentially budgetary measure."[27]

The powerlessness of AOF's government general to regulate the arrival of foreigners stands in contrast to global trends toward the increase in the regulation of migration. During World War I in France, fear of foreigners and wartime emergency meant greater scrutiny and regulation of their entry and stay in France, a task accomplished especially through the use of identity cards.[28] Throughout the 1920s and 1930s, fueled by fears of espionage and rising xenophobia, French nationality in the metropole continued to be defined, crystallized, and restricted by amendments on the regulation of foreigners and the foreigner's card.[29] Paris's police in particular undertook a massive effort to identify, monitor, and control foreigners through identity cards, but also raids, expulsions, and by sending out "inspectors throughout the city to check the legal status of every immigrant they could find."[30] France's strict policies toward immigrants were mirrored by the closing of borders to newcomers in other European countries and the United States. These countries established wartime measures to restrict entry of foreigners and then made the regulations permanent as an era of isolationism descended on Western states.[31]

One tool AOF authorities could use against "undesirable" foreigners was the threat of deportation—"expulsion" from the colony. Expulsions originated with an 1849 metropolitan law giving the Ministry of the Interior the right "to enjoin any foreigner traveling or residing in France, to leave French territory immediately and to have him taken to the border."[32] In 1874 the metropolitan law was officially adopted by the colonies.[33] The governor-general of AOF was required to have a legal basis for an expulsion, such as criminal activity or direct evidence of revolutionary agitation. In the interwar era expulsion became an expedient solution for removing foreign suspects from AOF, although it was most commonly used to expel criminals.

In a study of expulsions in interwar Marseilles, Lewis argues that race, class, and "undesirable" qualities like vagabondage were important factors.[34] In AOF suspicion of immoral activity was similarly an incentive to instigate the expulsion of a person who might conveniently have a criminal record. In 1918 Inspector Paoli conducted an investigation into the past of a Syrian, Antoine Henaine, and placed him under surveillance in Dakar. Henaine had served time in prison in Saint-Louis for fraud in 1914. Paoli's distaste for Henaine's lifestyle was evident. He wrote that Henaine had "always led a life of adventure," leaving Lebanon at the age of nineteen to work in Argentina and Paris before coming to Senegal. However, Paoli also indicted Henaine for "spending most of his time gambling in a café in the Place Protêt."[35] Judging the man "undesirable," Paoli had him expelled, technically on the basis of his criminal background, not his predilection for gambling.

In attempting to regulate the status of French colonial subjects from other colonies, authorities sometimes struggled with what they saw as a frustrating legal situation. These colonial migrants could avoid some of the legal restrictions placed on other foreigners. For example, Phan Cao Luo, a supposed "communist agitator" from Annam in Indochina, was suspected of planning a trip to AOF with his family. The director of APA noted with regret, "PHAN-CAO-LUO, being originally from a French colony, cannot be subjected to the obligation of a resident's permit [identity card] according to the decree of August 1, 1921 applicable only to foreigners. Our only action with regard to him, short of the refusal of the identity card which would be equivalent to immediate expulsion, can only be a tight surveillance, and if the case arises, placing him under arrest on the charge of speech, conversation, writing, or activities susceptible to damage our authority and trouble the public order."[36] French colonial subjects from other colonies enjoyed special privileges under the law but were always viewed as foreigners in terms of attracting suspicion. Catherine Coquery-Vidrovitch has argued that even as authorities grappled with the many laws surrounding the legal and civil rights of the originaires, a distinction was consistently made between citizenship and nationality. Even originaires, who had some of the most extensive rights in the colonies, were deprived of French nationality.[37] In a similar fashion, colonial subjects from outside AOF presented a conundrum. While they were not protected by the privileges of French citizenship, they could neither be forced to comply with demands placed on foreigners nor be punished under the *indigénat* or the customary laws of AOF. They were considered both "natives" and foreign yet were not subject to the laws that governed either natives or foreigners in AOF.

In addition to being subject to different laws, foreigners in French West Africa were also at the mercy of stereotypes inflected with racial overtones and exotic difference. Foreign French colonial subjects were more likely to be thought of and treated as "Asians" or "Africans" than as French colonial subjects once they entered AOF. In the early 1930s, for example, as communist activity grew in China and Indochina, officials in Paris and AOF began to perceive of Asians as threatening for their potential involvement in communist propaganda. As a consequence, in 1931 the director of APA in Dakar drew up a list of Chinese and Indochinese living in Dakar—just fourteen people—and forwarded it to Paris.[38] "Asian communism" and its connotations superseded the status of subjects of the French Empire.

### World War I, Enemy Spies, Nationality

The First World War ushered in a host of new fears about foreigners generally in AOF, inaugurating an era of close scrutiny of individual suspects. These fears, and subsequent surveillance and investigative measures, were directed primarily at enemy nationals: Germans, Austro-Hungarians, Turks, and any foreigner whose national origins appeared questionable. Foreign "enemies" would become nearly synonymous with "suspects" during the war as national origin defined entire groups of people as dangerous or suspect. Certain individuals then warranted greater scrutiny as suspects.

Enemy nationals in AOF were supposed to be interned, and other foreigners were identified by a color-coded system of identification cards (red for enemies, white for allies, gray for neutral, etc.).[39] These new technologies of surveillance facilitated the control of foreigners during wartime. However, one of the consequences of such a system was that it required officials to clearly identify and categorize people according to nationality. At a time when national origin was crucial to defining loyalty to France, French authorities directed anxiety toward people whose national origins were ambiguous, such as Alsatians. In 1915 a man named Anzemberger, interned as an enemy national in Bouaflé, Ivory Coast, claimed he was a French Alsatian but had lost his identity papers in a fire. The prefect of Meurthe and Moselle in France vetted his family connections in Alsace, including cousins at the front and an uncle who "is absolutely trustworthy. He is Alsatian, still French by choice."[40] As a result Anzemberger was released and permitted to join the Foreign Legion.

World War I also introduced the era of individual investigations of suspects by Inspector Paoli. All of the World War I suspects were foreigners. Foreigners of uncertain nationality were investigated and subsequently categorized as neutral, enemy, or, worst of all, spies. The case of Jaime Laredo Keslacy illustrates not only how narrowly national identity was imagined but also how unclear origins could generate enormous apprehension in wartime. Keslacy first came to the attention of the Civil Affairs Service in 1917, when he applied for a passport to travel to Sierra Leone and possibly Tenerife in the Canary Islands, apparently for business purposes.[41] He claimed to be Moroccan, born in 1880 in Casablanca, married, and working as a merchant in Dakar. Suspicion arose because as Keslacy was using his mother's Spanish-sounding name, Laredo, he appeared to be attempting to hide Austro-Hungarian origins that authorities associated with the name Keslacy. Furthermore he was "apparently not of the Moroccan race."[42] The delegate of Senegal raised the possibility that Keslacy might be a spy, writing, "The individual Keslacy, known as Laredo, is strongly suspected of certain grave intelligence work in favor of our enemies, but all of our research and surveillance have produced no results." A suspicion of hidden identity quickly morphed into an accusation of espionage. The delegate suggested the purpose of Keslacy's travel was not business but to conduct reconnaissance along the coast from Dakar to Port Etienne. He offered as further evidence of spy connections the fact that Keslacy "has relations with the crews of Spanish schooners coming from the Canaries to Dakar, on board of which individuals who appeared suspicious or did not have papers have been discovered."[43]

The commissaire in Dakar uncovered several facts about Keslacy. He had a "simple-minded" business associate named David Hatchvell, and Keslacy and his wife were of the "Israelite religion." Keslacy had one criminal infraction, an arrest for stealing from his own store. When the commissaire asked Keslacy about his national origins he said he never knew his father and did not know where he was born. As for the issue of his own nationality, Keslacy assumed he was Moroccan.[44] Keslacy himself seemed baffled by the mystery surrounding his national origins.

Local Moroccans told the commissaire that neither "Keslacy" nor "Laredo" was a Moroccan name.[45] Algeria confirmed that his parents were Jewish Moroccans and that after his father's death his mother remarried Laredo, a man of French nationality, living in Algeria. The governor-general of Algeria included a letter of recommendation from Keslacy's stepfather's brother-in-law in Oran.[46] Rabat responded that "Keslacy" was in fact a Jewish Moroccan name and that "Keslacy was born in Casablanca and is definitely of Moroccan nationality without any other origin."[47] Within two months of receiving this information, Civil Affairs cleared Keslacy of suspicion and granted him a passport for the Canary Islands.[48] Keslacy's story shows that in this period suspicion was provoked primarily when national origin was in doubt, but also that colonial authorities would go to great lengths to clarify this all-important category.

Concerns related to anti-French sentiment also characterized suspicion during the First World War. Karl Pedersen, a twenty-two-year-old Danish sailor, was working aboard a Norwegian ship passing through Dakar in late August 1917. The day his ship came into port, Pedersen was found drinking at the Café Cosmopolite with an African who worked as a guide for foreigners when, speaking "in German and English, and showing a provocative attitude toward the public, [he] said things such as 'Germany is my homeland' and struck up the song 'Deutschland über alles.'" The other customers present were "scandalized" and called the commissaire, who sent over the director of the Navigation Police. Pedersen, "over-excited and advancing toward the officer, insulted him and greeted him with these words: 'Do you think I am a German or is it you who is a German?'" Pedersen was arrested immediately and charged with "remarks of a nature to favor the enemy and to exercise an undesirable influence over the minds of the population."[49] Pedersen's defense was his "state of intoxication," and he claimed not to remember the incident. In November 1917 he was sentenced to a year in prison for his crimes. He made several requests for clemency, writing to the Danish ambassador in Paris and to the president of the French Republic.[50] A prosecutor reviewing his case denied the request, commenting that Pedersen was known to have traveled in Germany and that he had switched ships several times during the course of the war. His report also noted that a preliminary hearing had inquired whether "this individual, in any case undesirable, might have, under cover of his profession as a sailor, been a spy." The prosecutor admitted that this investigation had initially amounted to nothing but that later the Sûreté informed him that the name Pedersen had appeared on a list of potential spies, although whether or not it was the same man was unclear. Pedersen was forced to fulfill his sentence, and the prosecutor closed the case saying that even when he was sober he "must not be very Francophile, in that with the first whiffs of alcohol the German national anthem comes out of his mouth."[51]

During World War I, in a prelude of what would emerge much more definitively in the interwar era, authorities connected perceptions of immorality with political suspicion. Carmen Junkera, a Spanish woman, briefly passed through Dakar in 1915, working as a singer and dancer in a theater troupe. Within a month of having left the colony Junkera returned, now claiming to be a saleswoman, offering such wares as lace and women's toiletries.[52] As a transient and entertainer, she surely raised eyebrows. However, matters turned serious when in 1916 authorities suggested she could be involved in espionage given her proclivity for spending time with military men.[53] Although no evidence of espionage was discovered, various other details about her behavior were recorded in an investigation.

Junkera had befriended a European woman she met in a restaurant, inviting her new friend to the cinema. When the woman's husband, who had been out of town during their outing, returned and found out that his wife had been keeping company with a "woman of questionable virtue," he confronted Junkera and slapped her.[54] This brief violent incident later led to a fist fight between Junkera's new love interest, a wealthy French corporal, and her aggressor.

The accusation of espionage against Junkera, as in the case with Pedersen, was probably without merit. Investigators hardly pursued the allegations against her, instead repeatedly criticizing Junkera for her morality, once referring to her as a "vulgar prostitute."[55] Each time she left the colony, Commissaire Abbal thought he had "gotten rid of her," but he noted with chagrin that she returned several times. His main grievance was that "she seeks above all relations with military men" and that her morals are "excessively light and easy."[56] Finding no evidence of espionage, and with no criminal record to warrant expulsion, Abbal's only recourse was to keep Junkera under surveillance and wait until her passport expired in 1917, at which point he "invited her to return to her country of origin."[57]

Opinions on the morals and lifestyle of the foreigner Francis Blais also dominated characterizations of him as a suspect. Blais's file stands out not only because of his colorful life but also because he is one of the few World War I suspects who first came to the attention of authorities for an issue irrelevant to loyalty or national identity. Blais, a Luxembourgian, belongs to a cast of characters who would become more numerous in the 1920s and 1930s: expatriates who left criminal or moral indiscretions behind in Europe, took on aliases, and populated the cafés and dance halls of Dakar, much to the dismay of local authorities. In 1917 Blais's file was opened by the police because he made a suspiciously large bank deposit. He explained that the money came from his sister in Paris. The Sûreté Générale began looking into Blais's life and, not being able to establish the veracity of his claim, discovered a wealth of other information. Blais was already known to authorities as the owner of the Café des Alliés (a "café of ill repute") and the Parisiana Concert (a "house of debauchery") in Dakar.[58] The investigation revealed that his birth name was François Regis. While living in Paris, Blais was said to live off the prostitution of his wife and sister "and maybe even his own, his reputation for homosexuality having been established."[59] Blais's wife Françoise, known as Gaby, was an opera singer and had been living separately from her husband for several years in Spain and then Morocco. She planned to return to Dakar in 1917. Police deemed the extensive travels of Gaby and Francis Blais in Spain suspect.[60]

Research into Blais's past in Paris revealed a criminal record, including a 1907 condemnation for assault under the name Gaston Devilliers. Later that same year he spent fifteen days in prison for stealing. He was expelled from France but returned to enlist in the Foreign Legion. In 1907 his wife was arrested for prostitution.[61] His sister, Josepha, was also known to be a Parisian prostitute working under the pseudonym "Marcelle la blonde."[62] The French military got involved when Colonel Bernard asked for the expulsion of Blais from AOF, writing, "Although no proof of espionage has been raised against him, I believe that his presence in Dakar—where he manages a café-concert, frequented almost exclusively by non-commissioned officers . . . sailors and rather dubious individuals— presents a real danger."[63] Other than the "suspicious" travel to Spain with his wife, this was the first suggestion that Blais might have been involved in espionage. It seems clear that Blais presented no real security danger but that his lifestyle and his past made him an "undesirable" figure in Dakar. In November 1917 he was reported to be on his way back to Dakar with a performer named Mlle. Simonet, alias "Simone Hott," and his illegitimate son. When he arrived in Dakar he was greeted with an expulsion notice, and he returned once again to France.[64]

### Interwar Political Suspicion

In the interwar era suspicion became linked more directly to radical political activity and less to national origin. Police investigations expanded to include French and AOF-born suspects as well as foreigners. The archival organization itself recognized this change when, in 1917, the title of files for "surveillance of foreigners" was changed to "surveillance of foreigners and suspects."[65] In the interwar period the focus moved from wartime concerns to fears about communist propaganda and other potentially anticolonial political activity. Thus institutions created for the surveillance of foreigners were now mobilized for surveillance of not just foreigners but "foreigners and suspects."

This expansion of surveillance meant that foreigners were not the only suspects, but they were still prime suspects, and their stories continued to dominate suspects' files. These foreigners accused of anti-French activity were diverse; they came from Morocco, the Dutch East Indies, Martinique, and Argentina as well as Europe, including Austria, Scotland, Sweden, Denmark, Switzerland, Italy, and Germany. Suspected communist activity does not appear in the suspicious persons' files until 1925, but it is a common, although often loose, thread linking files on foreigners, Africans, and French suspects in the late 1920s and 1930s. Pan-Africanism and pan-Islamism, although appearing less frequently in colonial rhetoric, also emerged to define radical foreign political ideas that could take hold in AOF. Officially authorities most feared that the "native" African population would be susceptible to radical ideas spread by foreigners. Closely mirroring many of the fears expressed by the Colonial Ministry and governor-general described in chapter 1, interwar investigations of radical political activity reveal a colonial state gripped by fears of the influence of foreigners.

One of the earliest threats to emerge on the colonial radar was pan-Africanism. The Pan-African Congress was held in Paris during the peace talks of 1919, and several pro-black political organizations were created in metropolitan France in the early 1920s.[66] The possibility that pan-African organizations could infiltrate AOF's population suddenly seemed a valid and pressing threat. When Governor-General Merlin received word that an agent of Marcus Garvey's Black Star Line shipping company in Dakar was operating as a propaganda agent for the UNIA, he alerted the Colonial Ministry. Merlin judiciously considered the possibility that "this could be the work of an isolated individual looking to take advantage of this propaganda enterprise with the complicity of a few crooks." However, he also wrote, "the hypothesis of his affiliation with a revolutionary association is equally plausible."[67] In fact he would soon discover that there were legitimate Garveyists living in Dakar.

The government general was aware that the UNIA maintained its headquarters in New York with branches in the Belgian Congo, Liberia, and Lagos, Nigeria.[68] As explained in chapter 2, in 1922 new information emerged about a Garveyist organization in Dakar led by two Sierra Leoneans named Wilfrid Wilson and John Farmer.[69] Wilson's and Farmer's homes were searched and their friends interrogated by police. Although the men themselves denied involvement with the UNIA, documents, including propaganda tracts, meeting minutes, and a notebook detailing lists of members and dues, were discovered at their homes and offered evidence to the contrary.[70] Their possessions included flyers from New York announcing speeches by Garvey urging people to contribute five dollars to the "African Redemption Fund" as well as five copies of the *Negro World*, the UNIA's newspaper.[71] They also possessed publications from the UNIA translated into French, apparently for distribution in Dakar.[72]

Wilson had been living in Rufisque since 1916, where he was employed by various businesses, but had made frequent trips home to Sierra Leone. Farmer had arrived in Dakar in 1920 to work for the Elder Dempster shipping company until he was fired in March 1921. Other members of the local group included Francis Brown, Alpha Renner, Isaac Doherty, Amadou Jawabrah, Thomas Duck, David Brown, Clarence Randall, and Winston Williams, all from Sierra Leone save Duck, who was born in French Guinea to Sierra Leonean parents.[73]

In May 1922 John Kamara, a Sierra Leonean who was involved in the UNIA in the United States, visited the group in Rufisque. Farmer, Wilson, and others held a dinner in his honor prior to his departure. At the close of the dinner, Farmer made a speech which was later copied down by the UNIA members and translated by the French police. Farmer pointed out that Kamara was "commissioned to this West Coast of ours to spread the Garveism [*sic*] propaganda and affect organizations wherever possible." Farmer expounded on the goals of their group and the organization as a whole:

It's a marvelous realization that after hundreds of years of oppression, after such mighty sweeps by military nations into the oppressed territories of our beloved <u>Africa</u>, after great upheaval in <u>Europe</u>, <u>America</u>,

Asia and the Islands of the seas, the Black Race can rise to universal efforts to reclaim Africa—efforts which have seized the new Negro with unfailing grasp; an enthusiasm which has alarmed our oppressors, a goal that has now inspired us to the formation of a branch of the UNIA ... the only Negro organization that plans for the entire redemption of Africa, the complete evacuation of alien rulers from African territories.

It also exalted the international and pan-African aims of the UNIA: "Far on the other side of the Atlantic; far in foreign lands, in North, East West & South of America and in the West Indies, whither our ancestors were transported into slavery, the universal note has been raised: Africa has heard the call to unity. The whole Negro race is rising to a man and woe to them that shall sleep too long. We here can sleep no more. Ethiopia is stretching forth her hand and we believe in 'One God, One Aim, One Destiny.'"[74] The speech offered further evidence that the Garveyist group was indeed advocating the pan-Africanist goals of the UNIA.

The UNIA branches in Dakar and Rufisque appear to have been relatively isolated. According to police, Wilson and Farmer were "instigators of the movement" and had founded branches in Dakar, Rufisque, Thiès, Meché, and Bambey.[75] However, the lieutenant governor pointed out that the thirty-one names and addresses of people in Thiès, Meché, and Bambey were probably not all members of the UNIA; they were more likely signatories to a letter Farmer composed to Winston Churchill, secretary of state for the colonies, about the abuses of Gibbs, an employee at the British consulate.[76] Furthermore, although identified as suspects when their names were found in Farmer's notebook, searches of their homes turned up "no result."[77] One investigator even admitted, "It seemed to me that the members who joined the different sections were victims of swindlers because those that I questioned appeared rather as naïve people who believed they were joining a mutual aid society and not a political organization."[78] The lieutenant governor noted that the records of members and dues kept by the association were "completely anodyne and could lead one to believe it was a mutual aid society," exactly the impression that Wilson, Farmer, and others tried to give when they were questioned.[79] In any case, even if all the names listed in the documents were active and informed members of the UNIA, they were limited to "English subjects, originating in West African colonies," with one exception, a Dahoméen named Da Costa. The case was closed when the key members of the group, Wilson, Farmer, Doherty, Brown, and Renner, were expelled from AOF in July and August 1922, a simple solution given they were all foreigners.

What long-term impact did the Garvey group have on Senegal? In spite of the limited nature of the group, it appears that some interest in Garveyism continued despite the group's disbanding. Several months after the affair seemed to be closed, more people emerged with connections to the UNIA. Winston Williams, a Sierra Leonean who had been listed among the original adherents to the UNIA in Dakar, was questioned when a packet containing the *Negro World* arrived addressed to him. Williams shrewdly refused to accept his package, but Armand Angrand, also received, and accepted, a similar package. When questioned both men denied that they had requested the package from Garvey containing flyers, although Williams admitted he was socially acquainted with the Angrand family.

Angrand denied initiating communication with Garvey. He claimed instead that a friend of his named Horton in New York might have given the UNIA his name, knowing that Angrand spoke English.[80] Angrand's denials were put into doubt when a search of his home turned up more propaganda tracts and copies of the *Negro World*. More important, it was learned that Angrand, several of his family members, and others from the Dakar-Gorée area were creating a group called Comité de l'action Sénégalaise. Angrand claimed that the goal of the group was to collect subscriptions in order to publish a journal that would "defend the collective interests of the black race in Senegal."[81] The president of this newly formed committee, Massyla Diop, claimed when he was questioned by police that the group planned to publish a journal with the aid of Jean D'Oxoby, a French newspaper publisher.[82] The delegate of the government of Senegal in Dakar told the governor-general he believed the group to be "unauthorized and pursuing a political goal."[83] Although the UNIA in Dakar made few inroads into the Senegalese population, the links to Williams, Angrand, and the Comité suggest that the Garvey group had a continuing influence on Senegal.

The affair of the Garvey group made another impression on Dakar society. Although both the UNIA and the police hoped to keep the arrests hidden from the public, the newspaper *Eveil Colonial* (Colonial Awakening) described the matter at length and, according to the lieutenant governor of Senegal, "gave an exaggerated importance to the affair." The newspaper also failed to inform the public that foreigners, not Senegalese, founded the Garvey group.[84] Later, in August 1922 the pro-administration newspaper *L'AOF* reported that "a person from an honorably known family was apprehended at a street corner by two police inspectors: it was precisely at the moment when the mailman was handing him a letter."[85] The article explained that the envelope contained a copy of the *Negro World* and that the police had been tipped off by the postal service. Although not named, this recipient was clearly Angrand. A notable figure in Dakar, his arrest and its publicity as well as that of the expulsion of the Sierra Leoneans caused a stir. These newspaper reports had two notable results: the public gained knowledge of the UNIA and also became aware of the repressive actions of the police. *L'AOF* reported that the police had established a list of people involved in the Garvey group and "from now on a tight surveillance will be exercised around suspicious persons."[86]

Given the relatively few individuals actively involved in the Garvey group in Dakar, the danger of the group seems exaggerated by authorities.[87] However, the flurry of activity surrounding the disbanding of the group is suggestive of how the culture of suspicion functioned. Given that the administration was already convinced that an international threat lurked on the horizon, the first evidence of such activity in Dakar created considerable anxiety and inspired authorities to rapidly repress the group and institute broader surveillance.

If pan-Africanist ideas and groups achieved little, foreign African communists inspired even greater fear in authorities. The communist suspect who undoubtedly drew the most attention in French West Africa was a foreigner: the Gambian labor leader and journalist Edward Francis Small.[88] Unlike the embryonic Garveyist group of the early 1920s that failed to catch on in Dakar, Small's mission would have greater success in attracting interest among Senegalese.

Small was born in Bathurst, Gambia, in 1890, educated in Sierra Leone, and worked for the British administration at various administrative jobs, and as a teacher, a missionary, and for the French firm Maurel et Prom.[89] His activist career began in 1918, when he joined the National Congress for British West Africa, which advocated for greater influence of educated blacks in British African colonies.[90] Small founded a newspaper, the *Gambia Outlook*, and the Bathurst Trade Union. Through the union he led a strike in 1929 and succeeded in gaining concessions from British authorities.[91]

Syndicalism was illegal in AOF, but Small was more than just a union leader. His many visits to Europe to attend communist functions earned him the suspicion of French authorities. His communist connections were verified when customs officials in Bathurst searched his luggage and found two cases filled with brochures of Bolshevist propaganda.[92] He was indeed in touch with communists in London, Marseilles, and Berlin.[93] Small was equally involved with pan-Africanist movements. His close collaboration with George Padmore (at the time known by his birth name, Ivan Malcolm Nurse), the Trinidadian pan-Africanist, included working together on the *Gambia Outlook*.[94] Padmore contributed articles to the *Outlook* praising the Bolsheviks following a stay in the Soviet Union. Padmore also hoped to come to Dakar, but the French consulate in Bathurst, noting a Soviet stamp on his passport, refused him a visa.[95]

Small passed through Dakar many times on trips to Europe in 1930. In 1931 he came for a longer stay, arriving in Dakar with his secretary Boubakar Secka and making acquaintances among the locals and other immigrants from British African colonies. The French consulate in Bathurst warned the governor-general a couple of times that Nurse also had plans to come to AOF, but if Nurse showed up, the police had no record of it.[96] That summer Small conducted a political tour in the interior of Senegal, during which he encouraged rail workers to demand a salary equal to Europeans' and provoked some of them to threaten a work stoppage.[97] In Kaolack "many natives" had frequent and long talks with him. In Kaffrine he "tried to make connections with unhappy natives and with former native functionaries who had reason to complain about the authorities."[98] Small's influence appears to have reached widely into Dakar society too, as evidenced by the fact that a group of Europeans were overheard talking about his plan to "put up posters on the walls of Dakar for the occasion" of the "red day" of August 1 (referenced in chapter 2).[99] The fear of actual manifestations in the streets of Dakar meant the police chose to move decisively against Small. It was assumed that he had received direct orders at the Third International, which he had attended in Hamburg. Shortly thereafter it was discovered that Small and Secka had not applied for the requisite foreigners' card. Small protested, claiming the consulate in Bathurst never informed him of the law, but he was expelled in September 1931.[100]

Small has the most comprehensive file of all foreign suspects, and as a black African communist he clearly caused more anxiety than any supposed European Soviet agent ever did. French authorities were not wrong in estimating Small's power. Unlike other suspects, he was legitimately spreading radical ideas. The weightiness of his file is due not only to the suspicion surrounding him but probably also to his relative success in agitating in Senegal. He made connections both within and outside of Dakar, discussed unionization with workers, and also connected with local people involved in the international groups based in Paris and New York. His relations included French communists, and he was known among Europeans as well as Africans in Dakar. Small's story serves as a reminder that there were indeed communist political agents targeting AOF who were under surveillance by French authorities. Ideas about suspicious foreigners as communist agents, although driven by paranoia, were not entirely fantasy. And sometimes the government general could deploy an effective surveillance. In the case of foreigners such suspects could also usually be expelled easily.

Although African communists were perhaps most feared by colonial authorities due to their ability to easily connect with other Africans, suspected foreign communists of a variety of nationalities attracted the attention of police. The Lebanese Antoine Joseph Kredi, for example, was signaled as an agent of communist propaganda.[101] Moustapha Raden, subject of the Dutch East Indies, had recently embarked on a world tour, and authorities feared he might show up in AOF. The minister of colonies wrote that although Raden dressed as a "scout," in reality he "does not belong to any scouting organization, but appears to have close relations with Moscow and revolutionary milieux."[102] Or consider the Martinican Camille Saint-Jacques, a suspected communist who was supposedly planning to go on a tour of French West and Central Africa but never arrived.[103] These men were among the fifteen foreigners officials suspected of being communists between 1925 and 1937. About a dozen more foreigners originally from Gabon, Gold Coast, Lebanon, Poland, Tripoli, and Switzerland were described as being "anti-French" or "anti-European" propagandists.[104]

Other than Small, it is difficult to know if these suspects were legitimately anticolonial activists or falsely accused. Still, it is clear that the expanding culture of suspicion meant some foreigners were targeted who were quite clearly innocent of involvement in radical politics. This seems to be the case for the Vietnamese N'guyen Van Phu. Although N'guyen tried to help police by sharing information with them, he was placed under surveillance for nearly two years as a communist suspect. The suspicion cast on him stemmed from fears about Vietnamese communism, a topic discussed at length in the ministry's monthly propaganda reports. Authorities would have been aware that in 1924 Governor-General Merlin, who had recently taken up the position in Indochina after five years of service in AOF, was the target of an assassination attempt. They also knew that Ho Chi Minh founded the Vietnamese Communist Party in 1925 and that in February 1930 a nationalist group led the Yen Bay revolt, wherein Vietnamese soldiers serving in the French Army rebelled and killed two French officers.[105] These events undoubtedly stoked fears that such an event could occur in AOF and cast a shadow of suspicion on Indochinese in the colonies.

N'guyen, also known as Pierre Phu, was employed as head cook by the Hotel Métropole, a popular spot for foreign visitors to Dakar. Born in Hadong Province, he had lived in Marseilles for some time before he came to Dakar in 1928.[106] N'guyen was in the unusual position of being considered a suspect after having offered aid to the police. In August 1930 he received an unusual package in the mail from Marseilles: fifteen copies of the revolutionary communist journal *Lao Nong* (The Worker and the Peasant), written in Quoc ngu, the Latin script for Vietnamese.[107] The adjunct director of police wrote, "Nguyen, who claims not to know the name of the sender, spontaneously presented the journals to a police inspector saying that he did not read this type of journal." Less than a month later N'guyen received copies of a similar journal, *Vô San* (Between Us), and surrendered those as well. In spite of his loyal actions and the general opinion that "the few Indochinese living in Dakar are of a perfect correctness toward the administration and until now none of them seems to be interested in politics," N'guyen was placed under police surveillance.[108]

N'guyen's status as a French colonial subject was advantageous to authorities, who immediately communicated with their counterparts in Hanoi and Marseilles for background information. It soon became apparent that N'guyen had sent a suspiciously large amount of money to his brother in Hanoi and to some other Vietnamese in Marseilles. Nevertheless authorities in Dakar found nothing of interest in his present actions, writing, "The surveillance . . . and investigations have not uncovered any criminal or even suspicious act on the part of this individual." The police calculated that N'guyen's job at the hotel paid him 2,000 francs per month in addition to room, board, and laundry. The fact that he had sent a total of 80,000 francs to different members of his family did, perhaps, appear suspicious. N'guyen claimed that he had saved the money over the years working as a cook on different ships. He explained that he preferred to keep cash and not put it in banks and that he saved as much as he could. An administrator backed up this notion: "Nguyen Van Phu leads an extremely calm and regimented life. He never goes out and never spends any money; it is highly probable that the total of his earnings was saved."[109] More than a year after N'guyen received the first packet of journals, Inspector Gaston Braud reported to the director of the Sûreté, "Although at one time the actions of this individual seemed suspect, he appears to keep clear of all political agitation and has proven his loyalty toward us." Braud commented that N'guyen appeared to be a "serious and peaceful worker. Nevertheless he is held in observation."[110] In another light N'guyen Van Phu might have been understood as an informant, but fears of foreign, especially Indochinese, communism made authorities see him as a suspected propagandist rather than a valuable ally.

French authorities also feared the possibility of an anti-French Muslim conspiracy orchestrated by foreigners. Such fear was a key aspect of French Islamic policy dating from before World War I. Christopher Harrison writes, "Just as in metropolitan France there were numerous stories of Jesuit plots against the whole fabric of society, so too in West Africa in the decade before the First World War there were constant fears of a vast Islamic conspiracy orchestrated by malicious foreign agents."[111] Because of the French stereotype of "Black Islam" as strongly influenced by paganism, Moorish Islam was believed to be closer to Muslim orthodoxy.[112] "Black Islam" was therefore considered susceptible to outside influence and to have the potential to be shaped by nationalist and anticolonial movements.[113]

The Bureau of Muslim Affairs was charged with surveillance of Islam, especially of the marabouts, but the Sûreté Générale was occasionally involved in issues related to "Muslim propaganda," likely because of the perceived political implications of international Muslim movements in AOF. Youcef Ben Ali Haouda El Ghadamsi, from Tripoli, living in the Circle of Mao in Niger, had mailed "anti-European proclamations" to another Tripolitan in Niger in 1921.[114] An investigation located several other copies of the tract in Tripoli. It was further revealed that El Ghadamsi and other transmitters of the article were in close communication with powerful marabouts in Nigeria and Tchad.[115] The tract in question appears to be entirely religious in nature, warning of the consequences of the increasing sinfulness among Muslims. French authorities, however, interpreted the tract as "anti-European," suggesting, for example that "soon the sun will rise in the West" could mean "a general worldwide movement is in preparation."[116] All those foreigners who received the tract were expelled from AOF.

In 1929 the lieutenant governor of Niger reported that tirailleurs stationed in France and Tunisia were sending home "Arab books" and, as they were illiterate, reselling them to marabouts. In 1931 the minister of war described a similar scenario whereby African soldiers were buying Arabic books in the metropole and sending them back to Africa. The real threat, according to the minister, was that "among the books of a harmless or religious nature, there could be slipped in some tracts of Egyptian or oriental origin presenting a harmful and anti-French character."[117] The lieutenant governor of Sudan confirmed that Arabic books were being sent by soldiers stationed in North Africa and Syria, but thanks to a "rigorous surveillance by customs" he could assure the governor-general that the packages are "almost all made up of Corans and there had not been noted any suspicious or forbidden publication in mailings of this type."[118]

Moulay Mohammed Ben Othman El Alani, a Moroccan traveling merchant and member of the Tijaniyya brotherhood, came to Dakar once a year and was vaguely suspected of religious and political influence. His file mentions that he was "proud, talkative and insolent" and suggests that, like so many other itinerant travelers, the police were not exactly sure what to suspect of his travel and connections.[119] Such foreign Muslim travelers appear to be suspect for being precisely that. Surveillance apparently revealed no potentially threatening activity, but foreign Islam was enough of a threat to warrant investigation.

Paranoia about the influence of foreign Muslims seemed to be taking hold based on alarmism from the Colonial Ministry about international conspiracies. Another possible reason for the rejection of foreign Muslim proselytizers was a desire to maintain a positive relationship with Muslim leaders in AOF. Going back to the 1890s French administrators were careful to avoid antagonizing Muslim chiefs.[120] The administration also carefully maintained relationships with Muslim marabouts, even among those under surveillance by the Muslim Affairs Bureau. French administrators relied on leaders, especially Bamba, to maintain the labor force for the all-important peanut trade.[121] In addition to spreading an outside political doctrine, fears about foreign Muslim teachers might well have threatened this delicate balance.

If pan-Islam was frequently declared an official threat to the French Empire, it was not the only religion investigated by authorities for spreading propaganda. In 1935 the lieutenant governor of Dahomey wrote of Jehovah's Witnesses, "It is difficult to accept that the Jehovah's Witnesses are seeking only to proselytize."[122] Alfred Benjamin Weeks, a medical doctor, and William Roland Brown, a Jamaican of the Watch Tower Bible group, were evangelizing in Dahomey in 1935. Although all of the religious tracts that passed through Dahomey seemed to be entirely focused on religious themes, French authorities read between the lines to discover a "judeo-communist thesis" from references to "farmers and little workers" and to the "Kingdom of God," in which "there will be neither rich nor poor and everyone will work for the community."[123]

Christian evangelical preachers were also sometimes scrutinized as religious propagandists. The Scottish pastor Dugald Campbell was traveling through AOF selling religious materials to Africans. Although he appeared to be operating as a missionary, he had apparently had some adventures in Africa in the past as a salesman and an amateur ethnographer. An investigation revealed that an English subject named Campbell was in attendance at the Fourth Congress of the Communist Party in France. It was later decided that the communist in question was not this Campbell but another. One official described Campbell as "a poor devil, lacking resources and materials to get any information from the natives or to exercise any political action."[124] A Swiss Christian evangelist named d'Allmen also came under investigation when the director of APA used a January 1932 law that prohibited individuals from entering certain parts of AOF to forbid him from going to Mauritania. The APA bureau cited "the danger that evangelization could present . . . in certain Islamized regions of Mauritania."[125] Protecting d'Allmen was probably an important goal of this prohibition. Still, Christianity and Islam, promoted by certain suspicious foreigners, were understood as subversive.

### Shady Characters, Charlatans, and Swindlers

In the early 1920s prime suspects of suspicious behavior were black radicals, foreign communists, and sometimes pan-Islamists who hoped to spread their new ideas among the African population of AOF. Authorities sought and found suspects who fit this profile. What is surprising is how common it was for authorities to also identify suspects who did not closely fit the expectations outlined in the planning of security initiatives. In fact in many investigations of suspects, communism or anticolonialism was merely implied. Perhaps most surprising is the way suspicion expanded in the interwar era to include shady and enigmatic behavior. Among foreigners, authorities ultimately identified an unexpected cast of dubious international characters. These individuals were mostly Europeans who were affluent and well-traveled. Not necessarily involved in political radicalism but part of a vague and mysterious world of international intrigue, they too were identified as suspects.[126]

Eminently suspicious but more self-interested than political, best describes the story of Capt. Louis Gardiner, alias Col. Louis de la Garde, a British naval captain who had had an illustrious and notorious career as an international spy.[127] Gardiner had an international reputation for involvement in violent conflicts and political revolution. French authorities compiled information on his involvement in the Russo-Japanese War, the revolution in Chile, the Anglo-Boer War, and the unearthing of a sunken ship.[128] In the 1920s he was written up in the press for dealing arms to Abd el-Krim's revolutionary movement against the French and Spanish in the Moroccan Rif.[129] One newspaper described him as an "intimate advisor" to Abd el-Krim.[130] In 1925 the metropolitan press said the arrival of Gardiner in Tangiers had "raised a certain curiosity." Gardiner claimed to be there for commercial interests and that he had nothing to do with negotiations related to the "Rifian peace."[131]

When Captain Gardiner showed up on his yacht the *Silver Crescent* along the coast of West Africa in 1926, there was no doubt he was a suspicious character. He was traveling with his wife, a captain named MacLeane, and a fifteen-year old boy who was possibly his son. Gardiner claimed his trip was motivated by trade and that he planned to write an article for London's *Daily Mail* about his yachting expedition that would take him all the way to Australia.[132] Police who observed Gardiner reported that he was a man in his forties or fifties with a pince-nez and an "American" moustache who spoke Arabic, Spanish, and a little French.

Official visits aboard the *Silver Crescent* at different ports of call, including Port-Etienne in Mauritania and Conakry, found Gardiner eager to prove he had indeed taken up a career as a salesman, peddling watches, phonographs, razors, jewelry, and more.[133] Reportedly Gardiner had told people in Tangiers that he was willing to sell "anything from a razor to a railroad."[134] He was also eager to express his warm feelings for France. The circle commander of Port-Etienne wrote, "[He] does not forget to say several times that he represents French products [wine and champagne] although none of these products is present . . . also shows that he personally uses certain French merchandise (canned foods, rum, etc.) adds that he once lived in Paris near the Opera." Gardiner was not shy about telling tales of his past adventures, discussing his service in the Great War and his exploits as a spy in Germany, and claiming he had once owned a hotel in the United States and had worked as a doctor in hospitals in Tangiers.[135]

His entourage was equally subject to scrutiny. It was noted that Gardiner's supposed son did "not enjoy all of his mental faculties." As for Mrs. Gardiner, there was some doubt as to whether or not she was actually married to the captain. She appeared to be about twenty-five and was "susceptible to share confidences," revealing that she had lived among "the Arabs" for three months and showed photos of herself dressed "en arabe" as evidence.[136]

A circle commander in Mauritania cast doubt on Gardiner's claims to commercial enterprise, writing that while docked in Port-Etienne he "comes on land as little as possible." A merchant who was shown Gardiner's wares observed his lack of desire to sell, commenting, "A commercial traveler offers his services better than that."[137] Nevertheless authorities observed nothing else suspicious about Gardiner and his fellow passengers when they disembarked at Port-Etienne or Conakry. As is the case in many suspect files, if Gardiner did have ulterior motives they were never discovered. His direct past involvement in the Rif suggests there was legitimate concern that he might have engaged in revolutionary activity in AOF. However, unlike people suspected of pan-Africanism or communism, it was primarily Gardiner's mysterious and intriguing past that preoccupied French authorities.

A similar tale involving a hint of potentially radical politics, travel, and mystery emerges in the case of Rosie Graefenberg. A German woman in her early thirties, Graefenberg arrived in Dakar in 1929 aboard the *Brazza*. Her travels took her through Bamako, Ouagadougou, and parts of Ivory Coast, although a planned trip to Timbuktu was canceled. Graefenberg claimed she wanted to write a newspaper article for a Berlin paper about her travels and impressions of Africa. Prior to her arrival, however, the governor-general had been warned by the Colonial Ministry to "exercise a discreet surveillance on her actions."[138] She was described as a suspected communist agitator who wrote for a "known" communist paper called the *Voss Gazette* that, in reality, was not communist at all.[139]

Graefenberg was said to show considerable interest in the foreign population of AOF, especially the Russians. She also met with Blaise Diagne, the Senegalese deputy, with whom she discussed the recently published book *The Black Shame*, about the conduct of black soldiers in the French Army occupying the Rhine. One report proposed that Graefenberg was "a liaison agent for a German intelligence service." At one point she discussed her travels to Russia and "the cordial relationship she maintains with Stalin and the Soviet authorities." She was also generally positive in her assessment of French West Africa and expressed a desire to see a "Franco-German rapprochement."[140] Although she at first appeared to be a communist, her actions ultimately did not warrant any "unpleasant remarks."[141]

Graefenberg's adventures did not end with her AOF voyage. She went on to emigrate to the United States in the 1930s and marry a man named Waldeck. A few years later Rosie Waldeck published her autobiography, *Prelude to the Past*, which describes her 1929 voyage to AOF. Her description of her trip confirms that she was traveling for adventure and journalism. The chapter "Poker in French West Africa" focuses primarily on her travels in rural areas, or "the bush." Graefenberg's narrative of her travels is filled with stereotypes about naked "natives," oversexualized African women, and a "native King." According to Graefenberg, the Lobi people are "flawlessly handsome." She describes drinking lemonade made of green lemons and adopting a baby lioness.[142] A mixture of exotic escapade and mild criticism of the French, her memoir shows her to be a typical European adventurer, not a spy or a communist.

French authorities were not paranoid to investigate Graefenberg and Gardiner. He had connections with the revolution in Morocco and she sought out political leaders such as Diagne. Nevertheless Graefenberg's file also includes a significant amount of personal detail. For example, she was "of distinguished appearance, short of stature and physically agreeable."[143] Her maiden name, Goldschmidt, "seems to indicate that she is of Jewish origin."[144] Her file also includes a newspaper article describing her involvement in political scandals in Paris and her marriage to a man thirty-two years her senior, who was also the editor of her newspaper.[145] French authorities were far more interested in closely monitoring Graefenberg's speech for ulterior political motives for her trip than these personal facts, but these secondary details hint at the unusual position she occupied as a European woman traveling alone in AOF, which undoubtedly served to increase suspicion. Jennifer Boittin's analysis of Graefenberg's file, newspaper articles, and memoir leads her to conclude as well that Graefenberg was wealthy and eccentric, but certainly not a spy. Above all, Graefenberg was a German traveling at a moment when French authorities were actively seeking out suspicious characters and, Boittin argues, the "shadow of war" continued to draw special attention to Germans.[146] Graefenberg was a wealthy and internationally savvy woman traveling in the interior of West Africa with a vague connection to politics. Like Gardiner, she was suspicious not only because of her tenuous connection to radical politics but because she embodied a deeper mystery in which her presence and actions seemed inscrutable and uncontrollable.

Long part of romantic colonial lore and fiction, the European who fled his past and sought a new, hopefully lucrative life in an overseas imperial territory emerges as a reality among the suspicious persons of AOF. Because the culture of suspicion cast a wide net, European swindlers and charlatans inadvertently became enmeshed in a system created to seek out threats to imperial security. As we shall see in chapter 4, such stories were also common among French suspects, but because foreigners involved in shady activity could be expelled rather easily from the colonies, they were more vulnerable to police investigations.

One such individual was Bentinck Doyle, a British subject who had spent a few years in Dakar working as an independent merchant. Around 1918 Doyle was named an auxiliary agent at the British consulate, but his drinking problem led to his termination in 1920, something probably rather easily accomplished as he had never been officially accredited in the role by officials in London.[147] Shortly after losing his job, Doyle was arrested for embezzling from a British shipping company. Around the same time, it emerged that Doyle had also been illegally operating as the vice consul of Spain in Dakar since 1915, communicating directly with the consul general in Paris. Doyle had taken over the position when the vice consul of Spain left for Honduras and handed over his job to Doyle, who was clearly not accredited for this position either. Doyle claimed that Governor-General Angoulvant had known about his "irregular" position.[148] When he was convicted of embezzlement Doyle asked his wife to pass on his duties to a Mr. Yerby, vice consul of the United States. His prison sentence commuted, Doyle stayed on in Dakar selling milk, poultry, and eggs, but as this business was failing he became involved in what a police inspector referred to as "real swindling," landing him in jail and resulting in his expulsion in 1923.[149] Doyle's case reveals the casualness with which members of the European community sometimes wielded their authority, as one European felt qualified to slip his consular post to another. It also reveals how police investigations were not only concerned with political agitators but also targeted frauds and charlatans. Demonstrating some of the confusion that must have characterized the classification of Doyle's case, his file is found under the heading "Suspected Propagandists."

In a similar instance of fraud, the Swiss Jules Ernest created false credentials for himself as a chemist and claimed to be planning a glass factory along the Route de Rufisque in Dakar. A request to the French ambassador of Switzerland revealed that Ernest was not who he seemed. The ambassador wrote that Ernest had not even studied chemistry, let alone earned the doctorate he claimed to hold in the subject. His assertion that he worked in a Zurich chemistry lab was debunked as well when it was revealed that the company did not have a branch in Zurich. His only employment in Zurich seems to have been as a secretary at the municipal police.[150] Evidence suggests that Ernest ruffled feathers among the European business community, which was probably in reality what led to the investigation. It seems unlikely that he was ever considered a political threat. His case shows again that police authorities were sometimes more concerned with social misfits and troublemakers than with political propagandists.

Along with fraud, swindling, and generally crooked behavior, foreigners who did not seem to be overtly political but who engaged in unusual, that is, suspicious travel often came under the purview of the French colonial police. Travel to Moscow was, of course, duly noted, but depending on the circumstance, a trip to the United States could be as well if connections to the UNIA were made, or to Morocco, where the Rif uprising took place in the 1920s. In 1934, for example, a man from Gold Coast named Joseph Amon Kouame and his wife, "alias Robert and Rose," turned up in Ivory Coast. The Kouames had been students at the Stalin School in Moscow, and the governor-general warned his lieutenant governors several times of their potential arrival in AOF.[151]

But extensive travel alone, even to places that were not linked to radical politics, could be enough to arouse suspicion. Let us return now to the Austrian "Globe trotter" Joseph Riesinger, who planned a return trip to AOF in 1930 while traveling from Algeria to the Belgian Congo as his final destination.[152] Riesinger's travel companions included his wife, their two-year-old son, her mother, and the wife's brother. According to the Austrian legation, Riesinger's main goal of the voyage was to acquire a plantation in the Congo. His trip also included ethnographic studies of the Touregs and zoological studies of serpents in the Sahara.[153] The Riesingers seemed to crave adventure perhaps more than these practical plans. At one point during their trip, despite pleas from the authorities, Riesinger insisted on taking a road called "the path of death"—a thirty-five-day journey through the desert with minimal provisions, where his wife, two months pregnant, almost died from fatigue.[154] When the family arrived at the border of Niger in August, they were sent back to Algeria because they could not provide the deposit guaranteeing a return trip. In fact Riesinger did not have even have enough money to complete their proposed trip to the Belgian Congo.[155] This was the end of the Riesingers' travels in Africa, as a lack of funds forced them to abandon their dream of owning a plantation.

The Ministry of Colonies described Riesinger's attitude as "clearly anti-French."[156] But politics, as with the supposed spies Gardiner and Graefenberg, were a mere footnote in his story. The Riesingers were instead suspicious because of their disruptive behavior in Gao, their unwillingness to comply with orders, and their desire to travel through rural spaces usually off-limits to European tourists. They behaved in ways that were confusing, frustrating, and utterly abnormal for Europeans. They were threatening for their willingness to reject conventions, defy colonial authority, operate outside of administrative control, and disrupt the general order of things. Suspicious behavior, by 1930, now included unpredictable and antisocial behavior.

What accounts for the expansion of suspicion to include shady, crooked, immoral and generally enigmatic behavior? On the one hand, authorities now had experienced inspectors to investigate and monitor such people, who were perhaps mildly threatening and above all irritating. This fact surely provides part of the explanation. But long-term frustrations over the inability of the administration to regulate the entry of foreigners and the rapid transformations brought about by the end of the war, including the arrival of more European women in the colony, increased opportunities for évolués, and a more cosmopolitan set of foreign visitors, may have prompted authorities to use surveillance to limit foreign influence, whether it be politics, religion, or pure rebelliousness. While some suspects might disrupt the colonial order with political agitation, others disrupted the economic and social order with fraud or by defying race and gender norms. Just as foreigners of unclear nationality generated anxiety during the First World War, highly mobile and inscrutable characters represented a risk to a colonial society that appeared unsettled. If categories such as French, African, citizen, and subject helped authorities make sense of the world around them, the foreign suspect as propagandist, agitator, and shady character disrupted this sense of order and called for surveillance and investigation.

## Summary

In the early twentieth century concerns about entire foreign nationalities, especially Lebanese and Syrians, came to the fore in AOF, and institutions and bureaucracies were established to manage their entry, although without great success. Adapting laws from the metropole, authorities in AOF could specifically target and sometimes expel foreigners from the colonies whose presence was deemed "undesirable." During the First World War suspects were described as enemy nationals, potential spies, and disloyal foreigners who came under more intensive and individual investigation. Authorities showed an increasing desire to know and control the actions of particular individuals who combined an alleged political threat with their status as foreigners, a transition that would continue into the interwar era.

In some ways the principal targets of the culture of suspicion that emerged at the end of the First World War were foreigners. The profile of suspicious political behavior established by the Colonial Ministry, governor-general, and other administrators described in chapter 1 emphasized communism, pan-Africanism, and pan-Islamism as particularly threatening ideologies. All of these potentially dangerous factions were connected to foreign elements. In seeking out suspects, colonial authorities identified foreigners who were engaged or potentially engaged in all of these ideologies.

But the interwar surveillance of foreign suspects ultimately turned out to involve more than the repression of radical propaganda. While globally migration was being regulated and borders were closing due to the disruptions of the First World War, AOF's port was growing, and administrators found themselves helpless to control the entry of foreigners who, drawn by business, exoticism, or adventure, kept arriving, especially in Dakar. Lack of control over migration, alarmist rhetoric from the ministry about radical propaganda, and an empire generally in crisis seem to have led the administration to expand the use of surveillance. Colonial authorities discovered that the people who caused them the greatest consternation and problems were not necessarily political radicals but shady characters, potential frauds, itinerant travelers, or even crooks. Interwar foreign suspects introduced an unknowable and uncontrollable element into a colonial society that was already unstable and vulnerable. Foreign suspects were mobile, dynamic, inscrutable, and elusive—all things to be feared by authorities who had a looser grip than ever on colonial power. The predominance of foreigners in police files suggests that foreignness was an essential characteristic of the colonial suspect, a category constructed by authorities grappling with a society that was increasingly dynamic, mobile, and international.

Foreign suspects too participated in the culture of suspicion, although unintentionally. As Dakar become a key node of the French imperial network, it attracted foreigners from around the globe seeking the emerging possibilities of this increasingly cosmopolitan locale. The transient nature and diversity of the foreigners who arrived and departed from AOF confirm the arrival of new ideas and exchange with various parts of the globe. The stories of foreign suspects are glimpses into a small and often marginal segment of society. But their stories help reveal the dynamic and diverse society that emerged under colonialism in AOF. Captured by the records of the French police, they were powerful players in public scenes. Foreigners arriving in AOF for short stays often engaged the population, shared ideas, spread propaganda, and created networks—marking the colonial culture that was emerging through the interaction of French, Africans, and foreigners. The history of the role of foreigners in this story suggests that the political and cultural scene of AOF was one of domination, struggle, and accommodation between French and Africans and one that was also greatly influenced by international politics, ideas, and culture.

# 4

# "Powerless with Regard to Our Nationals"

*Policing Frenchness and Redefining the Civilizing Mission in AOF*

In 1925, while traveling in French Equatorial Africa, the writer André Gide came upon a shocking site: "After an hour's march through a monotonous steppe . . . we met a great quantity of porters; after them came a file of fifteen women and two men, tied round their necks by one and the same cord and escorted by guards, carrying five-thonged whips. One of the women had a baby at her breast. They were the 'hostages' who had been taken from the village at Dangolo, where the guards had been to requisition forty porters by order of the administration."[1] This and other examples of abuse by French colonial administrators fill Gide's account of his travels, which primarily took him through the other French African federation, but also to the fringes of AOF. However, Gide's account was more than just a critique of the colonial regime. His anger toward the administration was tempered by his interest in the exotic appeal of Africa and the hope that colonial policies could be improved to benefit Africans. Gide occupied an ambivalent stance toward the French state, as both critic of and adviser to colonial rule.

Gide was never described as a suspicious person in AOF, but many of his fellow French men and women were identified as suspects for behaving in ways that seemed to oppose the state or threaten the reputation of the French in Africa. Like Gide, they occupied an awkward position. They were at times in conflict with the French state but also took advantage of their status as French and appeared confident in their superiority as Europeans to decide what was best for Africa. This chapter explores the lives of French men and women investigated by police as suspects to consider how they were viewed by the administration and how these often marginal members of the French community understood their own place in French colonial Africa.

The culture of suspicion stoked fears among French authorities that African elites might turn against them, especially under the influence of nefarious foreigners with radical political agendas. Authorities quickly discovered that metropolitan French were just as likely as foreigners to propagate communism or other radical political ideologies. Investigations of suspicious French men and especially women can also be understood as part of a larger project of policing French identity and behavior. Like many white European foreigners, French suspects were viewed as dangerous because they were mobile and uncontrollable. But French suspects in particular earned extra scrutiny when they behaved in ways that suggested they might usurp state authority or provoke negative images of Frenchness. I argue that the culture of suspicion embraced by the colonial administration led to the investigation of French suspects in order to thwart political radicalism but also to condemn and shape undesirable behavior on the part of white metropolitans in Africa. Communist French were investigated by police, of course, but so too were royalists and anticlericalists. Impoverished and criminal French were sometimes labeled suspicious as well. When it came to investigations of French women as suspects or spouses of suspects, reports highlighted an official interest in criticizing and controlling white women's sexuality, a concern that surfaced in metropolitan France as well. Ultimately investigations of French suspects show how narrow a range of appropriate political and social behavior on the part of French residents and visitors was deemed acceptable by colonial authorities.

An analysis of French suspects under investigation in the interwar period also reveals that some elements of French colonial society envisioned French colonialism and their place in overseas territories. The French administration was the official face of a civilizing mission that had deep roots in French colonial ideology and rhetoric. Although it had changed over time, the civilizing mission still exalted France as a superior civilization and called upon the French to model European progress, especially in terms of democracy in the interwar era. Yet French populations inhabiting the colonies did not always espouse the same goals as the French government. Much as Gide differed in his assessment of the role of France in Africa, Catholic missionaries claimed quite divergent goals from those of the colonial state, which officially promoted republican and civilizing ideas but was more likely to opt for pragmatic solutions.[2] If nothing else, the French suspects of the interwar era confirm how fragmented French white society was in AOF and how frequently French metropolitans in AOF embraced goals that diverged from the official policies of the state. Nevertheless I argue that, like Gide, many suspects, through their words and actions, appeared to be critics or opponents of colonialism, but ultimately they too sought to reshape the French mission overseas within their own visions.

## The French of AOF

French people had much in common with other Europeans in AOF, so instead of looking at the category of French men (and women), it might make sense to focus on the category of whites in AOF. The status of whiteness, of course, carried enormous benefits in a society that was fundamentally organized by race. Also, white Europeans tended to create a community among themselves and were often generally regarded in similar ways by the French administration. Nevertheless there are good reasons for looking closely at the French as a singular group of suspects. French men and women had a unique relationship with the administration. First, their passage in the colonies was virtually unregulated. For a long time, to the great frustration of colonial officials, the French were not required to have passports or even identity cards to travel in AOF, making the use of false identities easier and the movement of French people more difficult to monitor. Concerns about the regulation of French migration were finally addressed in 1925, when Minister of Colonies Édouard Daladier required minimal verification of identity from French migrants; thus while foreigners had to obtain a foreigner's card and present a medical certificate, a judicial record, and other documents, French citizens only had to present a simple of identification and declare their arrival.[3] In addition, up until 1932 French were not required to submit a deposit for the cost of their return trip, meaning that anyone who could afford the trip could settle in AOF.[4] This relative lack of regulation certainly benefited those French who wished to evade entanglement with authorities. Second, French metropolitan citizens could and often did cultivate important personal relationships with administrators that might be to their advantage. However, along with such benefits came a closer scrutiny of the administration. Ultimately French people profited from looser restrictions on movement and the benefits of citizenship but were also subject to the scrutiny of the colonial state.

Although AOF was not a settler colony, there was a substantial French community made up of a combination of permanent settlers, including administrators, wealthy Bordeaux merchant families, small-time traders and their employees, workers, and a more transient population of missionaries, tourists, adventurers, and prospectors.[5] Dakar, the administrative and business capital of AOF and point of transit for most who entered French Africa by sea, had the highest concentration of French in the colony.[6] Within this community, colonial authorities identified people who appeared to be promoting political doctrines that could potentially endanger French sovereignty in West Africa.

### Dangerous Politics

As in the case of foreigners, even small hints of political radicalism among the French could draw the attention of colonial police. Metropolitan French were among the earliest communist suspects investigated in AOF. The Alsatian Henri Wagner, said to be affiliated with Moscow, was supposed to be headed for Senegal and Niger in 1922 on a propaganda mission.[7] In Zinder authorities were advised to look out for Wagner distributing propaganda and were told, "In the case where he becomes guilty of a criminal act . . . you need to refer him immediately to the Prosecutor." It was noted with some frustration that "in view of his quality as a Frenchman it is not possible to apply any sanctions to him other than those permitted by the penal code and the 1881 law on the press."[8]

Unlike itinerant communist agitators, French communists who were permanently rooted in AOF could maintain extensive contacts. In 1930 the Customs Service of Dakar reported that a package containing a collection of the periodicals *L'Humanité* (Humanity, the French communist newspaper), *L'Appel des Soviets* (Call of the Soviets), and *La Vie Ouvrière* (Working Life) was addressed to Joseph Boismare, chief of the train depot at Thiès in Senegal.[9] The issues included "numerous articles on the revolutionary movement in Indochina" and a "study of the Red Army, including numerous photographs." Although Boismare had engaged in "no patent act of propaganda of a political order," he was placed on the suspect list for Senegal.[10]

Roger Roche, who owned a garage that did "repairs of all kinds," was also the head of a communist cell in Rufisque. His correspondence to the metropole showed that he promoted unions and was involved in spreading communist propaganda. Intercepted correspondence sent to his comrades in France described his opinion of colonialism and his work as a communist in AOF: "As for the education of the native, from the social point of view it leaves much to be desired, but it is the fault of slave drivers who came to the land of the blacks to exploit them, not educate them. But with a little propaganda and with patience, I am certain we will have the strongest of armies given that a lot of them are literate and know how to write, it is only this racial hatred that must be erased."[11] Roche was affiliated with another suspect, Raphael Guilloteau, who was also a communist and chief of the train station in Bambey. One of Guilloteau's compatriots and coworkers, Georges Nomis, denounced him to the governor-general in 1925, describing him in a letter as a "fierce communist" who, "not satisfied to spread propaganda for the communist line in Moscow, encourages the blacks toward rebellion and the soldiers to disobedience." Nomis claimed that Guilloteau was soon to receive tracts and brochures that could "push the blacks of French West Africa to rise up against our protectorate."[12] Shortly thereafter Guilloteau was fired, and he headed back to France in 1926. The commissaire of police in Bambey wrote, "Because he is in contact with Lamine Singor [*sic*] in particular and other natives in general, I think that a close examination of his luggage (exam easy to do at customs) could be extraordinarily useful to know exactly the nature of his colonial relations and his work here."[13]

Jean-Baptiste Valery, a Corsican communist, appeared to pose a different and possibly greater communist threat. Valery was a representative of the International Club of Sailors and was known to Sûreté services in Morocco and Marseilles.[14] His task, while sometimes working under the pseudonym "Charles," was to "go aboard foreign vessels and signal the existence of the Club to the crew of these ships." The prefect of the Bouches du Rhône, where Valery once worked as a sailor out of Marseilles, described him as "intelligent, friendly and serious," and added, "Valery possesses a certain culture and enjoys a strong influence among the sailors."[15] Valery worked the voyage between France and the ports of North Africa. Two of his colleagues, Etienne Christophini and Pierre-Jean Loverini, were also supposedly communist agents employed by the Compagnie Paquet, which docked its ships in Morocco and Senegal.[16] Loverini, also a Corsican, was a fugitive of justice and reputedly an agent of Moscow. Spreading unionist and communist propaganda among the ships that served the route between metropole and colony, Valery, Christophini, and Loverini were suspects because of their political affiliation but were also considered exceptionally dangerous because they had unique access to the unpatrolled space of the sea.

In addition to communism, colonial officials were on the lookout for French supporters of other forms of anticolonial politics in AOF. In late July 1933 the radical journal *Chains*, along with the *Bulletin of the Anti-imperialist League* was "distributed among sympathetic milieux in Dakar." The documents were apparently passed from a sailor to a European "worker" in Dakar.[17] By August 1933 the police felt certain they had identified the two Europeans who delivered *Chains* into the colonies. About one hundred copies of the journal had apparently arrived in Senegal, of which the government intercepted about ten. The ultimate source of the documents appeared to be a unionist named Leroy who had left AOF to return to France a year before.[18] In September 1933 the police came into the possession of correspondence of a Frenchman named Henri Henriot, "propagandist" for the Anti-imperialist League, and an unidentified person in Dakar who was "a habitual correspondent of extremist organizations in the metropole." The addressee of the letter was unknown, but based on the correspondence from Henriot, someone in AOF had initiated the correspondence with the League. Henriot asked his correspondent to provide information for the League, including descriptions of "the life of black workers, how they are exploited, how many hours of work they do, how much they are paid, how they are treated by the bosses and administrators, how much they have to pay in taxes, what do they do when they cannot pay because they are impoverished, etc. . . . We also want to know what the black workers think about the situation and how they think they could improve their fate."[19] It is unclear if the correspondent in Dakar was ever found, but the story surrounding *Chains* shows that colonial authorities were actively seeking Frenchmen engaged in anticolonial propaganda outside of communist circles.

Perhaps even more alarming than the spread of anticolonial material by French travelers was the possibility that colonial officials were themselves promoting radical propaganda. In 1922 the Colonial Ministry expressed concern that French administrators might actually be the most dangerous source of anticolonial ideas.[20] Police agents proceeded to investigate low-level colonial administrators and members of the military in order to keep watch on potential dissenters. A former official in Civil Affairs, M. Brumauld des Allées, apparently became engaged in anti-imperialist politics while on leave in France for his health. He printed a tract named for the group Martyrs of Africa and sent it to Africans and Europeans in Cameroon. The supposed reason for the tract was Brumauld des Allées's "vowed hatred" for Blaise Diagne and his hope that his tract and a later book on abuses by the French regime in Africa would help the case of Diagne's political opponent Galandou Diouf.[21] The Martyrs of Africa was listed as a "suspicious association" by French colonial police in 1929.

Authorities considered Brumauld des Allées somewhat of a curiosity and did not take his campaign very seriously. For example, in some correspondence he referred to himself as "Brumauld" while referring to "des Allées" as someone else in order to make his association seem larger. The tract explains that the goal of the league was "to group together under one flag all Africans—blacks and whites who have suffered injustices." The president of the association (Brumauld), who worked in commerce and as an official for ten years, promised to serve as an eyewitness to corruption within the administration. In addition to exposing colonial corruption, the group would come to **the defense of the Africans who are ridiculed and bullied.**" They would also aid officials mistreated by "all the **bastards** and **brutes** of Africa."[22] The director of APA called Brumauld des Allées "an agent of civil services long ago compromised in an affair of trafficking of influence in Senegal, and several times subject to disciplinary punishment."[23] Brumauld was derided by the administration, but the fear that their own administrators and employees would turn against them was real.

Anticlericalism was not a specifically anticolonial or radical doctrine. In fact it has usually been understood as an aspect of republicanism. However, it too was considered suspicious from a political point of view in interwar French West Africa. In 1932 authorities observed what they described as a "massive" distribution of the French anticlerical journal *La Calotte* (The Cloth) to "important personalities of the city [of Dakar]."[24] Lucien Blache, a recipient of *La Calotte* and a type worker for a printer on Gorée Island, "would boast about being an anarchist and would freely praise humanitarian theories."[25] The anonymous shipment was eventually traced back to Willy Frank, the son of a German man and a mixed-race woman born in Saint-Louis. Frank was an employee of the Compagnie des Chargeurs Réunis who became interested in anticlericalism after reading *The Failure of Religions* by a Uruguayan author. According to the investigation into his life, this contact put Frank in touch with the French writer and anarchist André Lurulot, who recommended the periodicals *La Calotte* and *L'idée libre* (Free Idea) to Frank. Authorities went on to describe Frank as an "active militant" determined to "intensify his free-thinking propaganda."[26]

Although not French himself, Frank had deep connections with politically active French and African residents of Dakar. His mistress, the French Mme. Saint-Paul, also subscribed to *La Calotte*, as did "his native colleagues Antoine Bocco and Boubakar Sene."[27] Bocco himself was a close friend of Arthur Beccaria, the erstwhile head of the Dakar branch of the League for Defense of the Negro Race.[28] Frank was also said to be connected to Macassé Niass, an aviation photographer who was suspected of flying in copies of *La Voix des Nègres*. *La Calotte* itself, dated 1931 as well as "Thermidor 139," in reference to the dating system of the French Revolution, included caricatures of the clergy and the pope. It featured articles on nudism and comical exchanges between saints and cherubim in heaven.[29] It was likely the final article, "Why and How I Became a Free Thinker," as well as the deeper political convictions of the subscribers that captured the attention of the French authorities.

Police concerned themselves with the full spectrum of extremist politics, including those of the right. Several groups sent tracts within AOF promoting French conservative politics, including royalism. Curiously the earliest investigation of royalism in AOF occurred in 1925, when a Senegalese man by the name of Diouba Sylla was found to be distributing royalist tracts for Action Française in Rufisque. The commissaire of Rufisque was baffled that Sylla was interested in such tracts and queried his superior administrator to find out if he should allow Sylla to continue with the distribution of "anti-government tracts in the indigenous milieu."[30] Just a year later the ministry warned that Action Française, a Catholic royalist metropolitan organization, had announced the creation of a bureau in Dakar, with a president, vice president, and secretary, and had urged their members to contact the president when they arrived in the colony.[31] The author of a police report claimed, "This group, which currently is of little importance, is bringing together its leaders . . . who will assure the day when the royalist movement of France gives the order for revolt."[32] In 1934 a Frenchman named De Lumley was believed to be providing addresses for mailing copies of the group's journal to Europeans living along the Dakar-Niger train line.[33] Also in 1934 a functionary in Grand Bassam received a form for a subscription to a group called French Solidarity that included a plea from the Duke de Guise begging for restoration of the king. The Duke advocated "the principle of MONARCHY on which was founded and perpetuated FOR CENTURIES the grandeur of France and which alone can assure PEACE, ORDER, JUSTICE, THE CONTINUITY OF DESIGNS AND ACTS."[34]

Politics of the extreme right were possibly less common but perhaps of less concern to police authorities than leftist radical politics. Right-wing political groups likely did not have the same motivation to propagate their ideas among the African population as leftist organizations did. Nevertheless authorities found right-wing politics threatening. Investigations of royalism suggest that the administration, although authoritarian, was itself not a right-wing government but instead had a very specific political inclination toward a very narrow description of French colonial republicanism. In ascribing to such a perspective, authorities tightly monitored politics on both ends of the spectrum.

## Images of Frenchness

Fears about dangerous politics were critical to the construction of the profile of suspects, including French suspects. The administration, however, frequently demonstrated a preoccupation with French people who appeared poor, immoral, or, in the case of women, sexually promiscuous. Why? The presence of such French people in the colonies threatened notions of the superiority of French civilization, a critical rationale underpinning the justification for colonial rule. In the nineteenth century the civilizing mission, predicated on the idea that France was an advanced and superior civilization, was to bring French language, culture, and values through assimilation policies. By the twentieth century most of those assimilationist efforts had been abandoned, and the civilizing mission had been revised to mean "the material and the moral improvement of Africans."[35] The idea that France embodied a superior civilization and culture that should be emulated still lingered. French settlers were supposed to model those qualities through "elegant" homes and proper behavior.[36] Immoral or unseemly conduct might damage the reputation of all the French in West Africa. The identification of French suspects was supposed to repress radical politics, but colonial authorities also increased policing efforts to investigate, scrutinize, and criticize French men and women who did not conform to the strict demands of bourgeois French values.

French civilization was to be exalted partially for its economic achievements. Poor French, who were numerous in West Africa, tarnished this image. AOF was not alone in facing the question of how to square the presence of impoverished Europeans with claims to higher status based on race. Poor whites in colonial empires around the world aroused considerable anxiety among European elites, not only because they were more likely to form relationships with "natives" but also because they presented a poor image of the colonists.[37] French in positions of power in the administration were themselves often social climbers, but they routinely scorned some of their fellow French whom they believed to come from among the worst elements of metropolitan France. They rebuked the poor French as criminals and prostitutes.[38] In 1922 an administrator complained about "the numerous debarkations to Dakar of certain undesirables and prostitutes, the presence of which in this city is the cause of frequent offenses."[39] One official explained that as a result of the admission of such people to AOF, a "European underworld which corrupts Dakar is tending to grow in upsetting proportions and I predict serious difficulties between employers and employees if we do not end this type of exploitation of the indigenous element."[40] In a 1922 letter the delegate of Senegal in Dakar urged the lieutenant governor in Saint-Louis to bolster the authority of the police who faced rising migration of metropolitan French: "The police remain . . . powerless with regard to our nationals. Currently, the number of individuals lacking in all resources grows in Dakar. The proximity of Morocco brings us people who did not succeed in their enterprises or who are escaping from the police of this protectorate. Dakar remains blessed ground for those marked individuals that justice in the metropole seeks in vain." The dreaded consequence of such migration was "growth in the number of undesirables creating a danger for public security."[41]

Disapproval of the French population for poverty, immorality, and crime appears in suspect files as well. In 1921 a twenty-four-year-old named Etienne Bertram surfaced while crossing through the Casamance, a southern rural area of Senegal, having fled Gambia, where he was threatened with deportation by British authorities. Correspondence between offices described Bertram as "traveling on foot, with no baggage, not a dime, no military papers. Is being fed by the villages he passes through."[42] He claimed to be looking for work and once proposed a fake name. Urgent telegrams about his whereabouts and situation focused not on politics or a false identity but the bizarre circumstances of a Frenchman traveling through rural areas while "absolutely devoid of resources."[43]

The case of Charles Lombardini illustrates how notions of criminality could be linked with suspicion. Lombardini, a Corsican, had engaged in various unsavory actions related to his business ventures, which included a travel agency. When the agency failed, Lombardini "brutally fired" his "native employees" without paying them. His subsequent ventures included an association with a man named Carrega, a "person no less dubious and having several criminal convictions," and a partnership with an Ivory Coast planter to sell a car. In a 1930 scheme Lombardini took over a debris-clearing business, but when he could not pay his employees the promised salary, one of them protested, and "Lombardini hit him with such brutality that it caused him injuries bringing about an inability to work for 15 days." He was convicted of a variety of offenses, among them assault, swindling, abuse of confidence, and speeding. Lombardini was an "undesirable" who emerged from the "underworld" of French society in AOF. His actions cast suspicion not only on him but on all of "this unhealthy element that revolves around the orbit of the grand port." He was also described as reckless, foolish, and violent, "a dishonest and brutal individual who left a detestable reputation everywhere he has been, in France, in Senegal, in Sudan and Dakar." Furthermore, "In 1928 he returned to Corsica after having wasted all of his money."[44] Lombardini's case went before the criminal court, but the Sûreté provided information on him from a file marked "Suspicious Persons."

The French, much like foreigners, were also found to be involved in scheming and swindling, deception, and fraud.[45] Dr. Gutbaud, a Parisian, was traveling through AOF in 1929, carrying a large amount of money with him; having already spent 200,000 francs, he was seeking to establish pharmacies. Authorities suspected that Gutbaud was not truly a medical professional.[46] Like Gutbaud, a Dr. Antoine Vignard engaged in a classic scheme of crookedness through misrepresentation. He visited Togo in 1930, where he claimed to be researching the possibility of establishing the Lobi Company in the area. However, the commissaire of Togo noticed

Vignard "making a big deal out of his projects, but lacking any administrative or commercial references."[47] Apparently Vignard presented himself to the administration of Togo as an official of the Lobi Company, while he told the Lobi Company operating out of Anvers that he was a former lieutenant governor of Upper Volta. Both claims turned out to be false.[48]

If criminality and fraud were associated with white European adventurers more broadly, dubious sexual behavior was much more closely linked to white French women at a moment when the ordering of race and sexual behavior was changing. French Africa had been known for interracial relationships between French men and African women going back to the earliest settlements in the seventeenth century.[49] However, during the interwar era both metropole and colony faced a profound crisis related to women's freedom, sexuality, and anxiety about reproducing the next generation of the nation.[50] The period also saw the increased arrival of white women in the colonies and the establishment of stricter boundaries between the races. In AOF concerns about white women's sexuality were mostly linked to fears about miscegenation. Conklin claims, "A crucial aspect of the interwar strategy for safeguarding colonial authority was a growing emphasis on managing relations between the sexes."[51] African soldiers who had married French women were discouraged from leaving the metropole, not only because relationships between white women and black men were taboo but also because they could have a negative effect on the way "natives" viewed France.[52] Literature from the metropole on "social hygiene" emphasized the separation between the races for the prevention of disease and the "preservation of the race."[53] Experts on colonial living in this era prohibited interracial sex and warned of the dangers of a growing *métis* population and the harm done to white Frenchmen who fell under the sway of African women. Manuals advised French women in AOF to maintain strict standards of food, dress, and homemaking in order to make colonial life more palatable. Of course a French woman's devotion to motherhood was also a significant part of her duties.[54] The racial and sexual codes of the interwar years echo the fears about reproduction of the nation in France, and also anxiety about the status of the French in West Africa and their role in maintaining sovereignty.

In AOF only a handful of French and foreign women came under police surveillance during the First World War and the interwar era. Thomas writes that in interwar North Africa and the Middle East "political surveillance was an overwhelmingly male occupation in terms of both the watchers and the watched."[55] In the few investigations of French women suspects, questions about sexuality and morality almost always appeared. Colonial authorities condemned interracial sex as well as prostitution, signs of adultery, and promiscuity. Even as some French female suspects were initially investigated in political terms, it was in the language of morality and sexuality that their suspicion was ultimately defined.

The case of the French woman Marcelle Hervé reveals the ways that political suspicion could be translated into moral and sexual terms. Hervé arrived in Dakar in November 1930 with the purpose of meeting up with her "lover," a French naval captain named Carretier. Unable to reach Carretier, who was stationed in Atar, Mauritania, she made a trip to Saint-Louis, Senegal, before returning to France just short of a month after her arrival. Carretier was believed to belong to a communist cell in France and to have an "accommodating attitude with regard to revolutionary cells." This news was alarming because, due to his important position in the navy, he could be called on to succeed a circle commander in case of emergency.[56]

Despite the connection to political activity, details on Hervé's personal life move quickly to the fore of her story. Hervé was in the process of divorcing her husband, a retired naval officer. Surveillance revealed that after arriving in Dakar aboard the *Brazza*, Hervé spent the night at the Hotel Métropole, where she received a visitor, a uniformed naval lieutenant who arrived at midnight and spent the night in the room with her. During her time in AOF Hervé also went to Saint-Louis, where she apparently burned her undelivered communist tracts in a porcelain bidet at the Hotel Colmar and received a visit from a Lieutenant Cornovot.[57] Another report named her visitor in Saint-Louis as Cornevaux and called their relationship "intimate."[58] Soon after her time in Saint-Louis she returned to Dakar, where she again spent just one night, this time in the Hotel du Palais. The next morning she took a steamship for a return trip to France. The personal details are striking, especially because no evidence of political activity was ever obtained. Hervé did not give any hint of a communist agenda during her trip. The author of a report on her wrote, "We did not learn . . . that she openly displayed revolutionary opinions. Certain people who traveled in her company claimed she was on the contrary, non-communicative."[59]

When Emile Jean Minguin, a long-established French resident of Dakar who worked for many years at the port, was investigated for leftist politics, the sexual habits of his common-law wife attracted considerable interest as well. Minguin's "gross professional errors" and "bad character" aside, he was considered suspicious due to his involvement with syndicates, including fighting for an eight-hour workday at the port and the creation of the Syndical Association of Native Pilots. Minguin also wrote columns under a pseudonym for the newspaper *L'Ouest Africain* in which he criticized "the administration of the port, the colony and the rest" and "expressed his rancor and jealousy for his superiors." However, his personal life was also at issue in his file, and authorities were especially critical of his "concubine" Marguerite Jayet, called "Marcya." When the couple first met, Jayet was working as a "lyrical artist" with an engagement at the Dakar Casino and also, it was rumored, as a prostitute. Jayet seemed to have "numerous lovers" "other than Minguin," and while running a tobacco stand near the Café Metropole "continue[d] to engage in prostitution." Jayet's reputation was further sullied by the rumor that she sold drugs: "They say that she takes them herself and that it is she who supplies to Dakar a large part of the drugs that are consumed there." Minguin and Jayet were reportedly partners in the drug trade, as she sold what he was able to import on the sly through his job at the port.[60] While clearly Minguin's syndical activities and opposition to the administration were important, it appeared natural to authorities that such leftist politics would be linked with drugs and prostitution.

The case of Elizabeth Caton also revolves around the control of female sexuality and morality, but unlike the others barely hints at any political reason underlying the investigation. Caton, born in Saint-Louis, was living in Toulouse, where she worked as a typist for Radio Toulouse and was having an affair with her boss. But apparently she hoped to escape that life. She "claimed to her boss that her sister who was in Casablanca was gravely ill," and Caton planned to visit her. However, Caton did not go to Morocco; she actually went to Diourbel, Senegal, "to meet up with her former lover Robert Saunière," who was working for a French company. Caton and Saunière became engaged, but just a few days before the wedding she declared that she no longer wanted to marry him. Saunière convinced the reluctant bride to go through with the marriage. However, following a series of cables between Diourbel and Dakar, Caton claimed that her health required her to leave Africa. Saunière suggested a divorce, and Caton agreed and departed for the metropole less than three months after the wedding. She radioed her parents and claimed to be returning to France via Spain, where she would continue her journey by land. However, she did not follow through on this plan, instead staying aboard the ship until she reached Bordeaux and her "lover," presumably the boss from Radio Toulouse. From Bordeaux, Caton and her former boss traveled to Switzerland, Belgium, Luxemburg, Prussia, and Algeria and appeared to be leaving for Russia. The chief of the Sûreté in Senegal wrote that Caton's "travel appears suspicious and it would be interesting to know its goal."[61] Her actions were so interesting that authorities in Dakar alerted the Colonial Ministry in Paris of her return to Europe.[62] Caton's story ends there, and it appears that nothing further, at least nothing suspicious, was discovered about her voyages. Nevertheless the substantial interest in Caton's past in Toulouse and her relationships in AOF seems strange given that there is hardly a hint of politics or danger to her story (save the reference to Russia). It would ultimately appear that the vital problem with Caton was that she exhibited behavior in Senegal in the 1930s that was clearly unacceptable for a French woman. Like Hervé, Caton traveled extensively in Senegal without her husband and was believed to have multiple lovers.

In contrast to these stories, it is useful to consider the portrayal of a French woman who was investigated by police but was ultimately judged *not* to be a suspect. Audrée Delmas, born Hungarian but naturalized French, came to the attention of police because of her proclivity to undertake extensive travel alone. In 1931, despite warnings and poor health, Delmas traveled from Algiers through Morocco, then made many stops in AOF, including a trip to Timbuktu, and finally returned to Dakar by canoe.[63] Delmas's name suggests she was a member of one of the great Bordeaux merchant families established in Dakar, and her file confirms that she was "connected to well-known French families."[64] She also behaved as an upperclass person, for example, using a calling card to announce a visit to the administrator-mayor when she arrived in Timbuktu.[65] As much as Delmas irritated the administration by remaining "absolutely mute on the motive for her travels," she was not really considered a suspect.[66] In fact her file was not placed with other suspects' files but was archived in police records alongside them with the title "Mme Delmas." And despite the mystery surrounding her travels, Delmas was portrayed as an eccentric who was a bit crazy but not criminally or morally suspect. Although it was noted that she was a morphine addict. Delmas died of an unrevealed cause while traveling in Mauritania in 1932.[67] Her surveillance seems initially motivated by authorities' attempts to understand her unconventional actions, then later for her own safety, not because of any threat to the administration. Delmas's age, class status, and seeming lack of sexual adventure apparently protected her from the scrutiny Caton, Hervé, and Jayet received.

## Recasting the Civilizing Mission

While French authorities seemed to be using surveillance to police the morals, politics, and behavior of the French community, French suspects' files can also be used to tease out the ways some French imagined their own role in the colonies. Most suspects were not explicitly interested in the concerns of the colonial state at all, but were on a mission to enrich themselves, promote their political ideas, or find adventure. As such, they mostly sought self-reinvention. But in doing so they sometimes also reinvented the French civilizing mission on their own terms. Some suspects merely used the language of the civilizing mission, implying that their adventures were for the benefit of the Africans with whom they occasionally interacted. Others truly saw themselves as knowledgeable and righteous and aimed for moral or political interventions of their own design in African communities. In order to probe the various ways French people under surveillance reinvented their own version of the civilizing mission, I will take a close look at three suspects—an adventurer, an exile, and a communist.

Fortune-seeking individuals who set out for the colonies with hopes of adventure as well as profit operated on a particular set of fantasies about colonial spaces that mythologized the colonies as ripe for adventure and full of riches. French discourse on Africa often portrayed the continent as a blank space where Europeans had free rein to fantasize, invent, and explore.[68] Travelers were often as interested in experiencing the exotic landscape and wild animals of Africa as they were in witnessing the so-called premodern and primitive qualities of its inhabitants.[69] By the 1920s and 1930s literature about the colonies—from the works of Pierre Loti to those of Céline—had drawn a picture of colonial spaces as sensual and exotic.[70] Popular travel writers such as Geoffrey Gorer and Albert Londres also promoted exciting adventure in the colonies.[71] Films frequently featured plotlines in which metropolitan Frenchmen escaped tragic or criminal pasts by embarking on colonial escapades, especially by way of the romantic and mysterious Foreign Legion.[72] Metropolitan French sometimes came to AOF to play out a fantasy of colonialism that did not involve the upright bourgeois lifestyle advocated by the colonial administration but that of a hunter or fortune-seeker.

Frenchman Pierre Magard, initially investigated by the police for his alleged communist activities, typifies the seeker of fortune and adventure who defied convention as he carved out a new identity for himself far from the bourgeois moralizing images advocated by the colonial administration. In fact Magard's claims to grandeur and the outlandishness of his schemes led French authorities to believe he was insane. Magard had been stationed in AOF while in the military, only to return in the 1920s with various plans for making his fortune. His affiliation with the Communist Party, ostensibly the reason for suspicion, was actually a footnote to his life. By the time he became active in AOF in the mid-1920s, Magard was far more concerned with pursuing a personal fortune than spreading propaganda. He and his associate, the German Wache, reputedly a zoologist, traveled together "under the pretext of hunting and study . . . for several months through Upper Senegal and Sudan."[73] When they first arrived together in

October 1925, Magard listed "study and exploration" as the motive of their journey.[74] Magard had a connection with a German zoo and promised to deliver live wild animals, including giraffes and elephants, to Hamburg.[75] The pair had numerous other schemes going, such as prospecting for minerals and a fresh water spring.[76] They also claimed to be sketching out a route for a new railroad and seeking to create an "intellectual-cultural center" in Zinder, Niger.[77]

As time went on Magard's schemes became more complex and more incredible. In 1926 he made plans to go on a cinematographic mission with George Rostaing, who, "with the support of M. Poincaré and the Duchess of Uzes proposes to undertake a sort of 'anti-slavery and anti-cannibalism crusade.'"[78] Magard became well-known and widely doubted for his supposed connections to famous personalities and government figures. He claimed to have "recently visited Russia" and bragged about having "excellent relations with the governments of the principal European governments, notably Germany, England and Russia."[79] Officers present in Dakar in 1926 who had known Magard when he was in the army called him "violent, having a temper, and talkative."[80] Magard returned to Dakar, without Wache, in 1930 with plans to do some reporting, including an interview with the aviator Jean Mermoz.[81] He brought with him a letter of support from a Paris newspaper, Le Journal, asking that authorities "welcome" him and describing him as "an extremely serious man."[82]

Being labeled a suspect certainly did not mean Magard saw himself as opposed to French colonial state authority. On the contrary, he used his privileged status as a white Frenchman to request favors from the administration. After his 1925–26 trip to AOF he made plans to return to the colony, writing to the Ministry of Colonies under the name "Maquart" and describing a voyage in which he would personally lead a hunting expedition in AOF for a group of "about 15 young people from good families."[83] Magard had advertised the voyage in the periodical Le Chasseur Français (French Hunter), describing himself as "an old-time African" offering to take some young people "looking for some fine adventures" on a hunting trip.[84] Maquart was quickly unmasked as Magard, and it appears as if the hunting expedition never took place despite arousing some interest in the metropole. In a grotesque version of his zoo mission, Magard also petitioned the French authorities for permission to bring about sixty Africans to Germany as a kind of traveling spectacle. Administrators eventually denied this request after considerable deliberation.[85]

As much as his activities reveal him as a renegade, Magard was not anticolonial. In fact he sometimes seemed to ally himself with the French civilizing mission, sensing that such a connection would provide him some advantage. His schemes even occasionally adopted the terminology of the official civilizing mission. For example, he evoked nineteenth-century language when he discussed an "anti-slavery and anti-cannibalism crusade." His mention of the intellectual-cultural center in Zinder suggests a disingenuous desire to engage in altruism toward African people. In his zoo missions and railroad schemes Magard also expressed confidence that he possessed the authority to intervene in African societies.

But for Magard the civilizing mission was just a means to an end. He tried, and ultimately failed, to use such philanthropic projects to give himself a veneer of legitimacy. He talked of recruiting young men from "good families" and made claims of lofty acquaintances. In reality he came to French West Africa to live out an adventure of masculinity that cast him as the intrepid adventurer, artist, or entrepreneur. This self-reinvention was itself made possible by the opportunities provided by a colonial state that privileged the needs of white metropolitans and seriously considered even the most outlandish of requests.

While Magard's version of a civilizing mission was far from fully developed, other examples show that some French tried to engage in self-styled, independent civilizing missions. Owen White has described how the former French Catholic priest Auguste Dupuis-Yakouba was able to leave the mission and became a full member of the community of Timbuktu while remaining a Catholic and keeping his ties to the administration. Dupuis-Yakouba's life straddled the boundary of ideas about the "civilized" and "uncivilized," but he too offered an alternative imagining of the French mission in AOF by maintaining his faith and serving his community in new ways.[86]

Like Dupuis-Yakouba, the suspect August Eugène Greleau operated outside of the official context of the French administration and yet gave his own meaning to colonial intervention in Africa. Born in Paris in 1876, Greleau first came to the attention of colonial authorities when he crossed paths with a Dr. Heckenroth, who was accompanying the governor-general on a tour of the colonies. Heckenroth encountered Greleau, his illegitimate wife, and their three-month-old baby along a rural road near an encampment at Youpépaté in Sudan in 1921. Greleau claimed to have an affiliation with the French senator Anatole de Monzie and explained that he and his family were traveling along the Falemé River.[87] An investigation of these unusual circumstances followed, and the picture of Greleau that emerges combines criminality, subversive politics, immorality, and a dubious past left behind in the metropole.

Greleau's considerable criminal, military, and marital history allowed metropolitan authorities to access a significant amount of information about his past. Greleau claimed he was an architect by profession and had earned a degree from a mining school, but it was discovered that he did "not exercise, in reality, any profession." He had been married legitimately three times but was accused of tricking his second wife into marriage by hiding his past from her, which included an illegitimate son and a mistress. He was apparently an abusive and deceitful husband who had been convicted of attempted murder of his mistress Miss De Menard and her mother. His checkered history included prison time and different stints in the military, one of them with a regiment in Africa. During his mobilization for the First World War in the Cher "his behavior was so deplorable that his unit had him sent to Algeria as a measure of discipline until his demobilization in February 1918." After the war Greleau made his way to Lille, where he met Miss Ellbroult, the woman presumed to be with him in Africa. Ellbroult had a bad reputation of her own, as she was known to have "consorted with our enemies." Her family only added to this perception of "bad morality," for her mother was in the middle of a divorce and her sister "had a child with the Germans." The report, which was written by the Ministry of the Interior and sent by the minister of colonies, also noted that Greleau had departed France with false identity papers and that when he was demobilized from the military he took some blank leave-of-absence forms on which he filled in a false name. To complete this tale of deceit, abuse, and criminality, the author of a Paris report added that Greleau held socialist opinions and was "boastful, lying, lazy and violent."[88]

When Greleau first came to Dakar, in September 1920, it was to work for a branch of the Morosini Company, based in Paris. The commissaire of police in Dakar soon received an anonymous letter from Paris detailing Greleau's notorious past. The letter depicted Greleau as a criminal, convicted of robbery and murder, who had spent five years in prison in Melun and was forbidden to live in the Department of the Seine for ten years. It further accused him of being a "fervent libertarian" who should be "watched closely," as he had been caught "spreading brochures." "[He has] a facility of speech, his conversations have the style of a conference in which he exposes his revolutionary ideas, his profound hate for all that appears to his eyes to have an authoritarian character. Also, I warn you, pay attention to him, he is for strikes, in a word, all that can bring disorder." After these political accusations, the anonymous letter writer finished with comments on Greleau's personal character: "His private life is also infamous, married into an honorable family, which he outrageously deceived, he now cohabits with a girl." The letter arrived after Greleau had already been fired by the Morosini Company. When the police summoned him to headquarters, he named his estranged wife as the anonymous letter writer and assured authorities he would leave AOF on the next boat. Greleau did not keep his promise to leave, however, and while the commissaire was alerting the Sûreté Générale in Paris, Greleau and his "very blond" new wife left for the interior.[89] Greleau was trying to escape a criminal past and his domestic troubles by starting anew in AOF. When Dakar did not provide enough of an escape, he moved farther into the interior.

Reports from a local administrator in the Circle of Kayes stated that Greleau and Ellbroult had been living in Farabana for three months after having left Youpépaté. They were housed in rudimentary conditions but were given lodgings within the main square of the village near the chief, a man named Sega Madi, with whom Greleau was said to be "on excellent terms." Greleau and his wife hunted and lived off the land. A later report found the situation of the Greleaus to be slightly more difficult, claiming, "He lives off of public charity and the generosity of the people of the village." It was "thanks to [Madi's] intervention that the people of the village, each in their turn, supply him with the grain necessary for his diet." Madi also was responsible for building and furnishing the hut and straw verandah that provided shelter for Greleau, his wife, and a "young domestic who prepares their food."[90] Despite his apparent dependency on the village for food and shelter, Greleau asserted a range of activities as his motive for living in Farabana, including prospecting for gold, seeking land for cotton cultivation, and researching gold mines for Senator de Monzie.[91] Greleau's stay in Farabana suggests the curious combination of an adventurer and a refugee.

While his material situation seemed to cast Greleau as a beggar, his for-eignness and whiteness allowed him to elevate his status as he befriended Madi and others in Farabana. Greleau and Madi made "long excursions in the bush" together, speaking with the aid of an interpreter, Madi's brother Fily, who was a former tirailleur in the French Army.[92] Greleau worked to form relationships with other members of the village, although he had little knowledge of the local language and relied on a Bambara dictionary to communicate. He avoided discussion of politics, and his speech was "exempt from tendentious remarks." Instead Greleau preferred to discuss "commercial and industrial questions" as well as stories of a recent stay he had in Morocco.[93] The people of Farabana were described as impressed by Greleau. One report asserted that the villagers were "surprised and frightened by his gestures and actions, say that he is the descendant of the whites who, long ago were the masters of Makhana and Farabana and that he has returned . . . to recover control of the territory."[94] Greleau even went so far as to suggest that he had divining powers to impress people. Among his new neighbors in Farabana, he showed "cards that he consulted frequently, the natives having seen him spread them out."[95] He actively cultivated a persona that suggested a deep and old connection to Farabana, considerable knowledge of technical and commercial matters, and travel experience. His attempts to ingratiate himself showed a desire, not to live as the "natives," as Dupuis-Yakouba did, but to gain status and prestige within this community as an exceptional person. His actions suggest a desire to reinvent himself by creating a powerful new role for himself, not among the French but in a Sudanese village.

Madi perceived Greleau as having a direct and powerful relationship to French authorities. Madi had important connections of his own to the Devès family in Saint-Louis but "represented [Greleau] as a powerful boss who could make him an important territorial commander." Whether or not Greleau made such a suggestion or Madi inferred he had power because of his position as a white man is not clear. In fact Greleau tried to convince the people of Farabana that he was not French. He said he came from "a country 'behind France' that the Germans invaded first and ravaged during the war."[96] Greleau was willing to capitalize on his white, foreign status, but his denial of French nationality suggests a rejection of the official colonial project, perhaps hoping this would secure the trust of Madi.

Ironically, while Greleau vocally rejected the French colonial state and denied that he was French, he also directly approached French officials for help and revealed that he had created a civilizing project to aid the people of Sudan. In early April 1921 he presented himself to the administrator of the Cercle of Kayes, claiming to be an "engineer on a mission" and asked for medicine for himself, as he was destitute.[97] Greleau followed up this request by writing a letter in April to the delegate of the governor-general in Sudan asking for medical supplies.[98] An administrator had already noted that Greleau had some medicine and "would often treat the natives without ever asking to be paid."[99] He asked for "some remedies that would be indispensable for treating the natives of the villages I cross, and to my regret . . . am obliged to refuse, considering the somewhat onerous expense this has caused me until now." Greleau claimed his motivation was to prevent the spread of smallpox in the area, and he asked for vials of vaccine to administer to the locals. In addition to his request, perhaps in order to ingratiate himself with the administration or to solve a personal issue, he reported a theft to the administration committed by an African circle guard.[100] Greleau deftly presented different faces to the French state and to the people of Farabana. Like Dupuis-Yakouba, he forged an individual path that expressed both acceptance of and distance from the French colonial state. Co-opting the prestige of the French administration and engaging in actions that at times mirrored French authorities by providing medicine and forming alliances with leaders, Greleau seemed to endorse aspects of the civilizing mission, especially when they could be used for his own purposes. For Greleau the colonies were a place to go to flee his criminal past and domestic complications. Yet his vision of the colonial experience also provided a chance for him to create his own version of the civilizing mission, with himself as the hero.

To return to the all-important issue of communism, we may also find here evidence of an alternate kind of civilizing mission among French suspects. Camille Champeau, adjunct administrator, second class, was reported to harbor communist opinions in 1925. Champeau, who had served in the military and then reenlisted as a colonial administrator, worked in Fada and Ouagadougou in Upper Volta before returning to France for a convalescent leave. He was described as "married, father of a young girl, from a modest background because he says he is the son of a shepherd."[101] Champeau was first signaled as having communist tendencies when an Inspector Coste observed at the library of his post at Fada works by Lenin and Liebknecht.[102] The lieutenant governor of Upper Volta, upon hearing of this library, immediately contacted the circle commander at Fada to advise of the "immediate need for suppression of these volumes." The lieutenant governor then proceeded to speak personally with Champeau in order to "address remonstrance, to tell him what I thought of his opinions and make him understand how these tendencies were incompatible with his functions as a colonial administrator." Champeau defended himself by saying he "recognized that with regard to our colonial politics, and our task of civilization and progress, the application of the communist program in our colonies would create disastrous effects and would be diametrically opposed to the best interests of our indigenous populations." This response seemed to satisfy the lieutenant governor, who declared Champeau to be "more of a doctrinarian idealist and an utopist than one who will eventually take action."[103]

The characterization of Champeau as a mere "idealist" was wrong, however. Although it was considered a minor mention on his record, Champeau was said to "enjoy himself in the company of the natives whom he frequents." He was also "reproached for 'too great a camaraderie with the natives with whom he lacks firmness.'" Champeau appeared to be interested in the former tirailleurs, whom he approached to discuss their experiences in France and to hear their "impressions" and "any complaints they might have." It was even reported that he took the side of his domestic servants when they argued with his wife. Champeau was described as "incontestably a lover of natives who pushes praiseworthy feelings to excess." A report also explored the ambivalent feelings of the lieutenant governor about Champeau's politics. On one hand Champeau was criticized for his relationships with natives; on the other hand, his service in recruiting Africans for the First World War was seen in a positive light. Champeau appeared to display moral uprightness, patriotism, and faith in the civilizing mission, yet his communist beliefs were clearly at odds with his role as a colonial administrator.[104]

The most negative information about Champeau came from the circle commander at Fada, who said plainly, "M. Champeau is a communist, and naturally holds the political ideas of this party. He received here *Humanité*, *Le Bulletin Communist*, and *Bretagne Communiste* and he sent his membership dues to the party in France." According to the commander, Champeau had tried to convert people to communism, including the local teacher, M. Chevartzmann. However, the locals were "disconcerted and offended . . . by theories which shocked, distressed and brusquely rejected all their customs." He cited as an example of the disturbing nature of Champeau's theories that Champeau claimed a woman could leave her husband for a lover if she pleased, as women are "absolutely free." Champeau had succeeded in converting to communism Mamadou Taraoré, a writer in Fada and a man "of poor spirit, no scruples, and [who] is certainly entirely won over by communist theories." He concluded, "If the incontestable proselytism of M. Champeau has not had more success here, it is only because the country is not yet sufficiently evolved." Nevertheless, despite warning of the danger of Champeau to the colony, Lieutenant Governor Hesling prescribed a "discreet surveillance" of him during his convalescence in France, while also noting that Taraoré would be subject to local surveillance.[105] Champeau's situation made his life full of contradictions. Apparently although he saw the spread of communism as an effective way to uplift African people, he also saw fit to continue his duties as a colonial administrator. Even a proponent of radical politics might see his work as ultimately offering an alternative version of the civilizing mission.

## Summary

Above all, political policing in interwar French West Africa sought out people suspected of spreading radical political doctrines. Among French suspects this included communism and anticolonialism, but also anticlericalism and royalism. Communists and anticolonialists were uncovered even among French colonial administrators, demonstrating that administrators were not a monolithic group but individuals who sometimes prioritized personal political agendas over the goals of the French state. Ultimately, as politics of both the left and the right came under scrutiny, the culture of suspicion meant that only a narrow political point of view—one that embraced a moderate republican colonialism—was acceptable among the French in AOF.

But the surveillance of suspects reveals that more was at stake for the administration as they monitored their countrymen. Descriptions of suspects suggest that inspectors and other officials used surveillance tools designed to fight political dissidence to help shape a French community along specific class, legal, and moral lines. Representing France in West Africa, the French were meant to model civilization, and many suspects failed miserably at this obligation. Suspects included French who were impoverished, criminal, and fraudulent. In matters of sexual morality, authorities became distressed not only when racial lines were transgressed by sexual behavior but also when white Frenchwomen behaved autonomously outside the conventional protections of marriage.

The very fact that suspicious French came under surveillance by colonial authorities indicates that they were misfits living on the fringes of a European colonial society that expected a very particular set of behaviors. But even as authorities castigated suspects, called them troublesome, and attempted to control them, due to their legal status as French they could often operate independently, enjoying the protections of French citizenship and whiteness in West Africa. They could petition authorities and negotiate their situation, sometimes even gaining the assistance of the state.

French suspects' files are rich sources for understanding marginal elements of the French community. For most French settlers and travelers involvement in the official policies of the state was secondary to the pursuit of personal goals. French suspects rejected bourgeois notions of behavior and forged paths that recast the French colonial project in their own terms. Their priorities included personal prestige, financial reward, self-reinvention, adventure, and sometimes political proselytism. Colonialism was for these people not about modeling civilization as much as opening up a new world of opportunities. For those seeking the exotic appeal of Africa, it meant embarking on adventure and escaping European life. While colonial administrators tried to reconcile republicanism with imperialism in AOF, royalists, communists, and anti-imperialists used the colonial terrain to expand their reach.

Were French suspects truly at odds with French authorities? Did their actions undermine the civilizing mission? Most often they did not. Even as some French acted at odds with the state, they mostly still embraced the fundamental tenet of colonialism that viewed European civilization as superior and did not question their privileged status or the right of France to rule West Africa. Even as Magard and Greleau embarked on personal adventures, they reimagined and engaged in their own kinds of civilizing missions. They combined adventure and reinvention with distribution of medicine or rhetoric about ending slavery. Even Champeau, the committed communist, refused to give up on the French administration. Although they rejected bourgeois society and in some ways the state, these French suspects still had much in common with the official policies of colonial rule. Like André Gide, they opposed the colonial state in some ways, but in other ways they mirrored the state's aim of intervening and uplifting African societies.

Radical political ideas and reckless adventure conducted by the French in AOF were considered dangerous, but ultimately the most pressing fear that preoccupied colonial authorities was the possibility that radical politics would be spread among the African population. Some French helped form links in the connections that were surreptitiously built by African radicals. It is to these networks that I now turn.

# 5

# Creating Networks

## *African Suspects, Radical Politics, and Colonial Repression*

In the 1930s a Portuguese woman named Pieda Maria de Cardozo operated a café-restaurant on the rue Victor Hugo in Dakar that served as a "rendezvous point" for many "native" sailors who passed through the port.[1] One can only imagine that the café served as a place for the sailors to relax, eat, and drink after a long sojourn at sea and also a place to inquire about job opportunities, hear gossip about friends, and possibly receive news from family. French colonial authorities believed that Cardozo's café also served as a point of distribution for radical pan-African newspapers. In October 1931 John Soumah of French Guinea, employed as an assistant cook aboard a ship sailed by the Chargeurs Réunis shipping company, brought thirteen copies of the newspaper *La Race Nègre* to Dakar.[2] A month later a shipment of about forty copies of the same journal was smuggled by a sailor aboard the ship the *Touareg* meant for distribution in Senegal by Arthur Beccaria. The journal was likely sent from Marseilles by Diara Be, aka Pierre Togola, a Sudanese man who had served previously as an auxiliary guard for the Sûreté of Dakar.[3] In early 1932 the police launched an operation to catch Soumah in the act of bringing more copies of *La Race Nègre* to Dakar. However, the plan failed when Soumah did not arrive aboard the *Baoulé* as expected. In the meantime investigators had discovered that another former agent of the Sûreté, Sidi Oumar Kaba, a resident of Le Hâvre, was sending copies of *La Race Nègre* to Dakar "most often through the intermediary of native sailors embarking on the steamships serving the coast of West Africa." The investigation also determined that Cardozo was the "former mistress" of Kaba. Her café was placed under "tight surveillance" in an effort to finally snag the sailors smuggling in radical tracts, as it appeared to be a node in a radical network that brought clandestine copies of banned newspapers to French West Africa.[4]

In chapters 3 and 4 I addressed the role of foreign and French suspects under police surveillance and investigation. In this final chapter I turn to the stories of Africans from AOF and their engagement, real or supposed, with radical politics. As with foreigners and Frenchmen, the colonial administration took on a particular attitude toward African suspects. Compared to their European counterparts, African suspects were much more likely to be described solely based on their politics rather than their moral indiscretions. Of course "undesirable" qualities sometimes surfaced connected to criminality or immorality.[5] However, the intangible mystery of charlatans and adventurers and dubious sexual behavior that so often characterizes files of foreigners and French men and women remains largely absent from files on African suspects. Instead an African suspect was more likely to be described simply as "anti-French," "an extremist," or "likely to be rallied to communist or anti-French doctrines" or, in rare cases after an investigation was completed, "serious and respectful of Europeans."[6]

The racialization of Africans as represented in police files is subtle. On the one hand, authorities expressed profound fears that African citizens, évolués, and tirailleurs, all groups considered elites, would embrace radical politics. On the other hand, authorities were likely to oversimplify the ideas promoted by African political groups and to assume Africans might not fully understand the newspaper they read or the group they joined. Many files on African suspects are also distinctly brief; rare are files like those on Small or Kouyaté that contain voluminous pages of information. Many contain just a few pages, suggesting the difficulties authorities faced in penetrating African networks and enacting effective webs of surveillance, as described in chapter 2. As a result this chapter focuses more on the networks formed by African suspects than the background information compiled on the suspects themselves.

The history of politics in AOF, especially Senegal, has long been an interest for historians of West Africa due to the unique status of the originaires. Scholarly works on this topic include political histories of figures as Blaise Diagne, Galandou Diouf, Lamine Guèye, and Léopold Sédar Senghor.[7] Recent scholarship has also demonstrated ways traditional leaders were able to translate precolonial social and political power into colonial-era influence. Robinson argues that marabouts, in alliance with the French, took on new roles as political and economic leaders, especially in Senegal.[8] Rural elites, endowed with great authority as canton and village chiefs, worked for the state; they wielded enormous influence and accrued wealth.[9]

In spite of this proliferation of scholarship on African politics in the colonial era, radical politics in AOF have frequently taken a backseat to analysis of the active organizations in the metropole.[10] The reason for this emphasis on metropolitan black politics is that groups like the CDNR, LDNR, and Union des Travailleurs Nègres (UTN, Union of Negro Workers) were well-organized and attracted numerous members in France, yet they struggled to gain traction in AOF.[11] Some scholars have discounted the possibility that anticolonial politics could have existed at all in French West Africa before World War II due to the repression of the French colonial regime.[12] Others have assumed that the mere existence of such organizations in the colonies meant their success.[13] The reality is somewhere between these positions. Although black radical activity in metropolitan France influenced AOF deeply, a study of radical politics among blacks in France should not serve as a substitute for a careful examination of the politics of dissent in Africa, especially considering the very important differences governing life in the two places.

Although there was never any real danger of a communist or nationalist uprising threatening the French state prior to the Second World War, there were pockets of individuals, political networks, and organized groups among French West Africans who showed interest in communism, pan-Africanism, and, in the case of Dahomey, nationalism.[14] Jean Suret-Canale, in a study of the Dahoméen leader Louis Hunkanrin, writes that although a "genuine political life" did not exist in AOF until after the Second World War, there were "precursors: not only in armed resistance or religious movements . . . but in secular forms with an essentially modern character."[15] Suret-Canale qualifies his statement by writing, "What these precursors [of independence movements] achieved was undoubtedly of limited scope; in the objective conditions prevailing in this part of the French colonial empire, it could not have been otherwise."[16]

In telling the story of African suspects, I seek two interconnected goals. First, I use police surveillance files to reconstruct the networks that were the precursors to independence movements described by Suret-Canale. I describe several anti-French political networks: an armed Islam-inspired group, the Paris-based League for Defense of the Negro Race, a Dahoméen nationalist group, a Dahoméen teachers' union, and the network surrounding the communist and labor leader Edward Francis Small. Second, I chart the "objective conditions" referred to by Suret-Canale—that is, the ways French authorities used surveillance and investigations to repress political networks. While foreign suspects such as Small could be expelled from the colony, this option was not easily available for Africans. Surveillance and subsequent repression did not usually use violence; instead more insidious methods were chosen. Far from being tools simply for the collection of information, the ultimate consequence of the policing of suspects was the curtailing of political activity in French West Africa. Although repression was a real and legitimate problem, suspects made efforts to evade authorities through creative strategies. In the example described earlier, Soumah, Kaba, Togola, and Cardozo were apparently able to shuffle their smuggling plans enough to evade police authorities for several years.

## World War I Revolt in Ouakam

Policing of African politics of dissent did not begin with the interwar era. As in the case of foreigners, it is helpful to look at police files from the First World War if for no other reason than to draw a contrast to the interwar political scene. Significant African resistance to the recruitment campaigns of the war occurred in different parts of rural AOF.[17] The repression of these popular movements, which included both flight and armed resistance, was generally the domain of the military.[18] However, the police became involved in at least one case that highlights how African networks of resistance formed during that war.

In 1917 French colonial police investigated a seemingly well-organized plot in Senegal that combined antimilitary resistance with Muslim beliefs. Concerns about Muslim propagandists using the printing press to spread anticolonial ideas predate the First World War.[19] After the Ottomans entered the war on the side of the Central Powers, French West African authorities initially feared Muslim Africans would rally to their cause.[20] Their worst fears were soon allayed, but in 1917 a new resistance group focused on Islam took shape. The case in question centered on the theft of twenty rifles and bayonets from a military camp in Ouakam, just outside of Dakar. Military authorities received word from an officer stationed at the Medina camp of the Fourth Regiment of the tirailleurs sénégalais of meetings "convened by an unknown marabout" who committed "acts of propaganda to excite [the tirailleurs] to revolt against the Europeans." The meetings included both "tirailleurs and civilian natives" and were meant to result in "an attack on Dakar during the night of October 7–8 or the morning of the eighth." The discovery of the theft of rifles from the camp at Ouakam led authorities to suspect a link between the theft and a "plot against the security of the state." A Senegalese sergeant reported the activity and described a scene wherein a marabout tried to win over a group of people to the revolt: "A significant number of tirailleurs and some civilian natives were assembled at the foot of a baobab tree, in the countryside, near the Médina. With a production designed to stir the feelings of those assembled, a marabout, who seemed to come out of the trunk of the baobab and who they believed to be a Muslim saint having the privilege to go to Mecca every day . . . declared that he was the Mahdi, that the hour to rise up to defend Islam had come, that his all-powerfulness would easily conquer the resistance of the Europeans." By October 10 the investigation had succeeded in arresting Ibrahima Sow, who "knew too much about the affair not to be one of the leaders." A warrant issued for

Sow led to his immediate arrest by a military escort. However, "while en route, Sow disappeared in the night. The corporal and the escort soldiers claimed to have been threatened with a dagger." The governor-general was suspicious of the escape and suggested a "possible complicity of the men in the escort." These men were imprisoned as co-conspirators.[21]

The investigation continued (despite the "regrettable" escape of Sow) with searches of the homes of "suspicious" tirailleurs. These searches turned up letters "containing the clearest indications on the plot formed for holy war, the preparations in progress, the propaganda undertaken among the soldiers of Dakar, Thiès, Pout, in the name of marabout Mamadou Lamine and generally concluding with exhortations to action." The search led to an even greater number of arrests among those who were "suspects because they were in relations with the leaders" and those "who wrote or received letters proving their active participation in the plot."[22] The locus of the activity was found to be Thiès, Senegal, not Dakar, and a special administrator named Carera was designated to look into the plot.

Just as Carera set about his work, a "young native" came forward to denounce a meeting at Pout similar to the one described above. This meeting took place on the evening of October 4 upon the convocation of Alassane Dia, of Toucouleur ethnicity, who claimed to be a representative of Mamadou Lamine Dramé, a Tijaniyya marabout who had died while waging jihad against the French in 1887.[23] Dia called the meeting near the Keur Kamako tirailleur camp. A similar description of this meeting was given, including "the supernatural exit of the marabout from the trunk of the baobab. And, then the same propaganda was made for revolt against the White man, accompanied by the call to holy war, the announcement of a coming attack on Dakar and the request for participation of the crowd. Those attending, all tirailleurs, numbering around 50, had promised to turn their arms against the Europeans." The man who described the meeting turned Dia over to authorities at the train station in Pout. A search of his luggage found extensive documentation and names that "made the list of suspects grow considerably." His belongings also included a "curious mannequin in human form serving . . . to make people believe in the presence of Mamadou Lamine during the meetings." Authorities seemed surprised (considering that Lamine was dead) to learn "an investigation showed that [Lamine] was no more than a myth and that in reality Alassane Dia, veritable instigator of the plot, it seems, tried to add more weight to his exhortations by linking them with the name of a marabout who was well known in the area of Podor, named Mamadou Lamine, who appears to be unaware of the abuse made of his name and everything else about the affair."[24]

Twenty-eight individuals, all Toucouleurs, were arrested in the matter, and although their general strategy was to deny involvement or knowledge of the affair, French authorities concluded that by "contradictory depositions . . . their guilt is proven." On November 19 about a quarter of the stolen rifles were recovered.[25] The case was turned over to the military, and the police file was closed. It was later reported that the "principal guilty party, a civilian marabout," died in prison the following March. Among the others four were acquitted, and fourteen were given sentences that included prison time, expulsion from the colony, deportation, and military loss of rank.[26]

Having no sources on the Toucouleur soldiers' perspective on the theft makes it difficult to judge the relative accuracy of the French account. But the French point of view can be interpreted. This "revolt" in Ouakam coincided with the antirecruitment resistance of the First World War but also followed an era in which the French showed a remarkable tendency to conflate all reactions, threats, and actions of marabouts with an "Islamic conspiracy."[27] While Harrison identifies an "undoubted increase in millenarian Muslim activity in the first decade of the century," he also points to the tendency of French authorities to view Islam and marabouts with suspicion and cast much anti-French activity in terms of a Muslim "conspiracy."[28] It is indeed possible that the events surrounding the theft were filtered through a lens of Islamophobia. Nevertheless, because there is other evidence of simultaneous anti-French resistance to recruitment, the theft of arms indicates efforts to subvert French military power. And soldiers would be more likely to make a marabout their leader than a communist or other radical propagandist. In fact, as Governor-General Merlin made clear in 1921, the natives of West Africa had "only been preoccupied with commercial affairs, local politics and Muslim proselytism."[29] Islam was the most likely path for instigating rebellion at the time.

Perhaps the theft of rifles at Ouakam is most significant for highlighting the significance of the transition in political suspicion that occurred after the war. Muslim Affairs continued the surveillance of Islam, but police authorities who had only just recently been involved in the repression of a potentially violent uprising led by Muslims were increasingly obsessed with the unlikely possibility that international political radicalism would take hold in AOF. In the years after World War I, former tirailleurs were sometimes suspected of radicalism but usually not connected to Islam. Harrison writes, "The French administration in Dakar in the 1920s and 1930s saw less cause for alarm in Islam than they had done in previous eras."[30] Indeed in the 1920s Dakar's focus would turn to policing radical pan-Africanist groups such as the League for Defense of the Negro Race.

### The League for Defense of the Negro Race

The LDNR was the most important pan-African political movement to emerge from interwar Paris and find its way to AOF, although it was one among many radical, anticolonial, or literary movements in the metropolitan black community during that period.[31] A precursor to the LDNR, the Committee for the Defense of the Negro Race (CDNR), was founded in 1926 by the Senegalese Lamine Senghor. Senghor, a Serer, was originally from Joal and moved to Dakar to find work, eventually working for the French firm Maurel et Prom, before serving in the trenches in the First World War. He returned to France in 1921, where he found work at the post office. Disappointed by racism in France, Senghor soon joined the CGTU and the French Communist Party.[32] The CDNR, a communist-leaning group, lasted only one year; it was a year characterized by disagreement among the assimilationists, who hoped to work within the French administration, and the more radical members, who demanded independence for French colonies. Senghor and Kouyaté together founded the more radical LDNR in 1927.[33] With an office on the rue du Simplon in Paris, the LDNR published *La Race Nègre* and was more overtly communist than the CDNR.[34] After the death of Senghor in 1927, Kouyaté took over the direction of the LDNR and began forging a path closer to assimilationism. Yet he still differentiated his group from the cultural assimilationists who published *La Dépêche Africaine* (African Dispatch). Even with such overtures toward a more moderate cultural politics, Kouyaté still openly advocated for communist goals alongside pan-Africanism.[35]

Tiémoko Garan Kouyaté was Bambara, born in Ségou, Sudan, in 1902.[36] First educated at the primary school in Bamako, he spent 1918–21 at the famous École William Ponty on Gorée and graduated with the mention "assez bien." Kouyaté went on to serve as a teacher in Ivory Coast, then as an official (*fonctionnaire*) before being sent to study teaching at the École Normale in Aix-en-Provence in the metropole.[37] He failed to obtain the diploma he set out to earn in Aix and was expelled from the school. His teachers commented that he was "insolent and very undisciplined. . . . He makes clear his hostile sentiments towards the French administration in AOF."[38]

While Senghor's singular mission had been to "fight without mercy against colonialism, against all the imperialists of the world," Kouyaté embraced pan-Africanist ideas while also supporting anti-imperialism.[39] Under Kouyaté's leadership, the LDNR supported Garveyism and the National Association for the Advancement of Colored People of the United States. In 1927 and 1928 *La Race Nègre* published articles of cultural interest about blacks in the United States, cultural achievements of Africans throughout history, and eyewitness accounts of abuses committed by colonial administrators.[40] Kouyaté guided the LDNR along a complicated course, embracing cultural pan-Africanism and a rapprochement with Diagne and some of the other assimilationists, while still maintaining a communist stance yet resisting complete domination by the French Communist Party.[41]

In the mid-1920s the Colonial Ministry requested background information on Senghor and Kouyaté, then turned around and began dispatching information in the monthly propaganda reports about Kouyaté and other politically active colonial migrants in France.[42] The government general tracked his career and frequently disseminated information on him to the lieutenant governors by typing up excerpts of ministerial reports.[43]

Authorities were constantly on alert for Kouyaté's actions, tracing his movements in France and around Europe, including a visit to the Soviet Union, noting his connections within AOF and signs that he might return home. In October 1929, after a trip to Poland, Russia, and Belgium, at a meeting of the Seine section of the LDNR, Kouyaté declared he "had developed a taste for traveling." He announced that "next spring he would undertake a great propaganda world tour; he will visit America, the Antilles and will finish his trip with the English and French colonies of Africa."[44]

Although Kouyaté never returned to AOF, the LDNR, its members, and propaganda arrived there in 1927. When a pair of Dahoméen students who appeared to have connections with the LDNR passed through Dakar in April 1927, Police Inspector Lenaers reported on the two men and their acquaintances. Although he found no evidence of their political activity, he concluded, "There is no doubt that a connection has been established between the originaires of AOF living in the metropole who have joined the Communist group [the LDNR] and certain literate natives of Dakar."[45] In June 1927 a propaganda report announced that Kouyaté had sent a circular to "comrades in the provinces . . . and to friends in the colonies (in particular, those of Dakar)." Kouyaté himself claimed to be in correspondence with Tovalou and Doramy Liman, an administrative employee on leave in Dahomey, to encourage them to join the group.[46] Correspondence and the infiltration of propaganda tracts provided the earliest opportunity for the LDNR to reach AOF.

In 1927 the first chapter of the LDNR was created in Dakar by Beccaria, who established himself as treasurer of the new section.[47] An originaire born in Saint-Louis and a former sergeant in the French Army, Beccaria had been employed as a writer with the District of Dakar. He had also worked for the electric company and in a registry office.[48] His service in the war had led to a bad case of tuberculosis that left him disabled.[49] In a relatively unusual instance for Africans, Beccaria was indicted for his moral transgressions in addition to his politics. He was married to a "mulatto" woman from Casamance, but according to police, by 1927 he had spent his wife's fortune on "women of ill repute" and was separated from her. Police inspectors condemned Beccaria harshly, describing him as "one of these little young people, numerous in the country who thinks himself superior because he is an official [*fonctionnaire*]. He is sometimes listened to, but he will never be followed by a majority because he does not have the courage of his opinions."[50] In 1927 Beccaria was one of the most significant and reviled suspects in AOF, largely due to his important role in establishing the LDNR in Senegal.

Beccaria made ardent attempts to spread the propaganda of the LDNR but encountered various difficulties. When the League first established itself in Paris, he made overtures to the politician Lamine Guèye to persuade him to join. Guèye, who had earned a law degree in France, supported Diagne in the recruitment campaign but later became his political opponent.[51] Guèye was involved in the politics of the four communes and could not risk open affiliation with a radical organization. Beccaria, writing to Kouyaté, reported that Guèye said "he could not participate, and counseled me, rather, to give you moral and financial support in the battle you have undertaken."[52] Beccaria also complained about the lack of support for his branch from Paris, in spite of his efforts. He wrote, "I have sacrificed myself to a common cause, organizing meetings, engaging in endless discussions, without ever forming a section, not having received instructions from you."[53] He proposed several employees of the colonial administration as officers of the group as well as Joseph Angrand, a Dakar merchant who would serve as president. Joseph was the brother of Armand and a member of the early political action group the Young Senegalese.[54] In the meantime Beccaria promised to spread the word to "my disabled veteran friends, and others of this area, and those I meet in the bush while on periodic tours." In spite of obstacles he had succeeded in sharing information about the League as well as distributing copies of the journal to Ernest Chery in French Guinea, and in French Congo, where he had a contact in Leon Dervalle.[55]

Kouyaté eventually supported Beccaria by corresponding with individuals in AOF interested in the LDNR. In a typical exchange, Kouyaté wrote to Bakary Ba, the canton chief in Kédougou, Senegal, an acquaintance of Beccaria, in 1929. After giving Ba advice on how to be a fair administrator, Kouyaté urged him to show "that negroes can administer themselves." He ended his letter telling Ba, "Write me often. The price of a subscription to the 'Race Nègre' is 20 francs per year. And why don't you join the League?"[56] This kind of correspondence was Kouyáté's most effective means of building support for the League in AOF.

Adherents to the League surfaced in Sudan, Ivory Coast, and Togo. A man named Ackah in Grand Bassam, Ivory Coast, was put in charge of creating a section of the League along with Remi Peter Angovi as secretary and Paul Richemond as treasurer. Kouyaté wrote to Ackah urging him "to signal injustices and abuses. The hour is coming for our race to come out of its secular lethargy."[57] In 1928 Ackah was supposed to receive over six hundred copies of *La Race Nègre*, but when the Customs Service in Grand Bassam discovered them, he agreed to turn them over to the circle commander.[58] Another Ivoirian, Pierre Tournabia, a planter from Louga, subscribed to the League in 1928. After sending a money order of 60 francs to Paris, Tournabia received a membership card and copies of the journal, and after a year's membership would gain the right to vote in the election of officers. Meanwhile Kouyaté urged him, "Spread propaganda around you and let us know all the wrongs done to the interests of our compatriots."[59] The lieutenant governor of Ivory Coast admitted, "It is certain that the newspaper *La Race Nègre* is read by a large part of the literate native population along the lower coast and that an intense propaganda is underway to spread it throughout the colony."[60] The growth of the LDNR in Ivory Coast shows the ability of the networks it created to move the journals and other League materials out of Dakar and into other colonies.

The LDNR also made inroads in Kouyaté's home colony of Sudan. In 1929 Lucien d'Almeida, a court employee, was signaled by police as "engaged in propaganda in favor of the LDNR" when he lived in Bamako.[61] In 1930 an administrator identified d'Almeida as "having had relations with revolutionary organizations. This native figures in the police archives as a militant of said organizations. He is the object of a special surveillance by the Sûreté."[62] A letter intercepted in 1928 from Kouyaté to Amadou Thiam promised to send a League membership card and a newspaper and encouraged Thiam to form a group in Bamako and elect a president, secretary, and treasurer.[63] A 1929 report from the Colonial Ministry confirmed that Paris was aware of the LDNR's activities in Sudan.[64] Although surveillance probably prevented the success of the LDNR in Bamako, d'Almeida's and Thiam's activities provide evidence of another node in the LDNR's network.

In 1931 the League for the Defense of the Negro Race in Paris split again, this time with Kouyaté turning his energy toward syndicalism by creating the UTN and a new journal, *Le Cri des Nègres* (Cry of the Negroes). The new publication reached Dakar almost immediately, containing an article by the Guadeloupian communist Stéphane Rosso describing the Scottsboro rape trial in the United States and the deaths of Africans in the construction of the Congo-Ocean railroad.[65] A shipment of five hundred copies of *Le Cri des Nègres* dating from November and December 1931 was said to be on the way from Bordeaux to Dakar aboard *L'Amérique*.[66] *La Race Nègre* continued to be published under the direction of Emile Faure of Martinique, who directed the League after the split with Kouyaté. The paper also surfaced in Dakar in 1931.[67]

AOF did not absorb metropolitan propaganda only through the press and correspondence. Some LDNR agents came to AOF in person to agitate. Henri Jean-Louis, originally of Guadeloupe, who had spoken at a meeting of the Paris LDNR in 1929, came to Dakar in 1931, where he reported on the founding of *La Revue du Monde Noir* (Revue of the Black World), a metropolitan literary journal under the direction of the Haitian dentist and member of the Paris LDNR Leo Sajoux.[68] Jean-Louis was also a lawyer, formerly of the court in Brazzaville. While in the city he connected with Magatte Ba, who provided him with lodging, and Beccaria.[69]

As the LDNR grew, police surveillance and repression followed. Attempts to eradicate the group and their ideas included monitoring mail and searching homes to identify members of the organization. Kouyaté's mail was constantly under surveillance. In 1930 a search of the home of his brother Moudou Kouyaté turned up a letter from him. While describing the home search, Special Inspector of Police Jean Barreyre took the opportunity to comment on the situation of the movement as whole in Sudan: "The center of pan-negro agitation is located in Sudan and particularly in Kayes and Bamako among those called the 'intellectuals' of the country—teachers, postal workers, medical students, and typist-secretaries of the commercial houses. The Wolof element makes up a good part of it. Although for the moment this turbulent youth maintains a discreet reserve, without a doubt for fear of this famous 'Sûreté' of which Kouyaté speaks so well in his letter addressed to Sory Maïga, it appears necessary and urgent to keep a very close surveillance over their actions."[70] Shortly after the home search the lieutenant governor claimed success: "No meetings of a political nature have been held in Bamako and in the course of conversations held between the young people under surveillance no anti-French remarks have been noted."[71] This single incident is quite telling about the way surveillance and investigations repressed the activity of the LDNR. The investigation combined a home search with monitoring mail and surveillance. In this case, a discreet surveillance was not accomplished, nor does it seem to have been the goal. The investigation itself clued in Moudou Kouyaté and his comrades that they were being watched by the police, and so they ceased their activity.

Knowledge that one was under surveillance was itself probably sufficient deterrent for many others as well, especially after a police search took place. Public knowledge of surveillance and searches was an important part of repression. Nicole Bernard-Duquenet interviewed Amadou Sibi, a member of the LDNR in Saint-Louis in the 1930s, and believes that public knowledge of surveillance was quite widespread.[72] Thomas concurs that "objects of state interest" mostly knew they were under surveillance and "adjusted their behavior accordingly."[73] Merely knowing one was being investigated or monitored by the police likely prevented the expansion of activities of the LDNR.

Many adherents of the LDNR were also employees of the colonial administration. Once discovered, their employment could be threatened as a way to repress their activity. Angovi, an employee in Ivory Coast, canceled his membership in the LDNR for an unnamed reason in 1928, although it seems likely it was because he received a reprimand for receiving the League's journal. In a letter Kouyaté referred to Angovi as a "brave compatriot," expressed "real regret" at his departure, but also suggested he might have overreacted: "[He] made a tragedy out of things because, like all our subscribers, we have always sent his journal hidden in an envelope."[74] Beccaria found his job with the city of Dakar threatened. Police files indicate that his employer knew he was the leader of the LDNR. When Beccaria was informed he would be reassigned by the government to rural Kédougou, over nine hundred kilometers from Dakar, where his political agenda would be useless, he knew he was the victim of an insidious repression. But this was more than an attack on his political life. In Kédougou Beccaria would not be able to receive lifesaving treatment for his tuberculosis. However, his refusal of the transfer would mean dismissal. Beccaria considered the reassignment an excuse to destroy his career and halt his political activities. He asked Diagne and Vadier, the administrator of the District of Dakar, to intervene on his behalf as a war veteran in need of medical care and access to hospitalization.[75] But he ended up leaving his job, and authorities confirmed, "[He] claims that he voluntarily left the offices of the district [of Dakar] because he was under surveillance by the police."[76] Beccaria continued his political work, although he found himself more and more isolated: "This effort, made by me alone, without help in the midst of frequent attacks, has only augmented my courage [and my] devotion for my racial brothers."[77]

The administration also transformed policies to respond to the growing movement of the LDNR and prevent its spread. In 1928 the government general changed an existing law regulating the press to respond directly to the growth of the LDNR and other groups that were managing to distribute anti-French materials in AOF. The new decree extended a 1921 law targeting the foreign press that forbade periodicals "likely to cause damage to the respect due to French authority" to also include "local and metropolitan press in the French language." Under the law Governor-General Carde described the government general as the "unrestricted master" of all local, metropolitan, and foreign publications entering the colony. The government could forbid the sale or distribution of any journal found to be "of a nature to attack our authority." However, publications edited and printed in the metropole could not be forbidden outright: "Only the putting up for sale, the distribution or the exposition of these publications is punishable." Although "circulation" of such documents was technically legal, its legality was restricted to the publication's arrival at its destination in the colonies; the recipient could not redistribute or sell any publication considered subversive.[78] The timing of the shift (and the fact that a document describing it is found in the LDNR file) suggests that the change in law came in direct response to the level of alarm resulting from the arrival of LDNR propaganda in AOF in 1927.

In response to repression members of the LDNR as well as other political groups worked to maintain their connections in other ways. In Senegal the LDNR used the railroad to spread materials, and pockets of adherents appeared along the rail lines. Sailors were hired to smuggle newspapers aboard ships when the mail was tightly monitored. If they were lucky, sailors deposited the newspapers at their destination port and then departed aboard ship again before being identified. In one instance in 1927 sailors passed out cards displaying a hammer and sickle to dock workers unloading a ship at Dakar's port, presumably as a way to spread communist ideas without distributing illegal newspapers. The LDNR also asked their members to copy out articles in LDNR publications and pass the copies to a "trustworthy friend," then report back to the LDNR with the friend's name.[79] Such novel strategies allowed the LDNR to move information and locate new members while avoiding police observation. Togola, Soumah, Kaba, and Cardozo, mentioned in the opening to this chapter, testify to the complex networks and knowledge that made infiltrating AOF with suspicious newspapers possible, at least for a while. Kaba and Togola could exploit their knowledge as former employees of the Sûreté while also mobilizing forces within the metropole. Soumah used his position as a ship's cook to enter ports undetected, at least initially. Kaba, and surely others as well, maintained and utilized contacts in the colonies through the ideal position of Cardozo, a European owner of a restaurant catering to a clientele of African sailors.

Some historians have claimed that political repression actually stimulated political dissidence. Wilder writes, "Official efforts to classify and control indigenous elites generated more regulatory ambiguity and provoked new transgressions, which in turn required stricter policing measures and yet more dissent."[80] Thomas surmises, "Whether in mainland France or in the empire, the imposition of a racially ordered authority imposed an increasing burden on the network of state intelligence gathering. Alienation of the wider population only increased as a result."[81] While the repression of a group like LDNR surely angered and alienated many elite Africans in AOF, there is no evidence that the repression increased dissent. In fact the repression seemed to be successful, at least until the Second World War. Police efforts to dismantle the LDNR were largely successful by the early 1930s. In 1935 the LDNR made new attempts to spread their propaganda in AOF, only to abandon these in less than a year. They began turning their energy and propaganda to other projects, such as supporting Ethiopia in defending itself against Italian aggression.[82] The difficulty in spreading the propaganda and correspondence of the LDNR in AOF made other projects that could best use the limited resources available to the League a priority. Radical pan-Africanist political networks would not reemerge with the same force in AOF until after the Second World War.

## The Voice of Dahomey

Dahomey's unique history as a colony within AOF, characterized by an active export trade, a powerful landed elite, connection to the Brazilian slave trade, and early exposure to Catholic missions, resulted in the creation of a cosmopolitan and educated elite.[83] Early on under French rule the Dahoméen elite attempted to cooperate with the Europeans to invest in land and labor in ways that would create an indigenous form of capitalism. The French rejected this effort, preferring to keep capitalist development firmly in their own hands.[84] From these origins a bourgeois nationalist movement emerged that would sometimes ally with the French state but remained a vigilant critic of land policies, taxes, and rights to elections, among other things. The only truly nationalist movement to take shape in interwar AOF, Patrick Manning emphasizes, "was reformist rather than revolutionary, and it never challenged the right of France to rule Dahomey."[85]

Dahomey was also home to one of the most important critics of French colonial rule, Louis Hunkanrin. Hunkanrin's political activity began with the founding of a branch of the French-based League of the Rights of Man in Dahomey in 1910, an infraction for which he lost his post as a teacher.[86] His extensive contacts in the metropole allowed him to publish articles critical of the serious abuses by Dahomey's lieutenant governor Charles Noufflard, who murdered and arbitrarily imprisoned people, including Hunkanrin. Hunkanrin was forced into various kinds of exile, due to both official and informal pressure.[87] He led a campaign against the *indigénat*, under the laws of which he was arrested several times. At first he opposed French wartime recruitment, but later he secretly allied with Diagne and enlisted in the French Army, although the two ultimately had a falling-out due to Hunkanrin's refusal to cooperate with the administration.[88] In 1920 Hunkanrin was demobilized in France and stayed in Paris for a short time to join the growing radical movements there. He soon returned to Dahomey, however, where he was sent to prison for falsifying documents.[89]

It was from prison that Hunkanrin would witness and help lead the famous Porto-Novo events of 1923. The nationalist movement had percolated under the pressures of World War I recruitment, but postwar dissatisfaction with the colonial administration led to the open outbreak of protests. Strikes, refusal to pay taxes, and riots characterized a six-week period of anti-French activism. Colonial officials responded by repressing their critics and exiling leaders of the group. But they also made concessions to some demands, including increasing representation of Dahoméens on the Administrative Council and the creation of municipal councils in cities. Electoral institutions were thus expanded, although only about five hundred people secured new voting rights under the reforms by producing credentials proving their citizenship, education, merchant status, or extensive property ownership.[90]

The bourgeois nationalists benefited from these reforms, and the movement continued to gain strength through the 1920s. An important turning point for the movement was the 1927 establishment of the newspaper *La Voix du Dahomey* (Voice of Dahomey), an "organ of the landed and commercial elite."[91] The paper criticized the administration, including African canton chiefs, the *indigénat*, and lack of access to education.[92] In addition to providing a voice for the bourgeois national movement, the *Voix* supported candidates for election to the Chamber and Administrative Council and to the Superior Council in France, where Dahomey had one representative. Among the leaders of the *Voix* were Pierre Johnson, a member of the business and landed elite who served on the Chamber of Commerce and the Administrative Council in Dahomey in spite of his opposition to the administration, and Jean Adjovi, who also came from a prominent family. Adjovi inherited the title of chief from his father, helped Diagne with recruitment, served with the tirailleurs in the First World War, and was one of the very few Dahoméens who was able to gain citizenship after the war.[93]

The government general kept a special file on Hunkanrin maintained by the Dahomey branch of the government, not the police or APA.[94] But the Sûreté and government general were especially concerned with keeping track of the *Voix* because the leaders were assumed to be connected to radical political movements. In 1931 the director of the Sûreté in Dakar began to compile "Renseignements" (reports) on the leadership of the paper. Johnson and Adjovi, along with Firmin Santos and Alexandre d'Oliviera, were listed as "extremist agitators" and "suspects of communist propaganda."[95] Gerard Avomassado, originally of Togo, was described as a "widely known communist" who had lived in Bordeaux after the First World War and worked as a mechanic in Togo, then in the boiler works of the railroads in Dahomey, and had spent some time in prison for assault and battery. In addition to being involved in the LDNR and having "dubious morality," Avomassado had himself been one of the leaders of a strike in Dahomey in 1927.[96] Adjovi, the editor of the *Voix* at the time, was described as a "reader of extremist journals, correspondent of Georges Tovalou Quénum, militant communist," and "the soul of a vast association of criminals."[97]

Of course as bourgeois nationalists the leaders of the *Voix* were not communists; the movement was eminently more complex than this. The leaders advocated economic reform for the benefit of the landed and propertied classes, but their movement was willing to ally with workers to promote reforms that would benefit all Dahoméens. Within the national movement there was also a place for a cultural nationalism promoted by the Catholic Church as well as the radical ideas of someone like Avomassado, who was affiliated with Kouyaté and the UTN.[98] They also allied with Hunkanrin, who connected with the *Voix* from exile in Mauritania and published articles there in 1932. The administration's characterization of the group as radical communists misrepresents what was clearly a dynamic and broad-ranging political paper.

The repression of the *Voix* was long and complicated. Its members were part of a vocal, visible, and elite organization, unlike many other suspects, who operated clandestinely. One way the administration sought to decrease the power of the *Voix* was by attempting to co-opt Dahoméens who might have been drawn to the movement. From 1929 to 1930 under Lieutenant Governor Jean-François Reste the administration of Dahomey worked to earn the allegiance of canton chiefs, an upwardly mobile group whose loyalty might have been swayed by the *Voix*. Reste increased their pay and prestige, effectively creating an enemy for the nationalist movement within the growing middle class of chiefs.[99]

Articles published in the *Voix* in 1931 drew the attention of the government general. H. Dirat, the director of APA, wrote to the lieutenant governor of Dahomey about the "tendentious, even anti-French content" of some articles and compared them to "extremist journals of the Levant, Tunisia and the Spanish zone of Morocco." Dirat suggested that the lieutenant governor consider how regulations might put a stop to this "press campaign." Dirat also somewhat cryptically suggested a review of the salaries and positions of native employees, implying that too could be a punishment for the *Voix*'s publishers.[100]

In 1934 a series of moves by French officials in Dahomey directly sought to repress the *Voix* by targeting its leadership and its rights as a newspaper. In March 1934 Adjovi wrote directly to the Colonial Ministry in Paris to complain about an incident in February of that year in which the commissaire of police of Ouidah broke into a religious sanctuary (*couvent fétichiste*) at Adjovi's home, disrupting religious ceremonies and stealing musical instruments.[101] Given that Adjovi was well known to police, it is possible the incident was a form of harassment. On the other hand, also in March 1934 Governor-General Brévié wrote to the minister about another case related to Dahoméen "fetishes" thrown into the sea, a case that Adjovi also seems to have protested. According to Brévié, Adjovi exaggerated the affair and "endeavors to revive the incident at any favorable opportunity."[102]

Whether the Dahomey police were harassing Adjovi or he was irritating them, he and the colonial administration were clearly at odds.

In September 1934 conflict between the *Voix* and the administration peaked when the *Voix* refused to retract an article and the police raided the offices. Subsequently the administration embarked on an unyielding attempt to destroy the paper.[103] Although the raids revealed little of relevance before the court, Johnson was convicted for his involvement in the women's tax demonstrations in 1932.[104] Eventually the *Voix* was charged with breaking the 1928 law regulating the press, but the judge sided with the *Voix*, chastising the prosecution for bringing the case and meting out small fines for some and acquittals for others. The nationalist movement seemed to be revived, but the *Voix* had lost crucial allies, including Hunkanrin and the canton chiefs. According to Manning, the bourgeois nationalist movement was split between those who still criticized the state and those who sided with the administration.[105] While the *Voix* and the nationalist movement survived the repression and gained further momentum under the Popular Front, the group turned its attacks more directly on the canton chiefs and less frequently on the colonial administration, a strategy now deemed "too costly" due to the court cases.[106] While the administration failed to destroy the *Voix* and the bourgeois nationalist movement as a whole, it was able to quiet their criticism.

### Dahomey and the International Workers of Education

Given the other political movements happening in Dahomey in the early 1920s it should come as no surprise that the colony was fertile ground for the emergence of a teachers' union. The International Workers of Education (IWE, Travailleurs International de l'Enseignement) developed in a fashion similar to the creation of the LDNR. Metropolitan tracts were sent to the colonies and members encouraged their colleagues to join. Although ultimately unsuccessful, the story of the IWE reveals another dimension of radical politics in Dahomey and again illustrates how police could quash a growing movement.

In 1927 two Dahoméens, Adotevi Kpakpo and Mensam Covi, who had studied in Aix-en-Provence alongside Kouyaté, "passed through Dakar on their way to Dahomey."[107] Principal Inspector Lenaers reported that the two students, who were making their way to Dahomey from France, "had been in touch with their compatriots (expelled students) who are currently members of the Comité de Défense de la Race Noire [*sic*]. Shortly after the passage of these two natives, the tract 'International Workers of Education' which is located at 35, rue de la Grange aux Belles in Paris and the brochure 'Official Organ of the International of Workers of Teaching' appeared in Dakar."[108] One of the friends whom Kpakpo and Covi visited while in Dakar was named Acbessy; he was a "close friend" of Adolphe Mendy, who had already been reported for distributing the *La Voix des Nègres*.[109] After Kpakpo and Covi arrived in Dahomey similar tracts surfaced there as well. Kpakpo and Covi thus provide a key link between the growth of the LDNR in Senegal and the political scene in Dahomey, where the IWE emerged. The IWE's publication was forbidden by authorities because it involved syndicalism, which was illegal in AOF, except for a brief period under the Popular Front in 1936–37.[110] Furthermore the IWE's own publications stressed the group's links with communism, leaving no doubt that such an organization would be considered undesirable in AOF.[111]

A 1928 propaganda letter addressed to the teachers of AOF asked for information about the colony. It declared, "Comrades! It is up to you to tell us about your material and moral situation, what you think of the organization of education in AOF." The letter described relations between teachers and local administrators as "a permanent state of hostility," including punishments such as beatings. Life for teachers, it claimed, is "close to prison." The letter boasted that the IWE had significant contacts in AOF: "A teacher comrade in Sudan has worked with us; we receive regular mail from Dahomey, notably Senegal and from the Ivory Coast."[112]

In March 1929 French authorities became aware that the IWE had achieved some initial success in its propaganda campaign. Carde explained, "A functionary of this type [teacher] maintains epistolary relations with this international organization of which I do not need to underline the undesirable tendencies." He described the IWE as "a new form of communist propaganda in the colony" and naturally recommended a "discreet, but tight surveillance" over its activities in all colonies. Carde urged the lieutenant governors of Dahomey, Ivory Coast, and Senegal (all places mentioned in the propaganda of the IWE) to report back on "all maneuvers you manage to detect as well as the measures you judge useful to take."[113] In September of the same year, the Colonial Ministry wrote to warn the governor-general of the propaganda of the IWE: "This propaganda does not only have a pedagogical reach, but its ultimate goal, which it calls 'the struggle against imperialism' is essentially political."[114]

The lieutenant governor of Dahomey reported that he had indeed found evidence of the infiltration of the IWE propaganda in the teaching milieux of the colony, as well as some interest on the part of targeted teachers. Lambert Lyncée, originally of Martinique, and Herman Ekoué, of Grand Popo, Dahomey, both of whom had teaching posts in Dahomey schools, were actively engaged in spreading propaganda for the IWE. Ekoué had also been sharing his beliefs about unions with drivers and mechanics in Niger. Three other Dahoméen teachers had "come together to respond with a collective letter to a tract of the International of Workers of Education."[115] By October 1930 eight teachers in Dahomey had been "signaled by their bad attitude and by acts of subversive propaganda." These included Kpakpo, Emile Poisson, and Isaac Foly, all of who had been students in Aix-en-Provence.[116]

The investigation of the IWE extended throughout the federation. The governor-general reported that in Niger, Upper Volta, and the District of Dakar "no hint was discovered to warrant any fear that the native milieux had been touched by the subversive activities of the teachers affiliated with the 'International.'"[117] In Ivory Coast an investigation did not discover much about the IWE but led to other information, for example, that the teacher Bertrand Amessan was an "assiduous reader of *la Dépêche Africaine* and *La Race Nègre*" and was acquainted with "a certain Richmond Ehiman signaled in 1927 for creating a communist group."[118] The governments of Senegal and Mauritania found no hints of propaganda among the teachers in their colonies.[119] Alarm over unions thus could help mobilize an investigation throughout the federation.

Having collected information regarding the depth of the IWE's infiltration into the teachers of AOF, the administration responded with a plan to destroy the group. The repression occurred mostly in Dahomey, where teachers were "remind[ed] of their administrative, professional and moral obligations; [warned about] these tendentious publications and encouraged to alert their Chief of Service of all attempts to divert them from their duty." Disciplinary action involved transfers of some teachers to remote outposts. Lyncée was transferred to Sudan and Ekoué was sent to a rural region of Dahomey, described as being "among very primitive populations, resistant to all propaganda." Augustin, who authored a joint letter to the IWE, was transferred to Djougou, where he would be under the watchful eye of a European teacher. The lieutenant governor was confident that having made an example of these men, he would have no further problems, as he was "convinced that these teachers did not spread propaganda in their classes, they addressed only their colleagues or the intellectual elite of the country."[120] In September 1930 the inspector of primary education in Dahomey requested the transfer of both Poisson and Kpakpo.[121]

Despite a few lapses, the lieutenant governor painted a generally positive picture of the teachers of Dahomey. However, he proposed a more long-term solution to diminish the appeal of propaganda: "The action of the communists in the colonies, at least in Africa, would lose the major part of its efficacy if it did not find young people not knowing what to do with their leisure time." He suggested that "the organization of libraries, music groups, stadiums, and sport groups would not fail to contribute to the fight against extremist propaganda in offering the intellectual youth distraction, which has been up until now totally lacking."[122]

The movement for involvement in the IWE in Dahomey came on the heels of the influx of propaganda from the LDNR. Although it captured initial interest in Dahomey, administrators were able to prevent its spread. The fact that Dahomey was already known as a site of intellectual and political agitation likely influenced the speed of the repression. Given the few number of people involved and the subsequent scrutiny to which all teachers became subject, the suppression of the IWE suggests the crucial role played by teachers in the power dynamics of French colonialism. Hunkanrin himself had been a teacher, and this group of educated elites with a captive audience—their students—was powerful. Authorities paid careful attention to see if propaganda was also disseminated among students or remained within the ranks of educators. French authorities first gauged the level of the threat, then went about using various repressive tactics, including warning people not to join the group, transferring teachers to places they were less likely to continue their actions or where surveillance of administrators was direct. Finally, in a somewhat unusual attempt at repression, authorities considered finding alternative outlets to contain the impulses that led to engagement in revolutionary activity.

*Small's Network*

The LDNR and IWE were official organizations with headquarters in the metropole. A smaller, more informal network also emerged in AOF around the same time. This political network was created by Edward Francis Small during his visits to AOF in the early 1930s. As explained in chapter 3, in June 1931 Small brought his mission to Dakar in the company of his secretary Boubakar Secka. Small's time in Dakar attests to the growing interest in communist and pan-Africanist movements in Senegal. According to a surveillance report, Small "met a great number of natives in this city, for the most part those already converted to extremist ideas . . . and many more have come to meet him in the room he rents on rue Félix Faure."[123] Small energetically spread his politics and succeeded in reaching Senegalese workers and African colonial employees in Kaolack and Kaffrine.[124] Among his AOF acquaintances were Ernest Chery, who was involved with the LDNR and affiliated with the French League against Colonial Oppression; Fofana Coulibaly, a former teacher from French Guinea who "demonstrated extremist ideas and anti-French opinions"; and Raphael Mensah, who was "on a list of individuals suspected of being sympathizers of the revolutionary movement."[125] Small also had relations with English-speaking blacks, including at least one involved in the Garveyist incidents of 1922, William Winston, the associate of Angrand. Europeans too were part of Small's circle, especially French communists, notably Lamotte, the chief of the train station in Khombole.

Small was eager to reach out to the other fledgling radical organizations in AOF. He was a member of the International Association of Negro

Workers and, like his close associate George Padmore (aka Nurse), was likely in touch with Kouyaté. According to police, Small met with a group of "members or sympathizers of the LDNR" in Dakar, where "he took an active part in the discussion."[126] He was in touch with Ibrahima Sow, founder of the publication *Rumeur Sénégalaise* (Senegalese Rumor) who, in 1931, had published "three incendiary articles against the Government General."[127] Small was observed at a drinking establishment in the company of Mapenda Diaw, "until recently one of the principal directors of the Dakar Section of the LDNR."[128] Small's acquaintances extended beyond communists and pan-Africanists to the politician Galandou Diouf and an "influential disciple of the deportee in Ségou, Cheikh Anta."[129] Small's presence helped fill AOF's roster of suspicious persons because so many people became suspect merely by associating with him.[130]

Unlike the Sierra Leone UNIA group of 1922, Small was able to mobilize individuals who participated in networks that emerged in the late 1920s, especially the LDNR. By the time he arrived in 1930 there were individuals "already converted to extremist ideas." Despite his relative success, Small's activity would not last long. Laws regulating foreigners forced his departure in September 1931. No long-term political legacy of his network appears to exist.

*From Network to Network*

The group that gravitated around Small demonstrates the flexibility of dissident political groups. Individuals involved in such networks did not maintain strict allegiance to one, but moved from group to group as political activity was repressed or new activity emerged. In fact more often than not involvement in one dissident network meant exposure to and involvement in others. Members moved with ease and fluidity between groups as one emerged, another folded, or yet another became available just as one disappeared. This flexibility can be considered both a strategy on the part of suspects who maintained interest in groups in spite of difficulty as well as a consequence of repression. Because of the small number of people involved in radical politics, individuals could likely quickly learn about a new group or publication from someone already in their network.

Amadou Sall, the Senegalese mentioned in the introduction to this book, was involved in a variety of groups. Sall came to the attention of French authorities in the early 1930s, revealing his communist tendencies when, at the post office in Dakar, he "asked several natives if he could receive *l'Humanité* without difficulty and if there was a control of letters in Dakar."[131] Another report on him claimed that he "boasted, many times, about having lived in the United States where he knew the principal leaders of the Garveyist movement."[132] Sall also revealed, apparently to an informer, that he was connected to the LDNR and that he had been friends with Senghor. His correspondents included many people in the United States, and his acquaintances ranged from Arthur Beccaria of the LDNR to the marabout Cheikh Anta.[133] Sall's case serves as a reminder that although networks and organizations were important to the promotion of radical politics, individuals were not necessarily tied to them. Sall devoted his time and interests to involvement in various groups in different countries.

*Summary*

Repression by the colonial state was not the only factor that influenced success or failure of an African political network. Division within groups could delay putting ideas into action; the constant battle in the LDNR over whether or not to have an explicit communist affiliation or to engage with the cultural assimilationist groups among the splintering metropolitan groups is one example of such an internal disagreement. Kouyaté reportedly once felt threatened by the activity of the Ligue française contre l'impérialisme (French League against Imperialism), accusing one of his correspondents of being disloyal to his Union of Negro Workers by associating with this group. Kouyaté wrote, "Has your group been transformed into the League for the fight for the independence of Senegal and Soudan? Are you in contact with the French League against Imperialism? You must suspend all other political relationships with the metropole until we are better informed."[134]

The history of African political networks reinforces themes central to the surveillance of all suspects. The culture of suspicion cast a wide net in identifying potential suspects, and fears of communism meant that a bourgeois nationalist group could be treated with the same repression as a group like the LDNR, which had more overt links to communism. The creation and growth of dissident political activity also shaped the French colonial administration. In response to the rise in publications entering the colonies from the LDNR in 1927 the government general strategized new repressive tactics, including strengthening the law restricting the press. The emergence of the bourgeois national movement and the activity of Hunkanrin in Dahomey caused authorities there to allocate resources and personnel to the repression of new political groups.

In the metropole, despite surveillance practices of the CAI, newspapers were published, pan-Africanist groups convened, unions formed, and alliances made. In French West Africa colonial repression drove such activities underground. In addition to laws that made certain newspapers, public gatherings, and political groups illegal, surveillance forced individuals to carry on their activism in radical politics in secret. The repressive surveillance of authorities clearly handicapped such groups even as they continued to share information and locate fellow sympathizers. Mail was monitored, homes were searched, and individuals were placed under surveillance for potentially incriminating speech. The subtlety of the repression can be observed in tactics such as posting suspect employees to new jobs or advising suspects in no uncertain terms to discontinue their engagement with politics.

This study is limited by its reliance on French colonial documentation. Sources for understanding the ways the African suspects in these files understood radical politics or police surveillance are not readily available. However, police documents provide a glimpse into how they responded to repression: by coming up with new tactics to evade colonial control and profit from the few advantages they had—connections with sailors and networks that reached out into Africa and to the United States and France. Individuals showed their flexibility by shifting between groups and joining various organizations out of necessity. Surveillance and repression did not always destroy networks or make it impossible for new groups to form. Police repression nevertheless severely restricted the burgeoning radical political scene of AOF.

# Conclusion

In June 1940, shortly after the fall of France to Germany, French West Africa fell in line behind Marshall Pétain and Pierre Boisson became the governor-general. The Vichy regime in AOF was concerned with terrorism and sabotage as well as the spread of communist propaganda, something they claimed occurred when a 1940 troop demobilization led to revolt.[1] Vichy urged the police of AOF to exercise surveillance over "administrative agents who had been known to belong to groups of the Third International."[2] In 1941 police services were once again reorganized, this time under the name Direction de la Sûreté Générale. Although this new organization had the same goals of "preventive and repressive policing" as prior versions, its methods appeared to be different.[3] Rather than surveillance conducted by individual agents, these police services used "mobile brigades" to repress "anti-nationalists, Gaullists and Anglo-Saxons."[4] Internment for political reasons was preferred over the use of surveillance.[5] Hunkanrin was interned in Sudan after having been caught helping Free French volunteers come and go from Nigeria.[6] Evidence that the surveillance of suspects was almost completely abandoned under Vichy is also clear in the lack of documents on the subject. Just two suspects' files in the archives are dated 1940, while none is dated 1941 or 1942, and only a few appear between 1945 and 1947. The Vichy regime officially ended in 1942, with the departure of Boisson in July 1943, when the Free French took over.[7]

As the war in Europe came to a close, French officials hoped to preserve the empire and prioritized the collection of political intelligence once again. In May 1945 a political information bulletin noted the following: "A Senegalese living in France, Léopold Senghor, professor at the École Coloniale maintains a continuous correspondence with native journalists. . . . As already indicated, this native is a supporter of the Union Française, but in terms of absolute equality; he wants universal suffrage in AOF with a single electoral college without distinction between citizens and non-citizens, proportional representation of colonial territories in the next constitutional assembly, equality between Africans and Europeans."[8] Senghor would become the first president of an independent Senegal, but in the days following the end of hostilities in Europe, he was a "native" who espoused somewhat radical political views about equality between Europeans and Africans. As the war ended, a new era of political surveillance was beginning.

In the immediate postwar era forced labor was abolished, syndicalism became legal again, and new political parties were allowed to form. Authorities attempted to keep up with political changes with the collection of information on groups through voluminous political bulletins. In 1946 political information multiplied rapidly. Information sheets indicated that new political groups were forming quickly and attracting many new members. In June 1946 a *renseignements* report commented on "a keen interest" among "native milieux related to the creation of a League for Defense of the Economic Interests of AOF." Advertised in the newspaper *Paris-Dakar*, the group had already signed up more than a hundred members.[9] A report on the Dakar-Niger railroad syndicate chronicled the details of a meeting attended by about eight hundred people.[10] A 1946 report on the Socialist Party documented a political speech made by Secretary-General Alexandre Angrand to a crowd of three hundred in Thiès.[11] In August 1946 rumors swirled that the youth of Senegal would accept nothing less than immediate independence.[12] Africans no longer kept radical politics secret but proclaimed them with enthusiasm and in great numbers.

Independence would not come to French West Africa definitively until 1960. But the end of the war meant that political surveillance changed profoundly. In this burgeoning political context the police still conducted surveillance to collect information. For example, they infiltrated the unions that called for the famous railway strikes of 1947.[13] Surveillance of suspicious French metropolitans and foreigners was carried forward too, especially of academic researchers. Although surveillance of suspicious persons continued, the culture of suspicion had changed fundamentally. It moved away from a model that primarily identified individual suspects and small groups for surveillance and investigation. Its goal now seemed to be to catch and filter as much political information as possible through detailed reports. Strategies shifted as well. Political reports now began with an indication of where the information came from and an assessment of its quality, usually described as a "good native source" or "good European source." Informants or observers copied the texts of political or union speeches word for word and authorities passed them on in their "original version."[14] In the interwar era suspects' reports were frequently shared in polite letters typed on double-spaced pages. In the mid-1940s reports on single-spaced pages abruptly titled "Renseignements" overflowed with information. The shift in style seemed to express a new urgency in compiling as much information as quickly as possible as political threats loomed much larger.

The mass participation of Africans in politics meant it would be useless for authorities to focus on observing the smuggling of newspapers or the formation of secret networks. As the era of decolonization began, the culture of suspicion and the prioritization of discreet and clandestine police surveillance ended. Although the French still sought to slow down the age of independence, the techniques changed and the interwar communist, pan-Africanist, and charlatan suspects seemed quaint compared to the emergence of legitimate nationalist movements that sought independence or at least complete equality.

In the era of high imperialism surveillance over populations was a key way to describe the collection of information that allowed for colonial rule to function. This was demonstrated in the spatial ordering of cities, the use of maps and censuses, and the practice of ethnography.[15] Direct forms of repression such as prisons and police also thrived under colonial rule.[16] But in AOF during the First World War a particular kind of surveillance developed that was aimed at individuals and monitoring their possible threat to the French state. Ideas about what constituted suspicious behavior changed over time, but the scrutiny of people and their actions as threatening to the French state remained a priority. Unlike surveillance that targeted colonial populations in a general way, surveillance of suspicious persons directly targeted individuals and the political associations they formed. It involved investigations that sought detailed information about suspects' personal and political lives. Surveillance aimed to repress politics, yet its subtlety, discretion, and anonymity in urban areas reveal it to be a more insidious form of repression than other, violent means of control.

The roots of surveillance of suspects can be found in the surveillance of Muslim leaders and Lebanese and Syrians that began in the nineteenth century. During World War I the surveillance of these and other foreigners was considerably expanded to monitor enemy nationals, designate threats to national security, and generally observe those disloyal toward France. World War I was a transitional period for surveillance in AOF. During the war officials still relied on lists of names with general comments on the attitude of foreigners toward France. They also began in-depth investigations of individual suspects. Paoli, special inspector from the metropole, introduced the use of individual surveillance and detailed reports, a strategy that would be carried over to the interwar period.

The era of peace would in fact bring new turbulent waves of change to France and French West Africa. The metropole emerged from the horrors of the Great War only to face a new set of crises. As artists and thinkers fundamentally questioned French values, the nation faced a prolonged period of mourning, the reintegration of veterans, economic turmoil, and an intensified demographic crisis. French authorities felt anxious about the condition of their empire, even as the end of the war added new colonial mandates to French territory. In the immediate aftermath of the war, metropolitan authorities reimagined the civilizing mission to include democracy in the form of power sharing and economic revival in terms of *mise en valeur*.

France became increasingly isolationist in this period, but global currents of change would not be ignored. The successful Communist Revolution in Russia combined with growing political doctrines such as pan-Africanism and anticolonialism meant the future of the French Empire became mired in doubt. Sarraut's Colonial Ministry responded to these fears by establishing a surveillance apparatus to monitor colonial populations in the metropole and urged governors-general around the empire to do the same. The ministry mobilized its imperial network to share information about "revolutionary propaganda" occurring within its realms and around the world. Thus reports on activities taking place in Paris, North Africa, and especially Indochina landed on the desk of the governor-general in Dakar. Acknowledging that little interest in radical activity existed in AOF and that such politics seemed unlikely to appeal to the population, successive governors-general still followed through by increasing surveillance over populations to seek out propagandists and agitators.

The government general also faced more immediate local concerns as the war ended. African veterans returned to AOF in massive numbers in 1919, and foreigners from all over the world arrived in Dakar; tourists, white women, entrepreneurs, and adventurers all contributed to a turbulent and uncontrollable population, especially in AOF's cities. The administration attempted to regulate the entry of foreigners, but mostly failed. The surveillance of a wide variety of cosmopolitan itinerants for shady activity suggests that the administration felt particularly vulnerable when faced with this increasingly mobile and international element shaping colonial society. Ultimately the culture of suspicion and the surveillance of suspects emerged as global fears about political radicalism coalesced with local fears about a turbulent and dynamic population. Gripped with anxiety about international flows of ideas and people, the administration created systems to identify and investigate political suspects. But they also used those tools to monitor misfits who appeared to disrupt the social order.

The culture of suspicion reflects the particular atmosphere that ruled the political and social environment of some parts of AOF. But why did colonial control in AOF emerge in terms of surveillance and suspicion? Why did this form of subtle coercion, which included casting a wide net of suspicion but using discreet methods of surveillance, become a preferred form of control? The colonial administration used violent means of repression on occasion, including exile and internment of dissidents and the armed repression of actions such as the Porto-Novo strikes of 1923. The answer lies partly in the new forms anticolonialism took. As interwar authorities became more concerned with the spread of ideas than with an armed or violent resistance, they were forced to respond in new ways. Authorities quietly intercepted forbidden newspapers and monitored suspects who joined radical groups in order to perceive and thwart the flow of ideas rather than disrupt plots to overthrow the government.

In cities political repression occurred in a discreet and sometimes secretive manner compared with rural areas, where more direct techniques were used. In these urban areas, French colonial police employed republican-style methods that prized discretion, showing that they were influenced by republican values even while they engaged in repressive action. Authorities may also have believed that secret surveillance would help them collect more and better information. However, it also seems to be a strategy particularly well-suited to the urban spaces where French authorities maintained an uneasy relationship with African elites. French law provided republican political rights in the four communes dating to the nineteenth century, and other cities began to benefit from interwar association policies that increased power sharing. The use of discreet political surveillance avoided further alienating the African évolué populations while still monitoring their political activity. Authorities believed they could quietly prevent African political engagement from veering into radicalism, while publicly lauding their own efforts to increase elite African participation in various consultative councils. Ultimately, although political freedoms for African urbanites appeared to be growing in the interwar era, the reforms of association amounted to little, while urban spaces were quietly becoming increasingly subject to political repression.

Republican methods aside, the full picture of the practice of colonial power that emerges from the story of suspicion is not one systematically defined by republican values. Instead surveillance practices show the weakness, fragmentation, and incoherence of the colonial state. The ideas that urged the use of surveillance reflected the paranoia of the state, but practices were frequently irrational and haphazard too. Shadowing suspects in public places was combined with the use of spontaneous denunciations and the collection of gossip. Colonial officials established postal controls and bureaucratic forms to organize and disseminate information that was collected. They relied on controls at the port and collected information in public space by police and political informants. Although these methods served to gather information, authorities often remained baffled by the spaces they tried to control and the activities of people under observation. And even when information of legitimate political activity was uncovered, no clear methodology allowed authorities to sort through what was and was not a true threat.

Three groups of people under surveillance stand out: foreigners, French, and Africans native to AOF. Each group had a different relationship to the French state, but although these people operated under different restrictions, divisions between them did not exist in everyday life. French and foreigners made important connections with each other and with the African population as networks crossed racial and national lines in politics and personal relationships. Alliances made for political, economic, or social reasons that traversed these three groups were often far more important than the distinctions made between them from a legal perspective. Africans involved in radical politics made connections with French newspaper editors and radical European sailors. Foreign and French communists came to AOF specifically to reach the local population. People considered suspicious surely did not imagine themselves as suspects but identified themselves in a variety of ways according to their personal and political goals. The division of these people into categories according to the way they were viewed by the French state should not obscure the way they actually moved fluidly within society.

The particular connection between foreignness and suspicion can be observed in the special concern for foreign suspects but also in the stories of French and African suspicion. Suspicion was closely connected to the maintenance of contacts in France, the United States, or the Soviet Union. Communists, pan-Africanists, and anti-imperialists were all affiliated with groups that had their headquarters outside of AOF. Travel to Moscow, the Middle East, and North Africa was viewed as particularly dangerous due to the potential of exposure to communism or pan-Islamism.

Extensive movement, whether international or within AOF, was in itself considered suspicious and dangerous. From fears of the spread of disease from traveling Syrian merchants, wandering marabouts, or eccentric Europeans traveling through the desert, movement generated mistrust. Sailors, soldiers who served abroad, migratory workers, students, and occasionally tourists were looked at with suspicion specifically because of their tendency toward displacement. This preoccupation with mobility reflects a desire among administrators for stability and fear of the transient and uncontrolled in an era when empire appeared to rest on a precarious foundation.

Foreign travel was just one way to deviate from colonial norms. Individuals whose nationality, appearance, occupation, or morality did not fit prescriptions for colonial society alarmed officials who aimed to create a clear and legible society. Although detection of political activity was the ultimate goal of surveillance, it was the potential for political activity among people who appeared strange or unusual that is perhaps a more accurate definition of suspicion. Unlike the surveillance of marabouts, the power of whom was believed to be known and understood by officials, suspects were people who were consistently inscrutable. Their motives and activities were frequently more mysterious than political, which helped proliferate suspicion.

In reporting on French suspects, officials revealed that the political goals of police surveillance were not the only aims of surveillance of the population. Officials were also highly suspicious of the ways metropolitan French transgressed the moral, political, and class boundaries that were set up to define Frenchness in the colonies. Colonial authorities had special relationships with French metropolitans and described them in ways to suggest that they prized bourgeois respectability and narrow political interests within the French community. The broader goals of surveillance and the policing of morality among some foreigners and Africans also indicate how the culture of suspicion widened its goals.

Foreign and French radical politics were of such great concern to authorities partly because of their potential to spread among the African population. In some ways, therefore, even the surveillance of European foreigners was part of a racially based colonial domination. Those few Africans who demonstrated an interest in radical politics were closely monitored. Colonial policing damaged emerging movements that aligned themselves with the pan-Africanism of the United States, Paris, British colonies, and occasionally communism. Despite the repression that caused considerable harm to emerging anticolonial groups, Africans showed they had diverse political interests that can be viewed as precursors to the flourishing of nationalist politics of the postwar era. They also displayed considerable resourcefulness, coming up with tactics to dissimulate their activity, spread newspapers and tracts, and reconstitute networks after being disbanded.

Who was a suspect, then? He or she was not defined solely by race, gender, ethnicity, nationality, or class. Nor was the suspect simply a political agitator. He or she could be a communist, but could also be a charlatan, a crook, a misfit, an undesirable, or an otherwise enigmatic figure. Suspects included people acting outside the bounds of colonial power, usurping colonial authority, making connections that crossed racial boundaries as well as those agitating for anticolonial causes. Investigations show that officials sought to police politics, but they also pursued knowledge about a wide range of people in an attempt to control what they viewed as an increasingly unwieldy society. This definition of the suspect helps us understand the context of the colonial state in French West Africa in terms of the chaotic changes taking place after the First World War. It also helps us interrogate the very useful concept of the colonial category. Suspects defy conventional categorizations and reveal that the colonial state, while constantly seeking to identify enemies and misfits, did not always prioritize race, gender, or nation in labeling people. Instead the state demonstrated concern about individuals across all categories who did not fall in line with expectations of political, social, and moral behavior.

I have argued that a culture of suspicion emerged in colonial AOF, especially during the interwar period and within the colonial administration.

This culture of suspicion was created by various players—administrators, low-level police agents, and informers. Importantly the suspects themselves were actors in the culture of suspicion; radical activists, charlatans, propagandists, and adventurers, all engaged in activities that drew the attention of authorities. As agents in their own lives they actively sought opportunity or adventure or to promote their ideas. Because the culture of suspicion and fear about radical politics made even the slightest hint of political activity worthy of scrutiny, people trying to learn about or actively promote radical politics were forced to hide their actions and come up with strategies for avoiding the gaze of the state. In this way too suspects shaped the culture of suspicion.

Above all, police surveillance in AOF teaches us something about how French authorities there viewed their place in West Africa. They believed, for the most part, in the righteousness of their mission and the need to weed out dissent. However, while French notions of superiority defined reasons for the civilizing mission in AOF, an undercurrent of anxiety and fear powerfully shaped colonial politics in creating an atmosphere of suspicion. Based on different worries, French authorities imagined what threatened them most in terms of suspicious activity. Contributing to the culture of suspicion was an anxious Colonial Ministry, a changing international climate, but also suspects themselves who crossed borders, engaged in spreading propaganda and political messages, or took on schemes of adventure and fortune. Once the culture of suspicion was set in motion, it perpetuated itself. Possessing the strategies, tools, and means to investigate and conduct surveillance, colonial authorities did not hesitate to use them on all kinds of colonial misfits: charlatans, crooks, travelers, adventurous women, and more. The initial fears about communism, pan-Islamism, and pan-Africanism bore fruit as some political suspects were identified, but in time authorities were suspicious of a variety of politics and investigated royalist, syndicalist, Christian, and anarchist suspects, in addition to the social nonconformists.

Suspicion can be used as a lens to understand French colonial rule, but the rich texture of stories that emerge from surveillance records also brings new understanding to the variety and complexity of French West African life. Suspicious persons, while a minority and marginal members of the population, attest to the complex and varied nature of the urban society that developed within the context of French colonialism, with its attractions for foreigners and its connections to the rest of the French Empire. The movement of travelers, tourists, and transients suggests a society constantly in flux and strongly connected internationally. The variety of intellectual interests, contacts, and travel among French, foreigners, and Africans in AOF reveals a particularly dynamic society even in the face of a colonial state that attempted to repress such diversity.

# NOTES

### INTRODUCTION

1. Note on "Personnages Suspects" Baron Paul Von Heinl, undated; Renseignements, July 24, 1937, FMOD 21 G 28.

2. "Les Folles Nuits de Dakar: Tabarin," *L'indépendent colonial* (Dakar, Senegal), May 1932; Cruise O'Brien, *White Society in Black Africa*, 58.

3. On the Peyrissac firm, see Suret-Canale, *French Colonialism in Tropical Africa*, 173–74.

4. Director of APA (Affaires Politiques et Administratives) to the director of Sûreté Générale, April 8, 1937, FMOD 21 G 28.

5. Administrator of the circonscription of Dakar to the director of APA, January 14, 1931, FMOD 17 G 70.

6. Untitled, Dakar, November 26, 1931, FMOD 17 G 58.

7. Untitled, Dakar, January 18, 1932, FMOD 17 G 58.

8. The terms *suspicious persons* and *suspects* are taken from the archival documents. I do not put them in quotes in subsequent uses, but that intent should be understood.

9. Bayly, *Empire and Information*; Thomas, *Empires of Intelligence*; Cooper, *Decolonization and African Society*.

10. Bayly, *Empire and Information*; Thomas, *Empires of Intelligence*; McCoy, *Policing America's Empire*; Hevia, *The Imperial Security State*.

11. Thomas, *Empires of Intelligence*, 2.

12. Robinson, *Paths of Accommodation*.

13. Thomas identifies disagreements about the most important security threat as one of the key disputes of the interwar empire. Thomas, *The French Empire between the Wars*, 7–8; Conklin, *A Mission to Civilize*, 161–65; Wilder, *The French Imperial Nation-State*, 142.

14. Ahire, *Imperial Policing*; Anderson and Killingray, eds., *Policing the Empire*; Arnold, *Police Power and Colonial Rule*; Clayton and Killingray, *Khaki and Blue*; Fourchard and Albert, *Security, Crime and Segregation*; Thomas, *Violence and Colonial Order*; Thomas, *Empires of Intelligence*.

15. On the role of paranoia in shaping perceptions of Islam see Harrison, *France and Islam in West Africa*, 5. On emotion and colonial society see Stoler, *Carnal Knowledge and Imperial Power*, 12.

16. Africanists have made this claim in other contexts. See Berman and Lonsdale, *Unhappy Valley*, 75–100; Cooper, "The Dialectics of Decolonization," in Cooper and Stoler, *Tensions of Empire*, 409–10; Berry, "Hegemony on a Shoestring."

17. Wilder, *The French Imperial Nation-State*, 76–117; Chafer and Sackur, *French Colonial Empire and the Popular Front* describe colonial humanism as a particularity of the Popular Front's rule.

18. Dirks, *Colonialism and Culture*; Cohn, *Colonialism and Its Forms of Knowledge*; Cooper and Stoler, *Tensions of Empire*.

19. Stoler, "Rethinking Colonial Categories," in Cooper and Stoler, *Tensions of Empire*.

20. Genova, *Colonial Ambivalence*; White, *Children of the French Empire*; Osborn, "'Circle of Iron'"; Arsan, *Interlopers of Empire*.

21. There is an extensive literature on the originaires. The classic work is Johnson, *The Emergence of Black Politics in Senegal*; see also Crowder, *Senegal*; Coquery-Vidrovitch, "Nationalité et citoyenneté en Afrique occidentale française"; Shereikis, "From Law to Custom"; Genova, *Colonial Ambivalence*; Diouf, "The French Colonial Policy of Assimilation."

22. Roberts and Sarr, "The Jurisdiction of Muslim Tribunals in Colonial Senegal."

23. Michel, *Les Africains et la Grande Guerre*; Conklin *A Mission to Civilize*, 148–50.

24. Genova, *Colonial Ambivalence*, 36.

25. Genova, *Colonial Ambivalence*, 39.

26. Mann, *Native Sons*, 39.

27. The French Empire in 1920 made up 9 percent of the globe. Thomas, *The French Empire between the Wars*, 1.

28. On French anxiety and crisis in the metropole just after the war and into the interwar era see Stovall, *Paris and the Spirit of 1919*; Roberts, *Civilization without Sexes*; Panchasi, *Future Tense*.

29. Thomas, *The French Empire between the Wars*, 5, 17.

30. Thomas, *The French Empire between the Wars*, 32–33.

31. Thomas, *The French Empire between the Wars*, 2–5.

32. Conklin, *A Mission to Civilize*, 6–7.

33. Conklin, *A Mission to Civilize*, 188.

34. Betts, *Assimilation and Association*, 12–16.

35. Thomas, *The French Empire between the Wars*, 54.

36. Conklin, *A Mission to Civilize*, 188–89.

37. Conklin, *A Mission to Civilize*, 192.

38. Conklin, *A Mission to Civilize*, 200.

39. Genova, *Colonial Ambivalence*, 101–4.

40. Thomas, *The French Empire between the Wars*, 61–62.

41. Conklin, *A Mission to Civilize*, 194.

42. Conklin, *A Mission to Civilize*, 192–93.

43. On some of the earliest alliances between French men and African women, see Brooks, "The Signares of Saint-Louis and Gorée."

44. Jones, *The Métis of Senegal*, 157–58.

45. Jones, *The Métis of Senegal*, 162, 172.

46. Genova, *Colonial Ambivalence*, 19–23.

47. Conklin, *A Mission to Civilize*, 159–65; Genova, *Colonial Ambivalence*, 63.

48. Conklin, *A Mission to Civilize*, 203–4.

49. Mann, *Native Sons*, 74.

50. Mann, *Native Sons*, 75–76.

51. Mann, *Native Sons*, 71.

52. Klein, *Slavery and Colonial Rule in French West Africa*, 217–19; Mann, *Native Sons*, 72–73.

53. Mann, *Native Sons*, 77–78.

54. Klein, *Slavery and Colonial Rule in French West Africa*, 218.

55. On limits of naturalization see Genova, *Colonial Ambivalence*, 59; on indigénat, Mann, *Native Sons*, 72.

56. Genova, *Colonial Ambivalence*, 60.

57. Conklin, *A Mission to Civilize*, 159–60.

58. Genova, *Colonial Ambivalence*, 81-n-1.

59. Manning, *Slavery, Colonialism and Economic Growth in Dahomey*, 20, 266-67.

60. Furlough, "*Une Leçon des Choses*," 461.

61. Coquery-Vidrovitch, "L'Afrique Coloniale Française et la crise de 1930," 416.

62. Arsan, "Failing to Stem the Tide," 450.

63. Cruise O'Brien, *White Society in Black Africa*, 57.

64. On anxiety over women see Conklin, "Redefining 'Frenchness,'" 76–82.

65. Betts, "Dakar," 197.

66. On the construction of the cathedral see Foster, "An Ambiguous Monument."

67. Echenberg, *Black Death, White Medicine*; Betts, "The Establishment of the Medina in Dakar."

68. Betts, "The Establishment of the Medina in Dakar," 144.

69. Betts, "The Establishment of the Medina in Dakar," 148.

70. Bigon, *A History of Urban Planning*, 232, 236.

71. Cruise O'Brien, *White Society in Black Africa*, 17.

72. Betts, "Dakar," 199.

73. On the administrative organization, see Suret-Canale, *French Colonialism in Tropical Africa*, 307–49.

74. "Numerical Survey by Grade of Police Personnel Planned for 1924 and Funded by Municipal Budgets," FMOD 21 G 130.

75. Circular, governor-general, direction of APA, to lieutenant governors, May 8, 1928, FMOD 21 G 44.

76. Circular, governor-general, direction of APA, to lieutenant governors, May 8, 1928, FMOD 21 G 44; governor-general to minister of colonies, June 1, 1937, FMOD 21 G 105.

77. Bernard-Duquenet, *Le Sénégal et le Front Populaire*, 37–39.

78. Bernard-Duquenet, *Le Sénégal et le Front Populaire*, 26.

79. Renseignements, July 1936, FMOD 21 G 137.

80. Untitled, Dakar, November 26, 1931, FMOD 17 G 58.

## 1. "A VIGILANT SURVEILLANCE"

1. Governor-general to Ministry of Colonies, February 14, 1921, FMOD 21 G 126.

2. Thomas, *Empires of Intelligence*.

3. Bayly, *Empire of Information*, 10–55; Thomas, *Empires of Intelligence*, 2.

4. Buignoz, president of tribunal of Première Instance, to governor of Senegal, 1825, FANC 21 G 1.

5. Buignoz, president of tribunal of Première Instance, to governor of Senegal, 1825, FANC 21 G 1.

6. Buignoz, president of tribunal of Première Instance, to governor of Senegal, 1825, FANC 21 G 1.

7. Robinson, *Paths of Accommodation*, 39, 53.

8. Robinson, *Paths of Accommodation*, 52.

9. Robinson, *Paths of Accommodation*, 94.

10. Robinson, *Paths of Accommodation*.

11. Robinson, *Paths of Accommodation*, 215–18.

12. Robinson, *Paths of Accommodation*, 222–24.

13. See files, for example, in Propagande Panislamique, FMOD 19 G 22; "Renseignements sur Islam et le Monde," FMOD 19 G 26; Seydou Nourou Tall, FMOD 19 G 43. The surveillance by the Muslim Affairs Bureau in the interwar years is outside the scope of this project.

14. Documents dating from as early as 1902 exhort administrators to communicate general information to the government general. Instructions from Roume to lieutenant governors of Senegal, French Guinea, Ivory Coast, and Dahomey,

November 11, 1902, FANC 18 G 2; circular, governor-general to lieutenant governors, June 4, 1914, FMOD 21 G 45.

15. Administrator Decressac-Villagrand to governor-general, July 14, 1900, FANC 21 G 32.

16. Freitas, "Les Étrangers en Afrique Occidentale Française," 26.

17. Instructions from Roume to lieutenant governors of Senegal, French Guinea, Ivory Coast, and Dahomey, November 11, 1902, FANC 18 G 2.

18. Circular, governor-general to lieutenant governors, June 4, 1914, FMOD 21 G 45.

19. Circular, governor-general to lieutenant governors, December 24, 1918, FANC 21 G 32. On the loosening of restrictions.

20. Central commissaire Abbal to delegate of the government of Senegal in Dakar, October 3, 1916, FANC 21 G 43.

21. Governor-General Angoulvant to minister of colonies, March 2, 1918, FANC 21 G 33.

22. Bernard to central commissaire, undated, FANC 21 G 39.

23. Bernard to central commissaire, undated, FANC 21 G 39.

24. Lieutenant governor of Senegal to delegate of the colony of Senegal in Dakar, June 6, 1916, FANC 21 G 39. Bernard said much the same thing in his own letter, Bernard to central commissaire, undated, FANC 21 G 39.

25. Bernard to central commissaire, undated, FANC 21 G 39.

26. Report to governor-general, March 1918, FANC 21 G 3.

27. Report to governor-general, March 1918, FANC 21 G 3.

28. Special Inspector Paoli to governor-general, April 19, 1918, FANC 21 G 3.

29. Governor-general, civil affairs service, to commander of the navy in Senegal, January 23, 1918, FANC 21 G 3.

30. Report from administrator of the circle Niani-Ouli, September 20, 1918, FANC 21 G 38.

31. Mayor of Rufisque to lieutenant governor of Senegal, September 26, 1918, FANC 21 G 38.

32. Special Inspector Paoli to governor-general, April 19, 1918, FANC 21 G 3.

33. Report by Special Inspector Paoli, May 23, 1918, FANC 21 G 3.

34. Governor-general, service of civil affairs, to the delegate of Senegal, August 1918, FANC 21 G 3.

35. Special Inspector Paoli to governor-general, April 19, 1918, FANC 21 G 3.

36. Note from the general prosecutor to chief of civil affairs, August 21, 1918, FANC 21 G 3.

37. Chief of service of civil affairs to the delegate of Senegal, February 7, 1919, FANC 21 G 3. It is not clear why Paoli was replaced and returned to the metropole. It

seems possible, considering the disastrous nature of his tenure, that he asked to be released or that he was fired. It is also equally likely that with the war over, his specific duties were not needed.

38. Genova, *Colonial Ambivalence*, 58.

39. Thomas, *Empires of Intelligence*, 209.

40. The United States even feared anticolonial activities by Indian Americans. Sohi, "Race, Surveillance, and Indian Anticolonialism."

41. Edwards, *The Practice of Diaspora*; Boittin, *Colonial Metropolis*; Matera, *Black London*.

42. Thomas, *Empires of Intelligence*, 83.

43. Rosenberg, *Policing Paris*, 7–8, 97.

44. Thomas, *Empires of Intelligence*, 92.

45. Mazower, *The Policing of Politics in the Twentieth Century*.

46. Thomas, *The French Empire between the Wars*, 32–33.

47. Conklin, *A Mission to Civilize*, 174–211; Wilder, *The French Imperial Nation-State*, 51–52.

48. Thomas, "Albert Sarraut."

49. Thomas, "Albert Sarraut," 918.

50. Dewitte, *Les mouvements nègres en France*, 21.

51. Rosenberg, *Policing Paris*, 134–35.

52. Rosenberg, *Policing Paris*, 65–70.

53. Rosenberg, *Policing Paris*, 141–50.

54. Rosenberg, *Policing Paris*, 160–64.

55. Circular from governor-general, direction of APA, to lieutenant governors of the colonies, May (day unreadable) 1922, FMOD 21 G 131.

56. Circular from governor-general, direction of APA, to lieutenant governors of the colonies, May (day unreadable) 1922, FMOD 21 G 131.

57. Dewitte, *Les mouvements nègres en France*, 98–101.

58. "Note on revolutionary action of interest to the overseas territories," May 6, 1922, FMOD 17 G 61.

59. "Note on revolutionary action of interest to the overseas territories," May 6, 1922, FMOD 17 G 61.

60. "Note on revolutionary propaganda of interest to the overseas territories," August 31, 1924, FMOD 17 G 61.

61. "Note on revolutionary propaganda of interest to the overseas territories," February 28, 1925, FMOD 17 G 62.

62. "Note on revolutionary propaganda of interest to the overseas territories," October 31, 1924, FMOD 17 G 61.

63. "Extrait de la Dépêche ministérielle," October 27, 1924, FMOD 17 G 61.

64. "Extrait de la Dépêche ministérielle," October 27, 1924, FMOD 17 G 61.

65. Minister of colonies to governor-general, April 25, 1925, FMOD 17 G 62.

66. "Note on revolutionary propaganda of interest to the overseas territories," June 3, 1922, FMOD 17 G 61.

67. "Note on revolutionary propaganda of interest to the overseas territories," June 3, 1922, FMOD 17 G 61.

68. "Note on revolutionary propaganda of interest to the overseas territories," June 3, 1922, FMOD 17 G 61.

69. "Note on revolutionary propaganda of interest to the overseas territories," June 30, 1924, FMOD 17 G 61.

70. "Note on revolutionary propaganda of interest to the overseas territories," August 17, 1922, FMOD 21 G 131.

71. "Note on revolutionary propaganda of interest to the overseas territories," March 15, 1923, FMOD 21 G 61; "Note on revolutionary propaganda of interest to the overseas territories," May 16, 1923, FMOD 21 G 61.

72. "Note on revolutionary propaganda of interest to the overseas territories," November 30, 1925, FMOD 17 G 62.

73. "Note on revolutionary propaganda of interest to the overseas territories," February 28, 1925, FMOD 17 G 62.

74. "Note on revolutionary propaganda of interest to the overseas territories," December 31, 1924, FMOD 17 G 61.

75. "Note on revolutionary propaganda of interest to the overseas territories," March 31, 1925, April 30, 1925, June 30, 1925, July 31, 1925, October 1925 among others, FMOD 17 G 62. On the actions of Bloncourt, Saint-Jacques, Gothon-Lunion, and Nguyen see Dewitte, *Les mouvements nègres en France*.

76. Dewitte, *Les mouvements nègres en France*, 17, 34.

77. Dewitte, *Les mouvements nègres en France*, 55.

78. "Note on revolutionary propaganda of interest to the overseas territories," March 31, 1926, FMOD 17 G 62.

79. "Note on revolutionary propaganda of interest to the overseas territories," June 30, 1926, FMOD 17 G 62.

80. "Note on revolutionary propaganda of interest to the overseas territories," July 31, 1926, FMOD 17 G 62.

81. Thomas, *Empires of Intelligence*, 98–101.

82. "Note on revolutionary propaganda of interest to the overseas territories," June 30, 1928, FMOD 17 G 63. The source of the reports on the black colonies appears to come directly from the Contrôle et Assistance des Indigènes en France, which filed detailed reports on meetings of black groups.

83. "Note on revolutionary propaganda of interest to the overseas territories," April 30, 1929, FMOD 17 G 64.

84. "Note on revolutionary propaganda of interest to the overseas territories," May 31, 1930, FMOD 21 G 42.

85. "Note on revolutionary propaganda of interest to the overseas territories," October 31, 1924, FMOD 17 G 61.

86. "Note on revolutionary propaganda of interest to the overseas territories," December 1, 1924, FMOD 17 G 61.

87. "Extrait de la Dépêche ministérielle," January 15, 1925, FMOD 17 G 61.

88. This practice of excerpting certain interesting facts and sending them on to the lieutenant governors continued into 1935, when the propaganda reports disappear from the archives. Although the "black colony" was always of interest, the excerpts also included reports on international groups like the Secours Rouge International and the revolutionary activities in Indochina.

89. Draft of report to governor-general, March 1918, FANC 21 G 3. The report cited here is a handwritten unsigned draft.

90. Draft of report to governor-general, March 1918, FANC 21 G 3.

91. Draft of report to governor-general, March 1918, FANC 21 G 3.

92. Draft of report to governor-general, March 1918, FANC 21 G 3.

93. *Journal Officiel de l'Afrique Occidentale Française*, 1923, 27; Arrêté, September 10, 1922.

94. *Journal Officiel de l'Afrique Occidentale Française*, 1923, 27; Arrêté, September 10, 1922

95. Conklin, *A Mission to Civilize*, 198–99.

96. Conklin, *A Mission to Civilize*, 199.

97. Conklin, *A Mission to Civilize*, 199-, 201.

98. Conklin, *A Mission to Civilize*, 201.

99. Conklin, *A Mission to Civilize*, 218–23, 227–29.

100. Secret circular, governor-general to lieutenant governors, July 20, 1925, FMOD 17 G 53.

101. Secret circular, governor-general to lieutenant governors, July 20, 1925, FMOD 17 G 53.

102. Conklin, *A Mission to Civilize*, 163.

103. Scales, "Subversive Sound."

104. Coquery-Vidrovitch, "L'Afrique Coloniale et la crise de 1930," 412.

105. Coquery-Vidrovitch, "L'Afrique Coloniale et la crise de 1930," 417–18.

106. Genova, *Colonial Ambivalence*, 108–9.

107. Coquery-Vidrovitch, "L'Afrique Coloniale et la crise de 1930," 417.

108. *Journal Officiel de l'Afrique Occidentale Française*, 1931, 104.

109. *Journal Officiel de l'Afrique Occidentale Française*, 1931, 104.
110. Annual police and Sûreté report, Dakar and Dépendances, 1932, FMOD 2 G 32/22.
111. Annual police and Sûreté report, Dakar and Dépendances, 1937, FMOD 2 G 37/33.
112. Circular, governor-general to lieutenant governors, February 19, 1931, FMOD 21 G 45.
113. Circular, governor-general to lieutenant governors, February 19, 1931, FMOD 21 G 45, emphasis by Brévié.
114. Conklin, *A Mission to Civilize*, 313n72.
115. Commissaire of the territory of Niger to governor-general, direction of APA, August 3, 1922, FMOD 21 G 131.
116. Circular, lieutenant governor of Niger Brévié to circle commanders, February 12, 1923, FMOD 21 G 45.
117. Harrison, *France and Islam in West Africa*, 127–30; Robinson, *Paths of Accommodation*, 94–96.
118. Conklin, *A Mission to Civilize*, 142–73.
119. Instructions from lieutenant governor of Niger Tellier to circle commanders, July 15, 1932, FMOD 21 G 45.
120. Circular, governor-general to lieutenant governors, March 7, 1934, FMOD 21 G 45.
121. Circular, governor-general to lieutenant governors, March 7, 1934, FMOD 21 G 45.
122. Circular, governor-general to lieutenant governors, March 7, 1934, FMOD 21 G 45.
123. Instructions from lieutenant governor of Niger Tellier to circle commanders, July 15, 1932, FMOD 21 G 45.
124. Lieutenant governor of Mauritania to governor-general, direction of Sûreté Générale, February 4, 1932, FMOD 21 G 45.
125. Files on "suspects" did not decline during this period and police practices did not appear to change. Certainly the policies of the Popular Front likely varied from colony to colony. For example, Patrick Manning writes that in Dahomey "the spy services set up in 1934 were abolished" (*Slavery, Colonialism and Economic Growth in Dahomey*, 274).
126. Cohen, "The Colonial Policy of the Popular Front"; Chafer and Sackur, *French Colonial Empire and the Popular Front*; Bernard-Duquenet, *Le Sénégal et le Front Populaire*.
127. De Coppet is widely cited as being symbolic of reform in the colonies. In fact historians generally refer only to his "reformist agenda" when writing about him. See Cohen, *Rulers of Empire*, 137; Conklin, *A Mission to Civilize*, 254.
128. Bernard-Duquenet, *Le Sénégal et le Front Populaire*, 83–84.
129. Bernard-Duquenet, *Le Sénégal et le Front Populaire*, 84.
130. Bernard-Duquenet, *Le Sénégal et le Front Populaire*, 91–104.
131. Lieutenant governor Dahomey to governor-general, direction of APA, September 7, 1933, FMOD 21 G 90.

132. Lieutenant governor Dahomey to governor-general, direction of APA, September 7, 1933, FMOD 21 G 90.

133. Governor-general, direction of APA, to Colonial Ministry, direction of APA, January 22, 1934, FMOD 21 G 90.

134. Governor-general, direction of APA, to Colonial Ministry, direction of APA, January 22, 1934, FMOD 21 G 90.

135. Cohen, *Rulers of Empire*, 131.

136. Indeed, the Popular Front governor-general de Coppet was in charge when strikers were killed by soldiers in demonstrations. Cooper, *Decolonization and African Society*, 106–7.

137. Cooper, *Decolonization and African Society*, 94–95.

138. Renseignements, July 1936, FMOD 21 G 137.

139. Thomas, *Empires of Intelligence*, 263.

140. Dakar et Dépendances police and Sûreté Service annual report, 1937, FMOD 2 G 37/33.

141. Quoted in Conklin, *A Mission to Civilize*, 190–91.

142. Scales identifies the "paranoia and pragmatism that colonial bureaucrats and the French security services displayed in the face of widespread Algerian record listening" ("Subversive Sound," 400). Thomas writes that authorities in French North Africa "were almost programmed to see a Communist threat, whatever the indications to the contrary" (*Empires of Intelligence*, 101). Rosenberg claims that the prefect of police in Paris "continued to fear unruly foreigners, especially after the massive postwar strikes. Despite the authorities' success in repressing any plausible revolutionary threat, and despite the relative absence of large-scale immigration until the mid-1920s, he continued to worry about foreign agents and terrorists fighting 'their' battles on French soil" (*Policing Paris*, 48).

2. "A DISCREET SURVEILLANCE"

1. *Pépé le Moko*, directed by Julien Duvivier, 1937; Slavin, *Colonial Cinema and Imperial France*, 177.

2. Secret circular, governor-general to lieutenant governors, July 20, 1925, FMOD 17 G 53.

3. The sources for this chapter include correspondence between various members of the administration, the Colonial Ministry, and other European governments. Reports from police or lieutenant governors are the most common source. Unfortunately it was not possible to locate daily logs of surveillance activity. Methods of investigation and surveillance must be gleaned from reports and correspondence.

4. Governor-general to the Ministry of Colonies, February 14, 1921, FMOD 21 G 126.

5. French police and administrators were not the only colonial rulers to consider assimilated Africans suspicious. Meghan Vaughan shows that British medical discourse understood "de-tribalization" of assimilated Africans as part of the pathology of disease and mental illness (*Curing Their Ills*, 81, 108).

6. "Report on propaganda among native teachers," April 2, 1927, FMOD 21 G 28.

7. Circular, governor-general to lieutenant governors, February 19, 1931, FMOD 21 G 45.

8. Director of APA DuChene, Ministry of Colonies, to governors-general of the colonies and commissaires of Togo and Cameroun, undated, FMOD 21 G 38.

9. Direction of APA to the director of the Sûreté, June 19, 1923, FMOD 21 G 133. Kojo Goyave Quenum (aka Kojo Tovolou Houenou) went to Paris to pursue studies in law and called himself a prince but was in fact the son of a Dahoméen who became wealthy due to commerce with the French. Dewitte, *Les mouvements nègres en France*, 33. For Quénum's actions observed by the CAI, see Dewitte, *Les mouvements nègres en France*, 72–77.

10. Thomas, *Empires of Intelligence*, 28; Alexanderson, "'A Dark State of Affairs.'"

11. Commissaire of immigration to commissaire central of Dakar and delegate of the government of Senegal in Dakar, January 30, 1919, FANC 21 G 46.

12. Cabinet personnel to governor-general of AOF, Sûreté Générale, November, date unreadable, FMOD 17 G 58.

13. Cabinet personnel to governor-general of AOF, Sûreté Générale, November, date unreadable, FMOD 17 G 58.

14. Dakar et Dépendances police and Sûreté annual report, 1922, 2G 32/22.

15. Dakar et Dépendances police and Sûreté annual report, 1922, 2G 32/22.

16. Commissaire of the port police to central commissaire, November 15, 1930, FMOD 17 G 70.

17. Commissaire of the port police to central commissaire, November 15, 1930, FMOD 17 G 70.

18. Chargé d'affaires in Stockholm Lagarenne to minister of foreign affairs, April 17, 1931, and minister of foreign affairs to minister of colonies, April 29, 1931, FMOD 21 G 38.

19. Governor of Ivory Coast Reste to governor-general, direction of APA, general prosecutor and judicial service, July 4, 1934, FMOD 17 G 58.

20. This was not an uncommon characteristic of policing institutions. Robert Gellately describes even the Gestapo of Nazi Germany as "primarily a passive organization" ("Enforcing Racial Policy," 46).

21. Lieutenant governor French Guinea to governor-general, May, 1931, FMOD 21 G 28.

22. Principal inspector of police Lenaers to central commissaire of police, June 12, 1929, FMOD 21 G 28.

23. Administrator at Tiendougou to unreadable, July 22, 1921, FMOD 21 132.

24. Police Moiret to central commissaire, December 16, 1925, FMOD 17 G 58.

25. Police commissaire to lieutenant governor of Senegal, January 20, 1926, FMOD 17 G 58.

26. French consul in Tripoli Terver to minister of foreign affairs, December 3, 1930, FMOD 17 G 58.

27. See chapter 3 for more on Riesinger and his family.

28. This technique was frequently used in North Africa as well. Thomas, *Empires of Intelligence*, 26.

29. Lieutenant governor of Ivory Coast to commander of recruitment bureau, August 1, 1922, FMOD 21 G 133.

30. Renseignements, July 24, 1937, FMOD 17 G 58.

31. Résidence general of Morocco, direction of native affairs, to governor-general, January 9, 1925, FMOD 17 G 70.

32. Dewitte, *Les mouvements nègres en France*; Thomas, *Empires of Intelligence*, 2

33. Report, Inspector Gaston Braud, to director of the general security service, July 25, 1931, FMOD 17 G 58.

34. Report, Inspector Gaston Braud, to director of the general security service, July 25, 1931, FMOD 17 G 58.

35. "Voice of the Negroes" was the newspaper of the CDNR. Untitled, Dakar, February 2, 1927, FMOD 21 G 38.

36. Brévié was especially concerned about recruiting good informants to deliver all kinds of political and social information. Circular, governor-general to lieutenant governors, March 7, 1934, FMOD 21 G 45.

37. Cablegram, governor-general to lieutenant governor of Dahomey, March 26, 1916, FANC 21 G 40.

38. Governor-general, military cabinet, to Ministry of Colonies, personnel service, November 7, 1917, FMOD 21 G 41.

39. Renseignements, December 21, 1933, FMOD 17 G 66.

40. Renseignements, December 21, 1933, FMOD 17 G 66.

41. Renseignements, October 31, 1933, FMOD 21 G 28; FMOD 21 G 44 LDNR.

42. Central commissaire of Dakar Pourroy to delegate of the government of Senegal, October 14, 1922, and diverse correspondence of Laurent Anchouey, FMOD 21 G 133.

43. Angrand hailed from a wealthy and prominent Catholic merchant family from Gorée. His father, Léopold Angrand, was important in Gorée politics. Armand

Angrand was interviewed by Johnson about his father in 1964 for his classic work on Senegalese politics. Johnson, *The Emergence of Black Politics in Senegal*, 111, 203, 231. Armand served as mayor of Dakar in 1934–39. Jones, *The Métis of Senegal*, 190. He also published a book on the Lébous in the 1950s: Angrand, *Les Lébous de la Presqu'île du Cap-Vert*.

44. Delegate of Senegal to governor-general, direction of APA, August 18, 1922, FMOD 21 G 132.

45. Delegate of Senegal to governor-general, direction of APA, August 18, 1922, FMOD 21 G 132.

46. Delegate of Senegal to governor-general, direction of APA, August 18, 1922, FMOD 21 G 132.

47. Report by Special Inspector Paoli, February 18, 1918, FANC 21 G 46.

48. Vice governor-general Belgian Congo to governor-general, November 4, 1920, FMOD 21 G 126.

49. Central commissaire of police to the delegate of the government of Senegal in Dakar, June 9, 1922, FMOD 17 G 52. Gibbs's story about accidentally finding the cigarette case is faulty. It appears he planted it, and documents obtained by police suggest that Gibbs had an ongoing feud with Wilson and Farmer. In his handwritten notebook Farmer drafted a letter to Winston Churchill, secretary of state for the colonies, to complain about Gibbs's work at the British consulate in Dakar. Notebook of John Farmer, FMOD 21 G 126.

50. Central commissaire of police to the delegate of the government of Senegal in Dakar, June 9, 1922, FMOD 17 G 52.

51. Central commissaire Pourroy to the delegate of the government of Senegal in Dakar, June 17, 1922, FMOD 17 G 52.

52. Procès verbal of John Farmer, June 13, 1922, FMOD 17 G 52. For more on the Sierra Leone Garveyist group in Senegal, see chapter 3.

53. Special Inspector Barreyre in Bamako to director of police and Sûreté, November 7, 1930, FMOD 21 G 44.

54. Circle commander of Baol to governor of Senegal, April 7, 1931, FMOD 21 G 38.

55. Circle commander at Baol to governor of Senegal, April 7, 1931, FMOD 21 G 38. Cheick Anta was the brother of Amadu Bamba, founder of the Mouride brotherhood and himself an important Mouride who competed to succeed Bamba; he was kept under surveillance and exiled by the French administration. Harrison, *France and Islam in West Africa*, 114, 166–68.

56. Circle commander at Baol to governor of Senegal, April 7, 1931, FMOD 21 G 38.

57. Berlière, "A Republican Political Police?," 41.

58. Berlière, "A Republican Political Police?," 27–30.

59. Berlière, "A Republican Political Police?," 35, 40.

60. Secret circular, governor-general to lieutenant governors, July 20, 1925, FMOD 17 G 53.

61. Delegate of Senegal to governor-general, direction of APA, August 18, 1922, FMOD 21 G 132.

62. Report of Inspector Gaston Braud, July 25, 1931, FMOD 17 G 58.

63. Administrator of colonies, circle commander of Baol, to governor of Senegal, August 2, 1929, FMOD 21 G 38.

64. Untitled, Dakar, March 15, 1929, FMOD 21 G 28.

65. Direction du Cabinet Civil to Paris, May 14, 1929, FMOD 21 G 28.

66. Director of police and Sûreté Générale to director of APA, November 24, 1930, FMOD 17 G 58.

67. Renseignements, Dakar, June 18, 1931, FMOD 17 G 58.

68. Report of Inspector Gaston Braud, July 25, 1931, FMOD 17 G 58.

69. Renseignements, Dakar, July 26, 1931, FMOD 17 G 58.

70. Renseignements, Saint-Louis, July 11, 1930, FMOD 17 G 70.

71. Conklin, *A Mission to Civilize*.

72. Lewis, *The Boundaries of the Republic*.

73. Wilder, *The French Imperial Nation-State*, 6.

74. Although the Medina was created as the "native" quarter in 1914, Africans also lived in the Plateau. By the end of the 1920s there were still twenty thousand Africans living in the city of Dakar. Betts, "The Establishment of the Medina in Dakar," 148.

75. Police commissariat of Dakar et Dépendances annual report, 1930, FMOD 2 G 30/59.

76. Bigon, *A History of Urban Planning*, 225–26.

77. Bigon, *A History of Urban Planning*, 276.

78. Thomas, *Empires of Intelligence*, 27.

79. On the limits of surveillance strategies in other French colonies, see Scales, "Subversive Sound," 415.

80. See, for example, Roberts, *Two Worlds of Cotton*.

81. Cooper, *Colonialism in Question*, 48–49.

82. Ponzio for general administration of Dakar to governor-general, February 29, 1936, FMOD 21 G 28.

83. Thomas notes that while rural and urban differences existed in the collection of intelligence in Syria, they also had much in common, given that religious and social structures in rural and urban areas were similar (*Empires of Intelligence*, 206–7).

84. Circular, governor-general to lieutenant governors, March 7, 1934, FMOD 21 G 45. Surveillance records of suspicious persons do not, however, corroborate Brévié's hope that marabouts would play an important role in weeding out political revolutionaries. Robinson, *Paths of Accommodation.*

85. Instructions from Captain Mehrle, commander of the detachment of the gendarmerie, to gendarmerie brigade commanders of the cercle gendarmerie, February 7, 1935, FMOD 21 G 38, emphasis in the original.

86. Police commissaire of the city of Kébémer to commissaire of police in Saint-Louis, May 28, 1921, FMOD 21 G 132; lieutenant governor of Senegal to the governor-general, direction of APA, March 27, 1922, FMOD 21 G 132.

87. Administrator at Tiendougou to unreadable, July 22, 1921, FMOD 21 G 132.

88. Bureau Politique to governor-general, direction of the Sûreté Générale, June 17, 1931, FMOD 21 G 58.

89. Administrator of colonies, circle commander of Baol, to governor of Senegal, August 2, 1929, FMOD 21 G 38.

90. Mamdani, *Citizen and Subject,* 18, 22.

91. Thomas, *Empires of Intelligence,* 298.

92. According to Conklin, "On January 15, 1921, Dakar created a federal service *anthropometrique,* to compile dossiers on suspect Africans throughout the federation. Although compliance was sporadic at the local level, Dakar claimed to have 100,000 fiches in 1930" (*A Mission to Civilize,* 163). The judicial police may have had thousands of files related to crime, but the APA and Sûreté never came close to reaching that number.

93. "D-Modele de Renseignements Individuels," FMOD 17 G 67.

94. Renseignements to provide, FMOD 17 G 67.

95. Berlière, "A Republican Political Police?," 43.

96. Annex no. 2 to Circular 334, "Local Groups to Keep under Surveillance," September 12, 1930, FMOD 17 G 67.

97. Annex no. 2 to Circular 334, "Local Groups to Keep under Surveillance," September 12, 1930, FMOD 17 G 67.

98. Instructions from Captain Mehrle, commander of the detachment of the gendarmerie, to commanders of gendarme brigades in the circles, February 7, 1935, FMOD 21 G 38.

99. Central commissaire of Dakar to the delegate of the government of Senegal in Dakar, September 8, 1916, FANC 21 G 41.

100. Lieutenant governor to governor-general, Civil Affairs Service, August 29, 1916, FANC 21 G 41.

101. Delegate of the government of Senegal to governor-general, June 28, 1917, FANC 21 G 41.

102. Telegram, Ministry of Colonies to governor-general, July 6, 1917, FANC 21 G 41.

103. Berlière, "A Republican Political Police?," 43

104. Most pieces of information are judged "A" or "B." FMOD 21 G 11.

105. Manning, *Slavery, Capitalism and Economic Growth in Dahomey*, 267.

106. Renseignements, December 9, 1931, FMOD 21 G 28.

107. Thomas, *Empires of Intelligence*, 103.

108. "État d'un militaire signalé comme suspect," Colonel Rapine, July 9, 1931, FMOD 17 G 69.

109. Chief of Sûreté to the administrator of the district of Dakar, December 20, 1931, FMOD 21 G 43.

110. A report referred to "former agent of the Sûreté Sidi Oumar KABA" now living in Le Havre, untitled, "A.P.A.," February 26, 193, FMOD 21 G 44.

111. Thomas, *Empires of Intelligence*, 36.

112. For example, Individual bulletin, personnel of police and Sûreté, on Issa Saidou Djermakoye, entered into service 1941, FMOD 21 G 233.

113. Many of the final reports that were sent from the APA or directly from the police have no signature. However, a few are signed by a police inspector, while other inspectors' names surface within the text of reports, allowing for research on some but likely not all police inspectors who worked on investigations and surveillance of suspects.

114. The following analysis relies on examination of seven police inspectors deployed to AOF in the interwar era.

115. Prefect of police to minister of colonies, December 9, 1937; individual bulletin, Tournois, Abel, FM EE II 4903 (4).

116. Prefect of police to minister of Colonies, director of personnel and accounting, Paris, Nov 28, 1939, FM EE II 4897 (1).

117. Report on the medical file of Charles Moiret, inspector of police, February 7, 1942; Certificat de visite, minister of colonies, Conseil de Santé, Porto-Novo, November 18, 1937, FM EE II 4878 (12).

118. Individual bulletin, Morère, Dorothé, FM EE II 4878 (12); individual bulletin, Moiret, Charles, FM EE II 4878 (1).

119. Minister of the interior to Ministry of Colonies, Direction of Personnel and Accounting, Paris, September 9, 1933, FM 4878 (7).

120. Notice of renseignements on Lenaers, Gaston, FM EE II 2523 (16); individual bulletin Moiret, Charles, FM EE II 4878 (1); individual bulletin, Morère,

Dorothé, FM EE II 4878 (12); (4) individual bulletin, Tournois, Abel, FM EE II 4903 (4).

121. Individual bulletin, Braud, Gaston, Adrien François, FM EE II 4897 (1).

122. Individual bulletin, Ponzio, Louis, Charles, Léonce, FM EE II 3024 (3).

123. Individual bulletin, Beurnier, Maurice, FM EE II 2224 (4).

124. Individual bulletin, Rougier, Ferdinand Louis, FM EE II 3026 (1).

125. Individual bulletin, Verges, Paul, FM EE II 4883 (2); Individual bulletin, Tournois, Abel, FM EE II 4903 (4); Individual bulletin Braud, Gaston, Adrien François, FM EE II 4897 (1).

126. Individual bulletin, Braud, Gaston, Adrien François, FM EE II 4897 (1).

127. Individual bulletin Braud, Gaston Adrien François, FM EE II 4897 (1); Individual bulletin Moiret, Charles, FM EE II 4878 (7); Individual bulletin Verges, Paul, FM EE II 4883 (2).

128. The divorced men were Tournois, Braud, and Pourroy, although Pourroy remarried twice. Individual bulletin Tournois, Abel, FM EE II 4903 (4); individual bulletin, Braud, Gaston, Adrien François, FM EE II 4897 (1); individual bulletin Pourroy, Jean Marie Arthur, FM 2576 (19).

129. Individual bulletin Braud, Gaston, Adrien François, FM EE II 4897 (1); notice of military renseignements, Larra, Ernest, FM EE II 2516 (8); individual bulletin Moiret, Charles, FM EE II 4878 (1); individual bulletin, Morère, Dorothé, FM EE II 4878 (12); individual bulletin, Tournois, Abel, FM EE II 4903 (4); individual bulletin, Verges, Paul, FM EE II 4883 (2).

130. Individual bulletin, Braud, Gaston, Adrien François, FM EE II 4897 (1); Individual bulletin, Morère, Dorothé, FM EE II 4878 (12).

131. Renseignements notice, Lenaers, Gaston, FM EE 2523 (16).

132. Prefect of the Somme to minister of colonies, direction of personnel and accounting, Amiens, November 10, 1922, FM EE 4878 (7); Dorothé Morere to governor-general of AOF, October 21, 1922, EE 4878 (12).

133. Special Inspector Gaston Braud to the governor-general of colonies, general secretary of minister of the interior, August 1, 1940, FM EE II 4897 (1).

134. Special Inspector Gaston Braud to the governor-general of colonies, general secretary of minister of the interior, August 1, 1940, FM EE II 4897 (1).

135. Jean Pourroy to the governor of Guinée Française, April 2, 1908, FM EE II 2576 (19).

136. Jean Pourroy to the director of personnel, Ministry of Colonies, November 25, 1913, FM EE II 2576 (19).

137. Société Crédit de la Place Clichy to the minister, February 6, 1908, FM EE II 2576 (19); individual bulletin, Braud, Gaston, Adrien François, FM EE II 4897 (1).

138. Jean Pourroy to the governor of Guinée Française, April 2, 1908, FM EE II 2576 (19).

139. Gandillon to the minister, January 20, 1908, FM EE II 2576 (19).

140. Mme. Jeanne Vareschal to the minister, November 10, 1914, FM EE II 2576 (19).

141. Special Inspector Gaston Braud to the governor-general of colonies, general secretary of minister of the interior, August 1, 1940, FM EE II 4897 (1); individual bulletin Braud, Gaston, Adrien François, FM EE 4897 (1).

142. Individual bulletin, Braud, Gaston, Adrien François, FM EE 4897 (1); prefect of police to minister of colonies, director of personnel and accounting, June 23, 1928, FM EE II 4897 (1).

143. Governor-general of Indochina to the minister of colonies, Direction of Political Affairs, Saigon, July 5, 1930, FM EE 4897 (1).

144. Minister of the interior to the Ministry of Colonies, January 6, 1931, FM EE 4897 (1).

145. Governor-general of AOF, Direction of Personnel, to the minister of colonies, Direction of Personnel and Accounting, March 2, 1931, FM 4897 (1).

146. Lefebvre, director of Sûreté Générale, to the director of personnel in Dakar, January 3, 1941, FM EE II 4897 (1).

147. Cohen, *Rulers of Empire*, 51–56.

148. Roberts, *Two Worlds of Cotton*; Spear, "Neo-Traditionalism and the Limits of Invention in British Colonial Africa."

149. On the failure of the police to be "ubiquitous and omnipotent" in India, see Arnold, *Police Power and Colonial Rule*, 147. On the weakness of the auditory surveillance web in Algeria see Scales, "Subversive Sound," 415. On the limits of surveillance in North Africa see Thomas, *Empires of Intelligence*, 28.

150. Grandhomme, "La politique musulmane de la France au Sénégal," 240.

3. ENEMIES, CHARLATANS, AND PROPAGANDISTS

1. Lieutenant governor of Sudan to governor-general, direction of APA, September 26, 1930, FMOD 17 G 58.

2. Governor-general of Algeria to minister of foreign affairs, March 19, 1930; lieutenant governor of Niger to governor-general, direction of APA, June 2, 1930, FMOD 17 G 58.

3. Lieutenant governor of Sudan to governor-general, direction of APA, September 26, 1930, FMOD 17 G 58.

4. Lieutenant governor of Niger to governor-general, direction of APA, June 2, 1930, FMOD 17 G 58.

5. Rosenberg, *Policing Paris*, 48.

6. Miller, *Shanghai on the Metro*, 1–3.

7. Miller, *Shanghai on the Metro*, 178.

8. Slavin, *Colonial Cinema and Imperial France*, 157.

9. *Sanders of the River*, directed by Zoltán Korda.

10. The European population of AOF made up about 10 percent of urban populations. The city of Dakar was home to about sixty thousand Africans and ten thousand Europeans. Manning, *Francophone Sub-Saharan Africa*, 38. It is difficult to calculate the number of non-European foreigners. One estimate suggests that the Lebanese and Syrian population, by far the largest group of foreigners, constituted 10 percent of the non-African population. Freitas, "Les Etrangers en Afrique Occidentale Française," 48. In other words, even if half of all Europeans were foreign, foreigners could never have been more than 15 percent of any population, even in cities.

11. Noiriel, *The French Melting Pot*, 46.

12. Noiriel, *The French Melting Pot*, 52.

13. Circular, governor of Senegal to circle commanders, October (unreadable), 1923, ACS 1 F 118.

14. Mayor of the city of Dakar to lieutenant governor of Senegal, February 20, 1906, FANC 21 G 36.

15. "Arrêté related to foreigners residing in Senegal," June 1906, FANC 21 G 36.

16. Lieutenant governor of Dahomey to governor-general, September 13, 1907, FANC 21 G 36.

17. Lieutenant governor of Dahomey to governor-general, September 13, 1907, FANC 21 G 36.

18. Governor-general to lieutenant governors, May 24, 1911, FANC 21 G 36.

19. "Arrêté regulating the stay and establishment of foreigners in French West Africa," August 1, 1921, ACS 1 F 118.

20. Circular no. 86, governor-general to lieutenant governors, November 19, 1921, ACS 1 F 118.

21. Circular no. 86, governor-general to lieutenant governors, November 19, 1921, ACS 1 F 118.

22. Governor-general to governors of colonies, May 6, 1922, ACS 1 F 118.

23. Arsan, *Interlopers of Empire*, 116–17.

24. Arsan, *Interlopers of Empire*, 117.

25. Arsan, *Interlopers of Empire*, 105–7.

26. Delegate of the government of Senegal in Dakar to lieutenant governor of Senegal, October 9, 1923, ACS 1 F 118.

27. Arsan, *Interlopers of Empire*, 116.

28. Noiriel, *The French Melting Pot*, 61.

29. Noiriel, *The French Melting Pot*, 62–66.

30. Rosenberg, *Policing Paris*, 44–75, quote on 53.

31. Torpey, *Invention of the Passport*, 116–21.

32. Law of December 3, 1849, on the naturalization and residence of foreigners in France, FANC 21 G 37.

33. Order, May 20, 1874, FANC 21 G 37.

34. Lewis, "The Strangeness of Foreigners."

35. Report of special inspector of police, August 1918, FANC 21 G 44.

36. Direction of APA to director of the Sûreté Générale, February 5, 1923, FMOD 21 G 133.

37. Coquery-Vidrovitch, "Nationalité et citoyennité en Afrique occidentale française."

38. Direction of APA to Ministry of Colonies, direction of APA, CAI, Paris, January 14, 1931, FMOD 17 G 67.

39. Civil Affairs Service to lieutenant governors and commissaires of the government general, August 12, 1917, FANC 21 G 41.

40. Lieutenant governor of Ivory Coast to governor-general, Civil Affairs Service, September 30, 1915, FANC 21 G 41

41. Delegate of the government of Senegal in Dakar to the governor-general, Civil Affairs Service, June 19, 1917, FANC 21 G 41.

42. Civil Affairs Service to the delegate of the government of Senegal in Dakar; report for the central commissaire of police and the delegate of the government of Senegal, July 19, 1917, FANC 21 G 41

43. Report for the central commissaire of police and the delegate of the government of Senegal, July 19, 1917, FANC 21 G 41.

44. Dakar police report to the central commissaire of police, July 3, 1917, FANC 21 G 4.

45. Dakar police report to the central commissaire of police, July 3, 1917, FANC 21 G 41.

46. Governor-general of Algeria to the Sûreté Générale in Dakar, August 11, 1917, FANC 21 G 41.

47. Résidence general of Morocco to governor-general, August 29, 1917, FANC 21 G 41.

48. Civil Affairs Service, October 8, 1917, FANC 21 G 40.

49. Report, January 1, 1918, FANC 21 G 39.

50. Karl Pedersen to Danish ambassador in Paris, November 22, 1917, FANC 21 G 39.

51. Report, January 1, 1918, FANC 21 G 39.

52. Commissaire central to delegate of the government of Senegal, December 18, 1916, FANC 21 G 41.

53. Commissaire central to delegate of the government of Senegal, December 18, 1916, FANC 21 G 41.

54. Commissaire central Abbal to the delegate of the colony of Senegal in Dakar, December 18, 1916, FANC 21 G 41.

55. Lieutenant governor of Senegal to Civil Affairs Service, August 10, 1917, FANC 21 G 41.

56. Commissaire central Abbal to the delegate of the colony of Senegal in Dakar, December 18, 1916, FANC 21 G 41.

57. Civil Affairs Service to the lieutenant governor of Senegal, August 25, 1917, FANC 21 G 41.

58. Governor-general to minister of colonies, December 1917, FANC 21 G 41.

59. Minister of the interior, inspector de la police mobile to commissaire central of Dakar, June 15, 1917, FANC 21 G 41.

60. Minister of the interior, inspector de la mobile police to commissaire central of Dakar, June 15, 1917, FANC 21 G 41.

61. Minister of the interior inspector of de la police mobile to commissaire central of Dakar, June 15, 1917, FANC 21 G 41.

62. Minister of the interior inspector de la police mobile to central commissaire of Dakar, June 15, 1917, FANC 21 G 41.

63. Bernard to governor-general, November 1917, FANC 21 G 39.

64. Colonies to governor-general, November 17, 1917, FANC 21 G 41; notice of expulsion, November 29, 1917, FANC 21 G 41.

65. "Surveillance of foreigners," FMOD 21 G 36; "Surveillance of foreigners," 21 G 37; "Surveillance of foreigners," 21 G 38; "Surveillance of foreigners and suspects 1916–20," 21 G 39; "Surveillance of foreigners and suspects, 1916–18," 21 G 40.

66. Boittin, *Colonial Metropolis*, 80.

67. Governor-general, direction of APA, to minister of colonies, politics, February 14, 1921, FMOD 21 G 126.

68. Note, undated, FMOD 21 G 126.

69. See chapter 2 on the planted evidence that led to the search.

70. For example, Farmer claimed that a cigarette case containing a receipt for a letter sent to the UNIA in New York belonged to him but that he had written the letter for John Kamara. He had sent the letter in his own name because "it is the custom in Sierra Leone that he who knows how to write sends the letter in his name, even though he is not concerned with it." Farmer also told police that the UNIA was "a group that teaches natives of Africa diverse professions and when they are educated returns them to their country of origin." Wilson said that the branches of the UNIA in Senegal "have no relation with the American organization." Procès verbal, June 13, 1922, FMOD 17 G 52. There is a clear contrast between what the documents obtained during the search reveal and the statements made by the individuals in their interrogations.

71. Central commissaire of police to the delegate of the government of Senegal, June 17, 1922, FMOD 17 G 52. The composite of letters, pamphlets, speeches, and notes that were obtained in the search of Wilson's and Farmer's homes provide

ample evidence that a section of the UNIA was formed in Dakar and Rufisque. However, in a private letter Farmer continued to insist that Gibbs had planted the copies of the *Negro World*.

72. One announced a 1922 convention in New York that would bring together representatives from every continent. "The Third Annual International Convention of Negro Peoples of the World," August 31, 1922, FMOD 21 G 126.

73. Lieutenant governor to governor-general, July 11, 1922, FMOD 17 G 52.

74. Speech, "Gentlemen, as proposed members of the Rufisque branch of the UNIA and ACL," John Farmer's handwritten notebook, FMOD 21 G 126. The quotations come directly from Farmer's journal, written in English, which was taken during the June 1922 search. The Garveyism file also includes French translations of the speech.

75. Central commissaire of police to the delegate of the government of Senegal, June 17, 1922, FMOD 17 G 52.

76. Lieutenant governor to governor-general, July 11, 1922, FMOD 17 G 52.

77. Lieutenant governor to governor-general, July 11, 1922, FMOD 17 G 52. In fact one search turned up a letter at the home of Amadou Jawarrah, who denied knowing Wilson but had called him "his dear brother" in correspondence.

78. Central commissaire of police to delegate of the government of Senegal, June 17, 1922, FMOD 17 G 52.

79. Lieutenant governor to governor-general, July 11, 1922, FMOD 17 G 52.

80. Delegate of the government of Senegal in Dakar to governor-general, August 18, 1922; Procès Verbal of Armand Angrand, August 16, 1922, FMOD 21 G 132.

81. Procès verbal of Armand Angrand August 16, 1922, FMOD 21 G 132.

82. Procès verbal of Massyla Diop, August 17, 1922, FMOD 21 G 132.

83. Delegate of the government of Senegal in Dakar to governor-general, August 18, 1922, FMOD 21 G 132.

84. Lieutenant governor to governor-general, July 11, 1922, FMOD 17 G 52. The lieutenant governor feared foreigners as a threat, but it was a relief that anti-French activity was being carried out by foreigners and not Senegalese.

85. "Garveismes," *L'AOF: Echo de la Côte Occidentale d'Afrique* (Dakar, Senegal), August 17, 1922.

86. "Garveismes."

87. The file on Garveyism in AOF is several inches thick and occupies its own *côte* in the archives, 21 G 126.

88. Information on Small is scattered throughout files FMOD 17 G 58, 17 G 67, 17 G 66, and 17 G 70.

89. Langley, *Pan-Africanism and Nationalism in West Africa*, 137.

90. Wright, *The World and a Very Small Place in Africa*, 212.

91. Adi, *Pan-Africanism and Communism*, 99–100.

92. French consular agent in Bathurst to governor-general, December 1, 1930, FMOD 17 G 58.

93. Adi, *Pan-Africanism and Communism*, 100.

94. Edwards, *The Practice of Diaspora*, 256–58.

95. French consular agent in Bathurst to governor-general, December 1, 1930, FMOD 17 G 58.

96. On Nurse's plans to come to Dakar, see French consular agent in Bathurst to governor-general, April 28, 1930, FMOD 17 G 70.

97. Note for governor general, July 2, 1931, FMOD 17 G 58.

98. Note for governor general, July 2, 1931, FMOD 17 G 58.

99. Report, Inspector Gaston Braud to director of the Sûreté Générale, July 25, 1931, FMOD 17 G 58.

100. Note from Sûreté Générale to the director of APA, July 27, 1931, FMOD 17 G 58; E. F. Small to the French consular agent in Bathurst, August 15, 1931, Decree of expulsion for Edward Francis Small, October 15, 1931, FMOD 17 G 58.

101. Résidence general in Morocco to the governor-general, June 26, 1925, FMOD 21 G 28.

102. Ministry of Colonies to governor-general of AOF, February 18, 1930, FMOD 17 G 70.

103. Cablegram from Minister of Colonies Maginot to governor-general, July 27, 1929, FMOD 17 G 58.

104. See various files in FMOD 17 G 58, 17 G 62, 21 G 28, 21 G 38, and 21 G 132.

105. Thomas, *The French Empire between the Wars*, 227.

106. Administrator of the district of Dakar to governor-general, direction of APA, January 14, 1931, FMOD 17 G 70.

107. Translation of *Lao Nong* from Goebel, *Anti-Imperial Metropolis*, 142.

108. Adjunct director of the police and Sûreté to director of APA, August 30, 1930, FMOD 17 G 70.

109. Administrator of the circonscription of Dakar to governor-general, direction of APA, January 14, 1931, FMOD 17 G 70.

110. Report, Inspector Braud to director of the Sûreté Générale, February 28, 1932, FMOD 17 G 70.

111. Harrison, *France and Islam in West Africa*, 42.

112. Robinson, "France as a Muslim Power in West Africa," 122.

113. Grandhomme, "La politique musulmane de la France au Sénégal," 243.

114. Colonel Ruff, commissaire of Niger, to governor-general, March 14, 1921, FMOD 21 G 143.

115. Colonel Ruff, commissaire of Niger, to governor-general, May 21, 1921, FMOD 21 G 143.

116. Translation, March 7, 1921, FMOD 21 G 132.

117. Minister of war to military governor-general of Paris, commander of the region of Paris, military governor-general of Metz and Lyon, commander of regions 1–5, 7–14, 15–18, 20, and superior commanders of troops of Morocco, Tunisia, the Levant, and colonial troops, April 16, 1931, FMOD 17 G 69.

118. Lieutenant governor of French Guinea to governor-general, direction of APA, June 10, 1931, FMOD 17 G 69.

119. Résidence générale of Morocco to governor-general, January 18, 1935, FMOD 17 G 70.

120. Elizabeth Foster describes the clash between Spiritan missionaries in Senegal who sought to convert animist Serer who were ruled by Wolof leaders (*Faith in Empire*, 43–67).

121. Robinson, *Paths of Accommodation*, 209.

122. Lieutenant governor of Dahomey to governor-general, direction of Sûreté Générale, April 29, 1935, FMOD 21 G 41.

123. Administrator Antoine to lieutenant governor of Dahomey, undated, FMOD 21 G 41.

124. Governor-general to administrator of the district of Dakar, July 11, 1928, FMOD 21 G 38.

125. Direction of APA to director of the Sûreté Générale, May 22, 1936, FMOD 21 G 38.

126. Miller, *Shanghai on the Metro*.

127. Gardiner was on the radar of the police in metropolitan France as well. Miller, *Shanghai on the Metro*, 73–75.

128. Note, undated, FMOD 21 G 28.

129. Note, Bulletin of the French Africa Committee, July 1926, FMOD 21 G 28.

130. "Arrivée d'un conseiller d'Abd el Krim," *Le Temps* (Paris), November 10, 1925.

131. "L'Anglais Gardiner à Tanger," *Le Temps* (Paris), November 11, 1925.

132. Lieutenant governor of French Guinea to governor-general, November 20, 1926, FMOD 21 G 28.

133. Circle commander of Baie du Levrier to lieutenant governor of Mauritania, July 3, 1926, FMOD 21 G 28.

134. "Les aventures d'un ancient ambassadeur du Rif," *Le Temps* (Paris), June 8, 1926.

135. Circle commander of Baie du Levrier to lieutenant governor of Mauritania, July 3, 1926, FMOD 21 G 28.

136. Circle commander of Baie du Levrier to lieutenant governor of Mauritania, July 3, 1926, FMOD 21 G 28.

137. Circle commander of Baie du Levrier to lieutenant governor of Mauritania, July 3, 1926, FMOD 21 G 28.

138. Radiogram, Maginot to governor-general, March 12, 1929, FMOD 21 G 28.

139. Untitled, Dakar, March 15, 1929, FMOD 21 G 28.

140. Untitled, Dakar, April 16, 1929, FMOD 21 G 28.

141. Direction du Cabinet Civil to Ministry of Colonies, May 14, 1929, FMOD 21 G 28.

142. Waldeck, *Prelude to the Past*, 239, 244, 242, 240, 243.

143. Untitled, Dakar, March 15, 1929, FMOD 21 G 28.

144. Untitled, Dakar, March 15, 1929, FMOD 21 G 28.

145. Newspaper clipping, "Un drame berlinois," undated, FMOD 21 G 28.

146. Boittin, "Adventurers and Agents Provocateurs."

147. Director of police and Sûreté Générale to governor-general, March 2, 1923, FMOD 21 G 133.

148. Central commissaire Jean Pourroy to delegate of the government of Senegal, July 23, 1920, FMOD 21 G 133.

149. Director of police and Sûreté Générale to governor-general, March 2, 1923, FMOD 21 G 133.

150. Ambassador of the French Republic at Berne de Marcilly to Minister of Foreign Affairs Brians, December 6, 1929, FMOD 21 G 38.

151. Circular, governor-general to lieutenant governors, April 23, 1935, FMOD 21 G 38; circular, governor-general to lieutenant governors, November 6, 1934, FMOD 17 G 58.

152. Governor-general of Algeria to governor-general, September 8, 1930, FMOD 17 G 58; governor of Niger to governor-general, direction of APA, June 7, 1930, FMOD 17 G 58; French consul in Tripoli Terver to minister of foreign affairs, December 3, 1930, FMOD 17 G 58.

153. Legation of Austria in Paris to minister of foreign affairs, March 14, 1931, FMOD 17 G 58.

154. Annexe des allers, March 14, 1931, FMOD 17 G 58.

155. Governor-general to minister of colonies, June 26, 1931, FMOD 17 G 58.

156. Minister of foreign affairs to minister of colonies, March 31, 1931, FMOD 17 G 58.

4. "POWERLESS TO OUR NATIONALS"

1. Gide, *Travels to the Congo*, 90.

2. Foster, *Faith in Empire*.

3. Report from Minister of Colonies Daladier to the president of the republic, January 24, 1925, ACS 1 F 118.

4. Annual Report, Dakar et Dépendances police and Sûreté Générale, 1932, FMOD 2 G 32/22.

5. By the 1930s colonial tourism had developed to the extent that group tours were being offered by a French traveling club. Furlough, "*Une Leçon des Choses.*" On permanent residents see Mercier, "The European Community of Dakar." According to Mercier's data from 1955, Europeans were just 7 percent of the population, a number that had grown sixfold since 1938 (287).

6. Cruise O'Brien, *White Society in Black Africa*, 17–18.

7. Minister of colonies to governor-general, January 6, 1922, FMOD 21 G 132.

8. Circular to lieutenant governor and commissaire of Niger, January 30, 1922, FMOD 21 G 132.

9. Adjunct director of police and Sûreté to director of APA, May 28, 1930, FMOD 21 G 38.

10. Governor-General Brévié to director of APA, December 26, 1930, FMOD 21 G 38.

11. Copy of letter written by Roche, transmitted to the colonial commission, June 1925 (date unclear), FMOD 21 G 134.

12. Georges Nomis to governor-general, October 11, 1925, FMOD 21 G 28.

13. Commissaire of police of the city of Bambey to circle commander of Baol, January 21, 1926, FMOD 21 G 28.

14. Thomas, *Empires of Intelligence*, 102.

15. Prefect of Bouches du Rhône to minister of the interior, Sûreté Générale, April 8, 1928, FMOD 17 G 58.

16. Prefect of Bouches du Rhône to minister of the interior, Sûreté Générale, April 8, 1928, FMOD 17 G 58.

17. Renseignements, undated, FMOD 17 G 66.

18. Renseignements, October 19, 1933, FMOD 17 G 66.

19. Renseignements, September 8, 1933, FMOD 17 G 66.

20. Note on revolutionary propaganda of interest to the overseas territories, June 3, 1922, 17 G 61.

21. Minister of colonies to governor-general, October 3, 1929, and Note from CAI, FMOD 21 G 38.

22. Martyrs d'Afrique, FMOD 21 G 41, emphasis in original.

23. Director of APA, July 24, 1929, FMOD 21 G 41.

24. Renseignements, undated, FMOD 21 G 38.

25. Director of APA to cabinet director, January 21, 1932, FMOD 21 G 38.

26. Renseignements, undated, FMOD 21 G 38.

27. Renseignements, undated, FMOD 21 G 38.

28. Renseignements, undated, FMOD 21 G 38.

29. *La Calotte*, August 1931, FMOD 21 G 38.

30. Commissaire of police in Rufisque to circle commander in Thiès, September 25, 1925, FMOD 17 G 52.

31. Telegram, minister of colonies to Dakar, November 30, 1926, FMOD 21 G 134.

32. Telegram, minister of colonies to Dakar, November 30, 1926, FMOD 21 G 134.

33. Renseignements, March 23, 1923, FMOD 21 G 132.

34. Brochure, "FRANCAIS!," FMOD 21 G 134.

35. Conklin, *A Mission to Civilize*, 38.

36. Conklin, "Redefining 'Frenchness,'" 81.

37. Stoler points out that colonial states worked hard to try to create middle-class respectability through various kinds of social intervention, from financial aid to restrictions on sexuality, a project threatened by increasing numbers of poor whites in the colonies (*Carnal Knowledge and Imperial Power*, 35–38).

38. Cohen, *Rulers of Empire*, 51–55.

39. General administration to governor-general, direction of APA, October 16, 1922, ACS 1 F 118.

40. "Renseignements à fournir" to the prosecutor, May 18, 1931, FMOD 17 G 58.

41. Delegate of the government of Senegal in Dakar to governor of Senegal, received June 22, 1922, ACS 1 F 118.

42. Telegram, lieutenant governor to governor-general, August 16, 1921, FMOD 21 G 132.

43. Telegram, governor-general to the consul of France in Bathurst, August 1921, FMOD 21 G 132.

44. "Renseignements à fournir" to the general prosecutor, May 18, 1931, FMOD 17 G 58.

45. "Renseignements à fournir" to the general prosecutor, May 18, 1931, FMOD 17 G 58.

46. Untitled Dakar, June 3, 1929, FMOD 21 G 28.

47. Commissaire of the republic of Togo to lieutenant governor of Upper Volta, September 20, 1930, FMOD 17 G 58.

48. Compagnie du Lobi, société anonyme français, January 15, 1931, FMOD 17 G 58.

49. White, *Children of the French Empire*, 7–62.

50. Roberts, *Civilization without Sexes*; Andersen, *Regeneration through Empire*.

51. Conklin, "Redefining 'Frenchness,'" 67.

52. Genova, *Colonial Ambivalence*, 61.

53. Conklin "Redefining Frenchness," 71-72.

54. Conklin "Redefining 'Frenchness,'" 77–82.

55. Thomas, *Empires of Intelligence*, 28.

56. Lieutenant governor of Mauritania to governor-general, October 30, 1930, FMOD 21 G 38. In the same letter the lieutenant governor of Mauritania claimed to

have "documents clearly establishing" the communist sympathies of Carretier and requesting his transfer.

57. Renseignements, December 27, 1930, FMOD 21 G 38.
58. Lieutenant governor to governor-general, direction of APA, January 9, 1931, FMOD 21 G 38.
59. Renseignements, December 27, 1930, FMOD 21 G 38.
60. Director of police and Sûreté to governor-general, March 2, 1925, FMOD 21 G 133.
61. Chief of Sûreté in Senegal to governor of Senegal, February 10, 1931, FMOD 21 G 38.
62. Governor-general, Sûreté Générale, to minister of colonies, to governor of Senegal, February 23, 1931, FMOD 21 G 38.
63. "Voyages de Madame Delmas," FMOD 21 G 43.
64. Minister of foreign affairs to minister of colonies, January 20, 1930, FMOD 21 G 43.
65. Commissaire of police, chief of Sûreté, Sudan, to governor of Sudan, May 27, 1931, FMOD 21 G 43.
66. Lieutenant Colonel Charbonnier, circle commander of Tombouctou, to lieutenant governor of Sudan, FMOD 21 G 43.
67. Copy of official telegram, governor of Mauritania to governor-general, February 22, 1932, FMOD 21 G 43.
68. Miller, *Blank Darkness*.
69. Driver and Martins, *Tropical Visions in an Age of Empire*.
70. Todorov, *On Human Diversity*, 311; Miller, *Blank Darkness*, 208; Matsuda, *Empire of Love*; Venayre, *La Gloire de l'aventure*.
71. Gorer, *Africa Dances*; Londres, *Terre d'ébène*.
72. Slavin, *Colonial Cinema and Imperial France*, 157, 164.
73. Slavin, *Colonial Cinema and Imperial France*, 157, 164.
74. Report by Brigade de Sûreté of Senegal March 13, 1926, FMOD 17 G 70.
75. Direction of APA to governor-general AEF, May 15, 1926, FMOD 17 G 70.
76. Report by Brigade de Sûreté of Senegal, March 13, 1926, FMOD 17 G 70.
77. Telegram, administrator at Tambacounda to governor of Senegal, April 20, 1926, FMOD 17 G 70.
78. Governor-general to minister of colonies, APA, October 1, 1926, FMOD 17 G 70.
79. Report by Brigade de Sûreté of Senegal, March 13, 1926, FMOD 17 G 70.
80. Untitled, September 19, 1926, FMOD 17 G 70.
81. Governor-general, direction of APA, to minister of colonies, direction of APA, July 31, 1930, FMOD 17 G 70.
82. *Le Journal* to governor-general, June 15, 1930, FMOD 17 G 70.
83. Minister of colonies to Governor-General Carde, September 20, 1927, FMOD 17 G 70.

84. *Le Chasseur Français*, October 1927, FMOD 17 G 70.

85. Direction of APA to lieutenant governor of Senegal, January 25, 1926, FMOD 17 G 70.

86. White, "The Decivilizing Mission."

87. Note from lieutenant governor of Senegal to delegate of the government of Senegal in Dakar, March 11, 1921, FMOD 21 G 28.

88. Untitled, Paris, May 10, 1921, FMOD 21 G 132.

89. Central commissaire to delegate of Senegal in Dakar, March 16, 1921, FMOD 21 G 28, emphasis in police copy of the letter.

90. Administrator first class to lieutenant governor of Sudan, May 5, 1921, FMOD 21 G 28.

91. Central commissaire to delegate of Senegal in Dakar, March 16, 1921, FMOD 21 G 28.

92. Administrator first class to lieutenant governor of Sudan, May 5, 1921, FMOD 21 G 28.

93. "Fiche de renseignements on Mr. Greleau, Circle of Kayes," April 20, 1921, FMOD 21 G 28.

94. Administrator first class to lieutenant governor of Sudan, May 5, 1921, FMOD 21 G 28.

95. "Fiche de renseignements on Mr. Greleau, Circle of Kayes," April 20, 1921, FMOD 21 G 28.

96. Administrator first class to lieutenant governor of Sudan, May 5, 1921, FMOD 21 G 28.

97. Administrator first class, delegate of the governor at Kayes to governor of Sudan, April 23, 1921, FMOD 21 G 132.

98. Eugène Greleau to delegate of the government general at Kayes, April 7, 1921, FMOD 21 G 132.

99. Administrator first class to lieutenant governor of Sudan, May 5, 1921, FMOD 21 G 28.

100. Eugène Greleau to delegate of the government general at Kayes, April 7, 1921, FMOD 21 G 132.

101. Lieutenant governor of Upper Volta to governor-general, August 27, 1925, FMOD 21 G 134.

102. "Extrait du rapport d'inspection du cercle de Fada," April 5, 1925, FMOD 21 G 134. Inspector Coste noted as well that the communist materials were purchased for the library from the local budget.

103. Lieutenant governor of Upper Volta to governor-general, August 27, 1925, FMOD 21 G 134.

104. Lieutenant governor of Upper Volta to governor-general, August 27, 1925, FMOD 21 G 134.

105. Lieutenant governor of Upper Volta to governor-general, August 27, 1925, FMOD 21 G 134.

### 5. CREATING NETWORKS

1. Untitled, handwritten "A.P.A.," February 26, 1932, FMOD 21 G 44.

2. Direction of APA to governor-general and lieutenant governors, December 12, 1931, FMOD 21 G 44.

3. Renseignements, December 1, 1931, FMOD 21 G 44.

4. Untitled, handwritten "A.P.A.," February 26, 1932, FMOD 21 G 44.

5. African authorities would make occasional references to drinking or family problems as asides in files on AOF that were primarily focused on political activity. A criminal record or bad reputation could also increase suspicion. See Amoibet and Amadou Moustapha Fall, FMOD 21 G 38.

6. Lieutenant governor of Sudan to governor-general of AOF, APA, February 2, 1934, FMOD 21 G 38; Consular agent of France in Bathurst to the lieutenant governor of Senegal, December 5, 1922, FMOD 21 G 133.

7. Johnson, *The Emergence of Black Politics in Senegal*; Johnson, "The Impact of the Senegalese Elite on the French," in *Double Impact*; Vaillant, *Black, French and African*.

8. Cruise O'Brien, *The Mourides of Senegal*; Robinson, *Paths of Accommodation*.

9. Conklin, *A Mission to Civilize*, 204.

10. A few notable exceptions on radical politics during the interwar era are Suret-Canale, "An Unrecognised Pioneer"; Manning, *Slavery Colonialism and Economic Growth in Dahomey*; Spiegler, "Aspects of Nationalist Thought."

11. On black radicals in France see Dewitte, *Les mouvements nègres en France*; Boittin, *Colonial Metropolis*; Goebel, *Anti-Imperial Metropolis*.

12. Bernard-Duquenet writes that even during the Popular Front, "all the sympathizers of the League [League for Defense of the Negro Race] were kept under a tight surveillance and could hardly engage in local activity" (*Le Sénégal et le Front Populaire*, 36). Dewitte writes, "With the Dakar section [of the CDNR] the hope was born to see a movement develop on the black continent, but neither the CDNR, nor the League for Defense of the Negro Race could really exploit this opportunity, and Beccaria, isolated, would soon be subject to repression" (*Les mouvements nègres en France*, 153).

13. Genova writes, "The Ligue's influence spread rapidly throughout West Africa and among migrants from the colonies in France. Sections of the organization were established in every colony of the federation and throughout the metropole.

Lamine Senghor and Kouyaté, aided by the Communist trade unions, traveled frequently between France and West Africa, and information was disseminated and actions planned by way of an expanding network of supporters." Genova, *Colonial Ambivalence*, 75–76. It is unlikely that Kouyaté ever traveled to AOF as the police were carefully observing him and show no record of his appearance.

14. Edwards, *The Practice of Diaspora*; Manning, *Slavery, Colonialism and Economic Growth in Dahomey*.

15. Suret-Canale, "An Unrecognised Pioneer," 196.

16. Suret-Canale, "An Unrecognised Pioneer," 197.

17. Michel, *Les Africains et la Grande Guerre*, 50–63.

18. Lunn, *Memoirs of the Maelstrom*, 43–44, 50.

19. Harrison, *France and Islam in West Africa*, 96.

20. Harrison, *France and Islam in West Africa*, 118–19.

21. Governor-general to delegate of the governor of Senegal, December 1917, FANC 21 G 39.

22. Governor-general to delegate of the governor of Senegal, December 1917, FANC 21 G 39.

23. Governor-general to delegate of the governor of Senegal, December 1917, FANC 21 G 39; Robinson, *Paths of Accommodation*, 132–33.

24. Governor-general to delegate of the governor of Senegal, December 1917, FANC 21 G 39.

25. Governor-general to delegate of the governor of Senegal, December 1917, FANC 21 G 39.

26. Telegram, cabinet militaire to colonies, undated, FANC 21 G 41.

27. Harrison describes a "Mahdist plot" in Upper Senegal and Niger. He suggests that evidence for a conspiracy was conveniently compiled by authorities who wished a greater military presence in the region anyway (*France and Islam in West Africa*, 45–47, 55). Harrison describes the "Goumba affair" in Futa Jallon in 1909, initiated by the murder of a French administrator. An elderly, blind marabout who was a "lifelong . . . supporter of the French" was subsequently accused of participating in the crime by inciting "fanaticism" (78, 74). The marabout, Tierno Aliou, was put on trial, and rumors of an "Islamic conspiracy" were rampant (85). Harrison suggests that by the end of the trial, during which Aliou was found guilty, the French knew they had overreacted in turning the murder into a frenzied fear of Islamic conspiracy. He writes, "To a certain extent the affair marked the end of a period in terms of French attitudes to Islam, a period characterised by exaggerated fears and belief in the 'permanent conspiracy' of Islam" (89).

28. Harrison, *France and Islam in West Africa*, 56; on "fear of Islam," 29–56.

29. Governor-general to Ministry of Colonies, February 14, 1921, FMOD 21 G 126.

30. Harrison, *France and Islam in West Africa*, 164.

31. On the black literary and culture scene see Edwards, *The Practice of Diaspora*; Stovall, *Paris Noir*, 25–129; Boittin, *Colonial Metropolis*.

32. Dewitte, *Les mouvements nègres en France*, 127.

33. Dewitte, *Les mouvements nègres en France*, 153.

34. Dewitte, *Les mouvements nègres en France*, 154. For example, the LDNR opposed naturalization of individuals as a way to obtain rights, claiming this was a practice that benefited only the elite (157).

35. Dewitte, *Les mouvements nègres en France*, 174.

36. Lieutenant governor of Ivory Coast to governor-general, September 21, 1926, FMOD 21 G 28.

37. Chief administrator of Sudan to governor-general, direction of APA, November 19, 1926, FMOD 21 G 28.

38. Report, April 2, 1927, FMOD 21 G 28. Edwards also tells the story of Kouyaté's early life and career as an activist (*The Practice of Diaspora*, 250–76).

39. Senghor quoted in Dewitte, *Les mouvements nègres en France*, 169.

40. Dewitte, *Les mouvements nègres en France*, 162–64.

41. Despite the diverse themes in the *Race Nègre*, the government general of AOF would consistently refer to Kouyaté as the "Sudanese communist" and perceived of his different "Negro" groups as instruments for spreading communist propaganda. In fact it seems that the notion of a black-centered political movement for independence was alien to administrators.

42. Chief administrator of Sudan to governor-general, direction of APA, November 19, 1926, FMOD 21 G 28.

43. "Note on séjour de Kouyaté en Russie," FMOD 21 G 28; Note of Agent Désiré, August 3, 1926, FMOD 21 G 28. The note describes Kouyaté's politics as "very advanced."

44. "Note on revolutionary propaganda of interest to the overseas territories," October 1929, FMOD 17 G 64.

45. Report of Principal Inspector Lenaers, April 2, 1927, FMOD 21 G 28.

46. "Excerpt of a note on revolutionary propaganda of interest to the overseas colonies," June 30, 1927, FMOD 21 G 28.

47. Renseignements généraux, January 14, 1931, FMOD 21 G 28.

48. Untitled, Dakar, February 4, 1927, FMOD 21 G 134.

49. Fiche individuel, undated, ca. 1930, FMOD 21 G 38.

50. Untitled, Dakar, February 4, 1927, FMOD 21 G 134.

51. Dewitte, *Les mouvements nègres en France*, 333.

52. Beccaria to the president of the LDNR, September 6, 1927, FMOD 21 G 44. Dewitte reports that while on a 1928 trip to Paris Galandou Diouf, Lamine Guèye, and Kojo Tovolou joined the LDNR, but upon return to Senegal they hardly corresponded again with Kouyaté (*Les mouvements nègres en France*, 181–82).

53. Beccaria to president of the LDNR, September 6, 1927, FMOD 21 G 44.

54. Jones, *The Métis of Senegal*, 190.

55. Beccaria to president of the LDNR, September 6, 1927, FMOD 21 G 44.

56. Secretary-general of the LDNR to Canton Chief Bakary Ba, May 17, 1929, FMOD 21 G 44.

57. Secretary-General Kouyaté to Marcel Ackah, December 5, 1927, FMOD 21 G 44.

58. Lieutenant governor of Ivory Coast to governor-general, direction of APA, February 8, 1928, FMOD 21 G 44.

59. Secretary-General Kouyaté to Pierre Tournabia, "planter of cocoa," April 20, 1928, FMOD 21 G 44. In 1929 Ali, a customs employee in Ivory Coast, sent a mandate to the LDNR in Paris requesting a copy of the journal be sent in an envelope. Minister of colonies to governor-general, September 16, 1929, FMOD 21 G 44.

60. Lieutenant governor of Ivory Coast to governor-general, direction of APA, February 8, 1928, FMOD 21 G 44.

61. Report of Sûreté Brigade in Senegal, December 19, 1929, FMOD 17 G 68.

62. General administration to the general prosecutor, November 20, 1930, FMOD 17 G 68.

63. Secretary-general to Amadou Thiam, "employee at Naja brothers," Bamako, March 24, 1928, FMOD 21 G 28.

64. "Note on revolutionary action of interest to the overseas territories," October 1929, FMOD 17 G 64. The Dakar copy of this report from Paris includes a handwritten "?" next to "Bamako (Ivory Coast)."

65. Untitled, marked "confidential," Dakar, August 24, 1931, FMOD 21 G 44.

66. Ministry of Colonies, CAI, to the governor-general of AOF, APA, January 26, 1932, FMOD 21 G 44.

67. Summary of *La Race Nègre* August 1931, October 27, 1931, FMOD 21 G 44.

68. Untitled, August 22, 1931, FMOD 21 G 44. The ministry described the *Revue du Monde Noir* as "clearly hostile to our influence in Africa." Minister of war, interim minister of colonies, to governor-general, September 17, 1931, FMOD 21 G 44.

69. Governor-general to minister of colonies, direction of APA, August 29, 1931, FMOD 21 G 44.

70. Special inspector of police in Bamako Barreyre to director of the police and Sûreté, November 7, 1930, FMOD 21 G 44.

71. Lieutenant governor of Sudan to governor-general, direction of APA, January 8, 1931, FMOD 21 G 44.

72. Bernard-Duquenet, *Le Sénégal et le Front Populaire*, 36.

73. Thomas, *Empires of Intelligence*, 28.

74. Secretary-general (of LDNR) to M Léon Binzeme, March 24, 1928, FMOD 21 G 28.

75. Beccaria to president of the LDNR, September 6, 1927, FMOD 21 G 44.

76. Note on Beccaria, February 4, 1927, FMOD 21 G 134.

77. Beccaria to president of the LDNR, September 6, 1927, FMOD 21 G 44.

78. Circular, governor-general, direction of APA, to lieutenant governors, May 8, 1928, FMOD 21 G 44.

79. Spiegler, "Aspects of Nationalist Thought," 130, 125, 126.

80. Wilder, *The French Imperial Nation-State*, 142.

81. Thomas, *Empires of Intelligence*, 225.

82. Spiegler, "Aspects of Nationalist Thought," 215.

83. Harrison, *France and Islam in West Africa*, 150.

84. Manning, *Slavery, Colonialism, and Economic Growth in Dahomey*, 263.

85. Manning, *Slavery, Colonialism, and Economic Growth in Dahomey*, 261.

86. Suret-Canale, "An Unrecognised Pioneer," 202.

87. Suret-Canale, "An Unrecognised Pioneer," 204–7.

88. Suret-Canale, "An Unrecognised Pioneer," 207.

89. Manning, *Slavery, Colonialism, and Economic Growth in Dahomey*, 265.

90. Manning, *Slavery, Colonialism, and Economic Growth in Dahomey*, 266.

91. Manning, *Slavery, Colonialism, and Economic Growth in Dahomey*, 267.

92. Manning, *Slavery, Colonialism, and Economic Growth in Dahomey*, 267.

93. Manning, *Slavery, Colonialism, and Economic Growth in Dahomey*, 263–64, 267.

94. Dossier Hunkanrin, FMOD 8 G 9 and 10.

95. Director of Sûreté Générale to director of political affairs, December 29, 1931, FMOD 21 G 28.

96. Renseignements, December 9, 1931, FMOD 21 G 28.

97. Renseignements, December 9, 1931, FMOD 21 G 28.

98. Manning, *Slavery, Capitalism and Economic Growth in Dahomey*, 267–68.

99. Manning, *Slavery, Capitalism and Economic Growth in Dahomey*, 269–70.

100. Governor-general, APA, Dirat to lieutenant governor of Dahomey, February 22, 1932, FMOD 21 G 28.

101. Jean Adjovi to minister of colonies, March 12, 1934, FM Aff Pol 529/102.

102. Governor-general to the minister of colonies, APA, March 7, 1934, FM Aff Pol 529/102.

103. Manning, *Slavery, Capitalism and Economic Growth in Dahomey*, 272.

104. Manning, *Slavery, Capitalism and Economic Growth in Dahomey*, 272.

105. Manning, *Slavery, Capitalism and Economic Growth in Dahomey*, 273.

106. Manning, *Slavery, Capitalism and Economic Growth in Dahomey*, 274.

107. Report by Principal Inspector Lenaers, April 2, 1927, FMOD 21 G 28.

108. Report by Principal Inspector Lenaers, April 2, 1927, FMOD 21 G 28.

109. Report by Principal Inspector Lenaers, April 2, 1927, FMOD 21 G 28.

110. When syndicates were permitted in 1936 "as a result of metropolitan legislation, the right to organize was extended to workers with a primary education certificate: the two main unions to formalize their existence were a civil service association, headed by Richard Johnson, and the railroad union" (Manning, *Slavery, Colonialism and Economic Growth in Dahomey*, 274).

111. Secretary-general of Internationale des Travailleurs de l'Enseignement, September 1928, FMOD 17 G 68.

112. Secretary-general of Internationale des Travailleurs de l'Enseignement, September 25, 1928, FMOD 17 G 68.

113. Direction of APA to lieutenant governors of Senegal, Ivory Coast, and Dahomey, administrator of the district of Dakar, March 11, 1929, FMOD 17 G 68.

114. Minister of colonies to governor-general, September 11, 1929, FMOD 17 G 68.

115. Lieutenant governor of Dahomey to governor-general, APA, inspection d'enseignement, February 4, 1930, FMOD 17 G 68.

116. Governor-general, direction of APA, to minister of colonies, service of CAI, inspection council of public instruction, October 24, 1930, FMOD 17 G 68.

117. Governor-general, direction of APA, to minister of colonies, service of CAI, inspection council of public instruction, October 24, 1930, FMOD 17 G 68.

118. Lieutenant governor of Ivory Coast to direction of enseignement, undated, FMOD 17 G 68.

119. Lieutenant governor of Mauritania to governor-general, direction of APA, June 20, 1930, FMOD 17 G 68; Renseignements of Brigade of Sûreté of Senegal, July 31 1930, FMOD 17 G 68.

120. Lieutenant governor of Dahomey to governor-general, direction of APA, inspection d' enseignement, February 4, 1930, FMOD 17 G 68.

121. Inspector of education, colony of Dahomey, to governor of Dahomey, September 13, 1930, FMOD 17 G 68.

122. Lieutenant governor of Dahomey to governor-general, direction of APA, inspection d' enseignement, February 4, 1930, FMOD 17 G 68.

123. Renseignements, July 26, 1931, FMOD 17 G 67.

124. Note for the governor-general, direction of APA, July 2, 1931, FMOD 17 G 58.

125. Renseignements, undated, ca. 1933, FMOD 17 G 58; Renseignements, July 26, 1931, FMOD 17 G 66.

126. Renseignements, July 26, 1931, FMOD 17 G 58.

127. Note from the governor-general, October 3, 1931, FMOD 17 G 58.

128. Renseignements, July 26, 1931, FMOD 17 G 58.

129. Renseignements, July 26, 1931, FMOD 17 G 58.

130. These include Abdoulaye Dione, FMOD 17 G 58; James-Francis Senegal of Gambia, FMOD 21 G 38; Philippe Nelson, FMOD 17 G 67.

131. Renseignements, December 7, 1931, FMOD 17 G 58.

132. Untitled, November 26, 1931, FMOD 17 G 58.

133. Direction of APA to director of economic affairs, December 5, 1931, FMOD 17 G 58; Renseignements, FMOD 17 G 58; Renseignements, December 7, 1931, FMOD 17 G 58; Untitled, November 26, 1931, FMOD 17 G 58; Untitled, January 18, 1931, FMOD 17 G 58; Untitled list, December 28, 1931, FMOD 17 G 58.

134. Renseignements, October 31, 1933, FMOD 21 G 28.

CONCLUSION

1. Ginio, *French Colonialism Unmasked*, 126.

2. Telegram, Ministry of Colonies at Vichy to high commissaire of French Africa, November 15, 1940, FMOD 21 G 53.

3. Order No. 3124, organizing the direction of the Sûreté Générale of French Africa, September 3, 1941, FMOD 21 G 170.

4. Fourchard, *De la ville coloniale à la cour africaine*, 346.

5. Direction of APA to the director of the Security Service, June 8, 1943, FMOD 21 G 207.

6. Manning, *Slavery, Colonialism, and Economic Growth in Dahomey*, 274.

7. Ginio, *French Colonialism Unmasked*, xv.

8. "Synthese d'information générale bimensuelle Activité Politique des Indigènes," May 16, 1945, FMOD 21 G 92. The use of comprehensive political bulletins had begun in the late 1930s but was the main way of communicating political information from 1945 onward.

9. Renseignements, June 6, 1946, FMOD 21 G 96.

10. Renseignements, August 19, 1946, FMOD 21 G 96.

11. Renseignements, August 16, 1946, FMOD 21 G 96.

12. Renseignements, August 8, 1946, FMOD 21 G 91.

13. Cooper, *Decolonization and African Society*, 244.

14. This method of reporting details of meetings is much more similar to the work of CAI in France in the interwar era than to the surveillance of suspects in interwar AOF.

15. Myers, *Verandahs of Power*; Anderson, *Imagined Communities*, 163–85; Cohn, *Colonialism and Its Forms of Knowledge*; Robinson, "Ethnography and Customary Law in Senegal"; Wilder, "Colonial Ethnology and Political Rationality."

16. Bernault, *A History of Prison and Confinement*; Thioub, "L'enfermement carcéral."

# BIBLIOGRAPHY

ARCHIVES

The main collection of original archival documents consulted for this book, the Archives du government général de l'AOF, are located at the Archives Nationales du Sénégal (ANS) in Dakar. The documents are divided into two main collections: Fonds ancien (FANC) includes documents before 1920; Fonds moderne (FMOD) includes documents after 1920. All files cited from the Government General Archives (FMOD and FANC) are available on microfilm at the Archives Nationales d'Outre Mer (ANOM) in Aix-en-Provence and at the Archives Nationales de France (ANF) in Paris. Documents from all three sets of the collection were consulted at the three sites, and no distinction is made between them as they all refer back to the same set of original documents. In addition to the Government General Archives I consulted documents of the Ministry of Colonies Fonds ministériel (FM) at the ANOM and Archives of the Colony of Senegal (ACS) in Dakar at the ANS.

Archives du Gouvernement Général de l'AOF
    Fonds ancien (FANC) before 1920
        2 D 13 Etat de guerre entre les puissances étrangères
        2 D 14 Contrôle de l'activité étrangère en AOF pendant la guerre
        17 G Affaires Politiques: AOF, 1895–1920
        21 G Police et Sûreté 1825–1920
    Fonds moderne (FMOD) after 1920
        2 G Rapports annuels
        13 G Affaires Politiques, Administratives et Musulmanes: Sénégal
        17 G Affaires Politiques
        19 G Affaires Musulmanes
        21 G Police et Sûreté
Archives Nationales d'Outre Mer (ANOM)
    Fonds ministériels (FM)
        Affaires Politiques (Aff Pols)
        Séries EE II: Personnel

Archives Nationales du Sénégal (ANS)
  Archives de la Colonie du Sénégal (ACS)
    Série F Police et Prisons, 1 F 118

PUBLISHED WORKS

Adi, Hakim. *Pan-Africanism and Communism: The Communist International, Africa, and the Diaspora, 1919–1939.* Trenton NJ: Africa World Press, 2013.

Ahire, Philip Terdoo. *Imperial Policing: The Emergence and Role of the Police in Colonial Nigeria, 1860–1960.* Philadelphia: Open University Press, 1991.

Alexanderson, Kris. "'A Dark State of Affairs': Hajj Networks, Pan-Islam, and Dutch Colonial Surveillance during the Interwar Period." *Journal of Social History* 47, no, 4 (2014): 1021–41.

Andersen, Margaret Cook. *Regeneration through Empire: French Pronatalists and Colonial Settlement in the Third Republic.* Lincoln: University of Nebraska Press, 2015.

Anderson, Benedict. *Imagined Communities: Reflections on the Origins and Spread of Nationalism.* New York: Verso, 1991.

Anderson, David M., and David Killingray, eds. *Policing and Decolonisation: Politics, Nationalism and the Police, 1917–65.* New York: Manchester University Press, 1992.

———, eds. *Policing the Empire: Government Authority and Control, 1830–1940.* New York: Manchester University Press, 1991.

Angrand, Armand, *Les Lebous de la Presqu'ile du Cap-Vert.* Dakar: F. Gensul, 1949.

Arnold, David. *Police Power and Colonial Rule, Madras, 1859–1947.* New York: Oxford University Press, 1986.

Arsan, Andrew. "Failing to Stem the Tide: Lebanese Migration to French West Africa and the Competing Prerogatives of the Imperial State." *Comparative Studies in Society and History* 53, no. 3 (2011): 450–78.

———. *Interlopers of Empire: The Lebanese Diaspora in Colonial French West Africa.* New York: Oxford University Press, 2014.

Bayly, C. A. *Empire and Information: Intelligence Gathering and Social Communication in India, 1780–1870.* Cambridge, UK: Cambridge University Press, 1996.

Berlière, Jean-Marc. *Le Monde des polices en France XIXᵉ–XXᵉ siècles.* Paris: Editions Complexe, 1996.

———. *Police et policiers en France, XIXᵉ–XXᵉ siècles.* Brussels: Complexe, 1992.

———. "A Republican Political Police? Political Policing in France under the Third Republic, 1875–1940." In *The Policing of Politics in the Twentieth Century*, edited by Mark Mazower, 27–55. Providence RI: Berghahn Books, 1997.

Berman, Bruce, and John Lonsdale. *Unhappy Valley: Conflict in Kenya and Africa.* Vol. 1. Athens: Ohio University Press, 1992.

Bernard-Duquenet, Nicole. *Le Sénégal et le Front Populaire.* Paris: L'Harmattan, 1985.

Bernault, Florence, ed. *A History of Prison and Confinement*. Portsmouth NH: Heinemann, 2002.

Berry, Sara. "Hegemony on a Shoestring: Indirect Rule and Access to Agricultural
Land." *Africa: Journal of the International African Institute* 62 (1992): 327–55.

Betts, Raymond. *Assimilation and Association in French Cultural Theory*. New York:
Columbia University Press, 1961.

———. "The Establishment of the Medina in Dakar, Senegal, 1914." *Africa* 41, no.
2 (1971): 143–52.

———. "Dakar: Ville Impériale (1857–1960)." In *Colonial Cities*, edited by Robert
J. Ross and Gerard J. Telkamp, 193–206. Boston: Springer, 1985.

Biarnès, Pierre. *Les Français en Afrique noire de Richelieu à Mitterand: 350 ans de
présence Française au sud du Sahara*. Paris: A. Colin, 1987.

Bigon, Liora. *French Colonial Dakar: The Morphogenesis of an African Regional Capital*.
Manchester, UK: Manchester University Press, 2016.

———. *A History of Urban Planning in Two West African Colonial Capitals: Residential Segregation in British Lagos and French Dakar (1850–1930)*. Lewiston
NY: Edwin Mellen Press, 2009.

Boittin, Jennifer. "Adventurers and Agents Provocateurs: A German Woman Travel-
ling through French West Africa in the Shadow of War." *Historical Reflections*
40 (2014): 111–31.

———. *Colonial Metropolis: The Urban Grounds of Anti-imperialism and Feminism
in Interwar Paris*. Lincoln: University of Nebraska Press, 2010.

Brooks, George E. "The Signares of Saint-Louis and Gorée: Women Entrepreneurs
in Eighteenth-Century Senegal." In *Women in Africa: Studies in Social and
Economic Change*, edited by Nancy J. Hafkin and Edna Bay, 19–44. Stanford:
Stanford University Press, 1976.

Chafer, Tony, and Amanda Sackur, eds. *French Colonial Empire and the Popular Front:
Hope and Disillusion*. New York: St. Martin's Press, 1999.

———, eds. *Promoting the Colonial Idea: Propaganda and Visions of Empire in France*.
New York: Palgrave, 2002.

Clancy-Smith, Julia, and Frances Gouda, eds. *Domesticating the Empire: Race Gender,
and Family Life in French and Dutch Colonialism*. Charlottesville: University
of Virginia Press, 1998.

Clayton, Anthony, and David Killingray. *Khaki and Blue: Military and Police in British
Colonial Africa*. Athens: Ohio University Center for International Studies, 1989.

Cohen, William B. "The Colonial Policy of the Popular Front." *French Historical
Studies* 7 (Spring 1972): 368–93.

———. *The French Encounter with Africans and the White Response to Blacks*. Bloomington: Indiana University Press, 1980.

———. *Rulers of Empire: The French Colonial Service in Africa.* Stanford: Stanford University Press, 1971.

Cohn, Bernard S. *Castes of Mind: Colonialism and the Making of Modern India.* Princeton NJ: Princeton University Press, 2001.

———. *Colonialism and Its Forms of Knowledge: The British in India.* Princeton NJ: Princeton University Press, 1996.

Conklin, Alice. *A Mission to Civilize: The Republican Idea of Empire in France and West Africa, 1895–1930.* Stanford: Stanford University Press, 1997.

———. "Redefining 'Frenchness': Citizenship, Race Regeneration, and Imperial Motherhood in France and West Africa, 1914–40." In *Domesticating the Empire: Race, Gender, and Family Life in French and Dutch Colonialism,* edited by Alice Conklin and Frances Gouda, 65–83. Charlottesville: University of Virginia Press, 1998.

Cooper, Frederick. *Citizenship between Empire and Nation: Remaking France and French West Africa, 1945–1960.* Princeton NJ: Princeton University Press, 2014.

———. *Colonialism in Question: Theory, Knowledge, History.* Berkeley: University of California Press, 2005.

———. "Conflict and Connection: Rethinking Colonial African History." *American Historical Review* 99 (1994): 1516–45.

———. *Decolonization and African Society: The Labor Question in French and British Africa.* Cambridge, UK: Cambridge University Press, 1996.

———, ed. *Struggle for the City: Migrant Labor, Capital and the State in Urban Africa.* Beverly Hills CA: Sage, 1983.

Cooper, Frederick, and Ann Laura Stoler, eds. *Tensions of Empire: Colonial Cultures in a Bourgeois World.* Berkeley: University of California Press, 1997.

Coquery-Vidrovitch, Catherine, ed. *Etre étranger et migrant en Afrique au XXième siecle: Enjeux identitaires et modes d'insertion.* Paris: L'Harmattan, 2003.

———. "L'Afrique Coloniale Française et la crise de 1930: Crise structurelle et genèse du sous-développement." *Revue Française d'histoire d'outre-mer* 63 (1976): 386–424.

———. "La ville coloniale: 'Lieu de colonisation' et 'métissage culturel.'" *Afrique Contemporaine* 168 (1993): 11–22.

———. "Nationalité et citoyenneté en Afrique occidentale française: Originaires et citoyens dans le Sénégal colonial." *Journal of African History* 42 (2001): 285–306.

Crowder, Michael. *Senegal: A Study of French Assimilation Policy.* London: Methuen, 1967.

———, ed. *West African Resistance: The Military Response to Colonial Occupation.* New York: Africana, 1971.

Cruise O'Brien, Donal. *The Mourides of Senegal: The Political and Economic Organization of an Islamic Brotherhood.* New York: Oxford University Press, 1971.

Cruise O'Brien, Rita. *White Society in Black Africa: The French of Senegal.* Evanston IL: Northwestern University Press, 1972.

DesBordes, Jean-Gabriel. *L'immigration libano-syrienne en Afrique Occidentale Française.* Poitiers: Imprimerie Moderne Renault, 1938.

Dewitte, Philippe. *Les mouvements nègres en France: 1919–1939.* Paris: Harmattan, 1985.

Diouf, Mamadou. "The French Colonial Policy of Assimilation and the Civility of the Originaires of the Four Communes (Senegal): A Nineteenth Century Globalization Project." *Development and Change* 29 (1998): 671–96.

Dirks, Nicholas, ed. *Colonialism and Culture.* Ann Arbor: University of Michigan Press, 1992.

Driver, Felix, and Luciana Martins, eds. *Tropical Visions in an Age of Empire.* Chicago: University of Chicago Press, 2005.

Echenberg, Myron. *Black Death, White Medicine: Bubonic Plague and the Politics of Public Health in Colonial Senegal, 1914–1945.* Portsmouth NH: Heinemann, 2002.

———. *Colonial Conscripts: The Tirailleurs Sénégalais in French West Africa.* Portsmouth NH: Heinemann, 1991.

Edwards, Brent Hayes. *The Practice of Diaspora: Literature, Translation and the Rise of Black Internationalism.* Cambridge MA: Harvard University Press, 2003.

Fall, Babacar. *Le travail forcé en Afrique Occidentale Française, 1900–1946.* Paris: Karthala, 1993.

Foster, Elizabeth A. "An Ambiguous Monument: Dakar's Colonial Cathedral of the Souvenir Africain." *French Historical Studies* 32, no. 1 (2009): 95–119.

———. *Faith in Empire: Religion, Politics, and Colonial Rule in French Senegal, 1880–1940.* Stanford: Stanford University Press, 2013.

Foucault, Michel. *Discipline and Punish: The Birth of the Prison.* New York: Vintage, 1979.

Fourchard, Laurent. *De la ville coloniale à la cour africaine: Espaces, pouvoirs et sociétés à Ouagadougou et Bobo-Dioulasso (Haute Volte) fin XIXᵉ siècle–1960.* Paris: L'Harmattan, 2001.

Fourchard, Laurent, and Isaac Olawale Albert, eds. *Security, Crime and Segregation in West African Cities since the 19th Century.* Paris: Karthala, 2003.

Freitas, Michèle. "Les Etrangers en Afrique Occidentale Française de 1900 à 1920." Thesis, Aix-en-Provence, 1968.

Furlough, Ellen. "*Une Leçon des Choses*: Tourism, Empire, and the Nation in Interwar France." *French Historical Studies* 25, no. 3 (2002): 441–73.

Gellately, Robert. "Enforcing Racial Policy." In *Re-evaluating the Third Reich*, edited by Thomas Childers and Jane Caplan, 42–65. New York: Houghton Mifflin, 1993.

Genova, James E. *Colonial Ambivalence, Cultural Authenticity, and the Limitations of Mimicry in French-Ruled West Africa, 1914–1956.* New York: Peter Lang, 2004.

————. "Conflicted Missionaries: Power and Identity in French West Africa during the 1930s." *Historian* 66 (2004): 45–66.

Gide, André. *Travels to the Congo*. New York: Modern Age Books, 1937.

Ginio, Ruth. *French Colonialism Unmasked: The Vichy Years in French West Africa*. Lincoln: University of Nebraska Press, 2006.

Girardet, Raoul. *L'idée coloniale en France de 1871 à 1962*. Paris: Éditions de la Table Ronde, 1972.

Goebel, Michael. *Anti-Imperial Metropolis: Interwar Paris and the Seeds of Third World Nationalism*. Cambridge, UK: Cambridge University Press, 2015.

Goerg, Odile. "From Hill Station (Freetown) to Downtown Conakry (First Ward): Comparing British and French Approaches to Segregation in Colonial Cities at the Beginning of the Twentieth Century." *Canadian Journal of African Studies* 32, no. 1 (1998): 1–31.

————. *Pouvoir colonial et espace urbains, Conakry et Freetown des années 1880 à 1914*. Paris: Harmattan, 1997.

Gorer, Geoffrey. *Africa Dances: A Book about West African Negroes*. London: J. Lehmann, 1949.

Grandhomme, Hélène. "La politique musulmane de la France au Sénégal (1936–64)." *Canadian Journal of African Studies* 38 (2004): 237–78.

Harrison, Christopher. *France and Islam in West Africa*. Cambridge, UK: Cambridge University Press, 1988.

Headrick, Daniel. *The Tools of Empire: Technology and European Imperialism in the Nineteenth Century*. New York: Oxford University Press, 1981.

Hevia, James. *The Imperial Security State: British Colonial Knowledge and Empire-Building in Asia*. New York: Cambridge University Press, 2012.

Hobsbawm, Eric, and Terence Ranger, eds. *The Invention of Tradition*. Cambridge, UK: Cambridge University Press, 1983.

Hodgson, Dorothy L., and Sheryl A. McCurdy, eds. *"Wicked" Women and the Reconfiguration of Gender in Africa*. Portsmouth NH: Heinemann, 2001.

Johnson, G. Wesley, ed. *Double Impact: France and Africa in the Age of Imperialism*. Westport CT: Greenwood Press, 1985.

————. *The Emergence of Black Politics in Senegal*. Stanford: Stanford University Press, 1971.

Jones, Hilary. *The Métis of Senegal: Urban Life and Politics in French West Africa*. Bloomington: Indiana University Press, 2013.

*Journal Officiel de l'Afrique Occidentale Française*, 1923.

*Journal Officiel de l'Afrique Occidentale Française*, 1931.

Klein, Martin. *Islam and Imperialism in Senegal, Siné-Saloum, 1847–1914*. Stanford: Stanford University Press, 1968.

———. *Slavery and Colonial Rule in French West Africa*. New York: Cambridge University Press, 1998.

Langley, J. Adoyele. *Nationalism and Pan-Africanism in West Africa, 1900–1945: A Study in Ideology and Social Classes*. Oxford: Clarendon Press, 1973.

Lebovics, Herman. *Bringing the Empire Back Home: France in the Global Age*. Durham NC: Duke University Press, 2004.

———. *True France: The Wars over Cultural Identity, 1900–1945*. Ithaca NY: Cornell University Press, 1992.

LeClère, Marcel. "Les Français sous surveillance: Naissance des Renseignements Généraux." *Histoire* 1981 (32): 83–86.

———. *La Police*. Paris: Presses Universitaires de France, 1972.

Lewis, Mary Dewhurst. *The Boundaries of the Republic: Migrant Rights and the Limits of Universalism in France, 1918–1940*. Stanford: Stanford University Press, 2007.

———. "The Strangeness of Foreigners: Policing Migration and Nation in Interwar Marseille." *French Politics, Culture, and Society* 20 (2002): 65–96.

Liauzu, Claude. *Aux origines des tiers-mondismes: Colonisés et anticolonialistes en France, 1919–1939*. Paris: L'Harmattan, 1982.

Londres, Albert. *Terre d'ébène*. Paris: Busson, 1929.

Lunn, Joe. *Memoirs of the Maelstrom: A Senegalese Oral History of the First World War*. Portsmouth NH: Heinemann, 1999.

Mamdani, Mahmood. *Citizen and Subject: Contemporary Africa and the Legacy of Late Colonialism*. Princeton NJ: Princeton University Press, 1996.

Manchuelle, François. "Assimilés ou patriotes africaines? Naissance du Nationalisme culturel en Afrique française, 1853–1931." *Cahiers d'Etudes Africaines* 35 (1995): 333–68.

Mann, Gregory. "Fetishizing Religion: Allah Koura and French 'Islamic Policy' in Late Colonial French Soudan (Mali)." *Journal of African History* 44 (2003): 263–82.

———. "Locating Colonial Histories: Between France and West Africa." *American Historical Review* 110 (2005): 409–34.

———. *Native Sons: West African Veterans and France in the Twentieth Century*. Durham NC: Duke University Press, 2006.

Manning, Patrick. *Francophone Sub-Saharan Africa, 1880–1995*. New York: Cambridge University Press, 1998.

———. *Slavery, Colonialism and Economic Growth in Dahomey, 1640–1940*. New York: Cambridge University Press, 1982.

Matera, Marc. *Black London: The Imperial Metropolis and Decolonization in the Twentieth Century*. Berkeley: University of California Press, 2015.

Matsuda, Matt. *Empire of Love: Histories of France and the Pacific.* New York: Oxford University Press, 2005.

Mazower, Mark, ed. *The Policing of Politics in the Twentieth Century.* Providence RI: Berghahn Books, 1997.

McCoy, Alfred W. *Policing America's Empire: The United States, the Philippines, and the Rise of the Surveillance State.* Madison: University of Wisconsin Press, 2009.

Mercier, Paul. "The European Community of Dakar." In *Africa: Social Problems of Change and Conflict,* edited by Pierre L. Van den Berghe, 283–300. San Francisco: Chandler, 1965.

Merriman, John. *Police Stories: Building the French State, 1815–1851.* New York: Oxford University Press, 2006.

Michel, Marc. *Les Africains et la Grande Guerre: L'Appel à L'Afrique.* Paris: Karthala, 2003.

Miller, Christopher J. *Blank Darkness: Africanist Discourse in French.* Chicago: University of Chicago Press, 1985.

Miller, Michael. *Shanghai on the Metro: Spies, Intrigue and the French between the Wars.* Berkeley: University of California Press, 1994.

Morlat, Patrice. *La répression coloniale au Vietnam, 1908–1940.* Paris: L'Harmattan, 1990.

Myers, Garth. *Verandahs of Power: Colonialism and Space in Urban Africa.* Syracuse NY: Syracuse University Press, 2003.

Noiriel, Gérard. *The French Melting Pot: Immigration, Citizenship and National Identity.* Minneapolis: University of Minnesota Press, 1996.

Osborn, Emily Lynn. "'Circle of Iron': African Colonial Employees and the Interpretation of Colonial Rule in French West Africa." *Journal of African History* 44 (2003): 29–50.

Panchasi, Roxanne. *Future Tense: The Culture of Anticipation in France between the Wars.* Ithaca NY: Cornell University Press, 2009.

*Pépé le Moko.* Directed by Julien Duvivier. Paris: Paris Film, 1937.

Roberts, Mary Louise. *Civilization without Sexes: Reconstructing Gender in Postwar France, 1917–1927.* Chicago: University of Chicago Press, 1994.

Roberts, Richard. *Two Worlds of Cotton: Colonialism and the Regional Economy in the French Soudan, 1800–1946.* Stanford: Stanford University Press, 1996.

Roberts, Richard, and Kristin Mann, eds. *Law in Colonial Africa.* Portsmouth NH: Heinemann, 1991.

Roberts, Richard, and Dominique Sarr. "The Jurisdiction of Muslim Tribunals in Colonial Senegal, 1857–1932." In *Law in Colonial Africa,* edited by Richard Roberts and Kristin Mann, 131–43. Portsmouth NH: Heinemann, 1991.

Robinson, David. "Ethnography and Customary Law in Senegal." *Cahiers d'Etudes Africaines* 32 (1992): 221–37.

———. "France as a Muslim Power in West Africa." *Africa Today* 46 (1999): 105–27.

———. "French 'Islamic' Policy and Practice in Late Nineteenth Century Senegal." *Journal of African History* 29 (1988): 415–35.

———. "The Murids: Surveillance and Collaboration." *Journal of African History* 40 (1999): 193–213.

———. *Paths of Accommodation: Muslim Societies and French Colonial Authorities in Senegal and Mauritania, 1880–1920*. Athens: Ohio University Press, 2000.

Rosenberg, Clifford. *Policing Paris: The Origins of Modern Immigration Control between the Wars*. Ithaca NY: Cornell University Press, 2006.

*Sanders of the River*. Directed by Zoltán Korda. London: London Film Productions, 1935.

Scales, Rebecca P. "Subversive Sound: Transnational Radio, Arabic Recordings, and the Dangers of Listening in French Colonial Algeria." *Comparative Studies in Society and History* 52 (2010): 384–417.

Shereikis, Rebecca. "From Law to Custom: The Shifting Legal Status of Muslim Originaires in Kayes and Medine, 1903–1913." *Journal of African History* 42 (2001): 261–83.

Slavin, David. *Colonial Cinema and Imperial France, 1919–1939: White Blind Spots, Male Fantasies, Settler Myths*. Baltimore: Johns Hopkins University Press, 2001.

Sohi, Seema "Race, Surveillance, and Indian Anticolonialism in the Transnational Western U.S.-Canadian Borderlands." *Journal of American History* 98 (2011): 420–36.

Spear, Thomas. "Neo-Traditionalism and the Limits of Invention in British Colonial Africa." *Journal of African History* 44 (2003): 3–27.

Spiegler, J. S. "Aspects of Nationalist Thought among French-Speaking West Africans, 1921–1939." Ph.D. dissertation, Oxford University, 1968.

Stoler, Ann Laura. *Carnal Knowledge and Imperial Power: Race and the Intimate in Colonial Rule*. Berkeley: University of California Press, 2002.

Stovall, Tyler. "Colour-blind France? Colonial Workers during the First World War." *Race and Class* 35, no. 2 (1993): 36–55.

———. *Paris and the Spirit of 1919: Consumer Struggles, Transnationalism and Revolution*. New York: Cambridge University Press, 2012.

———. *Paris Noir: African Americans in the City of Light*. New York: Houghton Mifflin, 1996.

Suret-Canale, Jean. *French Colonialism in Tropical Africa*. New York: Pica Press, 1971.

———. "An Unrecognised Pioneer of the Democratic and National Movement in Africa: Louis Hunkanrin (1887–1964)." In *Essays on African History: From the Slave Trade to Neocolonialism*, 196–219. London: Hurst, 1988.

Thioub, Ibrahima. "L'enfermement carcéral: Un instrument de gestions des marges urbaines au Sénégal, XIX–XXᵉ siècles." *Canadian Journal of African Studies* 37 (2003): 269–97.

Thomas, Martin. "Albert Sarraut, French Colonial Development, and the Communist Threat, 1919–1930." *Journal of Modern History* 77 (2005): 917–55.

——. *Empires of Intelligence: Security Services and Colonial Disorder after 1914.* Berkeley: University of California Press, 2008.

——, ed. *The French Colonial Mind.* Vols. 1 and 2. Lincoln: University of Nebraska Press, 2011.

——. *The French Empire between the Wars: Imperialism, Politics, and Society.* Manchester, UK: Manchester University Press, 2005.

——. *Violence and Colonial Order: Police, Workers, and Protest in the European Colonial Empires, 1918–1940.* Cambridge, UK: Cambridge University Press, 2012.

Todorov, Tzvetan. *On Human Diversity: Nationalism, Racism and Exoticism in French Thought.* Cambridge MA: Harvard University Press, 1993.

Torpey, John. *Invention of the Passport: Surveillance, Citizenship and the State.* Cambridge, UK: Cambridge University Press, 2000.

Vaillant, Janet. *Black, French and African: A Life of Leopold Sédar Senghor.* Cambridge MA: Harvard University Press, 1990.

Vaughan, Megan. *Curing Their Ills: Colonial Power and African Illness.* Stanford: Stanford University Press, 1991.

Venayre, Sylvain. *La Gloire de l'aventure: Genèse d'une mystique moderne, 1850–1940.* Paris: Aubier, 2002.

Wakeman, Frederic E. *Policing Shanghai, 1927–1937.* Berkeley: University of California Press, 1995.

Waldeck, Rosie Goldschmidt. *Prelude to the Past.* New York: William Morrow, 1934.

White, Owen. *Children of the French Empire: Miscegenation and Colonial Society in French West Africa, 1895–1960.* New York: Oxford University Press, 1999.

——. "The Decivilizing Mission: Auguste Dupuis-Yakouba and French Timbuktu." *French Historical Studies* 27, no. 3 (2004): 541–68.

Wilder, Gary. "Colonial Ethnology and Political Rationality in French West Africa." *History and Anthropology* 14, no. 3 (2003): 219–52.

——. *The French Imperial Nation-State: Negritude and Colonial Humanism between the Two World Wars.* Chicago: University of Chicago Press, 2005.

Wright, Gwendolyn. *The Politics of Design in French Colonial Urbanism.* Chicago: University of Chicago Press, 1991.

Wright, Donald. *The World and a Very Small Place in Africa: A History of Globalization in Niumi, the Gambia.* Armonk NY: M. E. Sharpe, 1997.

# INDEX

155; prison as, 155; public knowledge as, 162; reassignment as, 162–63, 172; responses to, 164, 174, 175, 185; successful, 162–65; surveillance as, 180, 218n12; of *Voix du Dahomey*, 168–69

republicanism, 67, 147; and surveillance, 54, 66, 67, 68–70, 84, 182

Riesinger, Joseph, 59, 87–88, 117–18

Roume, Ernest, 22–23

royalism, 129–30

rural areas, 43–44; and association, 9; and Great Depression, 41; surveillance in, 23–24, 27, 72–75, 85

sailors, 96, 126, 149–50

Saint-Jacques, Camille, 34, 107

Saint-Louis, Senegal, 21, 68

Sall, Amadou, 2, 17

*Sanders of the River* (film), 88

Sarraut, Albert, 8–9, 29–31

Senegal, 6, 7, 22, 46, 105; colony of, 46, 77; communism in, 33, 35, 48, 61, 68, 173, 175; Edward Francis Small in, 173; League for Defense of the Negro Race in, 55, 158–60, 162–63, 164; Lebanese and Syrians in, 25; revolt in, 152–56; regulation of foreigners in, 90–91; police in, 21, 25, 27; politics of, 151; socialist party of, 14. *See also* Dakar; four communes

Senegalese Action Committee, 63, 103

Senghor, Lamine, 33–34, 35, 36, 125, 156

Senghor, Leopold Sedar, 178

sexuality, 133–36, 147

shadowing, 66–68

singers. *See* performers

slavery, 102, 139

Small, Edward Francis, 17, 61–62, 68, 104–6; in Dakar, 173, 174; network of, 173–74; in Senegal, 173

soldiers. *See tirailleurs sénégalais*

Somalia, 57

sources, 14–16, 198n3, 204n113

strikes, 11, 105, 142, 166, 179

subjects (*sujets*), 7, 17; from other French colonies, 17, 93–94, 108

Sudan, 141–45, 160–62

Suret-Canale, Jean, 152

Sûreté Générale, 13, 14, 36–39, 41–43

surveillance, 3, 45, 47, 48, 51, 104; in Algeria, 40; in AOF, 3, 4, 13, 19, 50; association and, 50–51; of Christians, 110–11; as colonial mode of rule, 3, 21, 180; colonial security and, 3; discretion and, 54, 66–68, 69, 84, 182; of foreigners, 25, 93; in France, 26, 30–31, 34, 66–67; of general population, 23–24; of individuals, 25, 26–27, 180; knowledge of, 104, 162, 163; of Lebanese and Syrians, 23, 24, 71–72; limits of, 70–72, 202n79, 106n149; of Muslims, 4, 22–23, 44, 65–66, 83, 109–10; policies of, 4, 16, 20, 21–22, 36, 40–41, 44–45, 46–48, 49, 54; at ports, 60–61, 71–72; postwar, 77, 178–79, 224n14; practices of, 4, 16, 38, 54, 66–68, 72–75, 84, 224n14; republicanism and, 54, 66, 67, 68–70, 84, 182; in rural areas, 23–24, 27, 72–75, 85; rural vs. urban, 72, 74–75, 202n83; sources and, 14–15; in urban areas, 27, 54–55, 70–72, 84–85; World War I and, 24–28, 94–99, 180; World War II and, 177–78. *See also* informants; investigations; postal control; shadowing suspects, 2–3, 5–6, 16, 18, 49, 55–56, 122, 183, 185–86; administrators as, 127–28, 145–47; communism and, 185; investigations of African, 157–75; investigations of foreign, 26, 95–118; investigations of French, 124–30, 131–47; stories about, 15–16, 120, 184, 187; total number of, 14–15. *See also* suspicion

suspicion, 5; and anti-French sentiments, 96–97, 117; and appearance, 59–60; assimilation and, 199n5; elite Africans and, 55; of espionage, 95–96, 97, 98, 99, 111, 114; and foreignness, 89, 119, 183–84; and immorality, 141; and inscrutability, 184; and internationalism, 181, 184; and Islam, 109–10; and mobility, 45, 46, 61, 78, 99, 113–14, 116–18, 136–37, 184; and money, 98; and mystery, 113, 115, 118; and poverty, 131–32; and radical politics, 99–100, 113–14; and speech, 59–60; and unclear nationality, 95–96; and unions, 135. *See also* anarchism; anticlericalism; anticolonialism; communism; crime; fraud; pan-Africanism; royalism

suspicious persons. *See* investigations; suspects

syndicates (unions), 14, 43, 48, 105, 135, 178, 179, 223n110. *See also* International Workers of Education

Syria, 21, 78; communism in, 29

Syrians. *See* Lebanese and Syrians

teachers, 146, 157, 169–73

Tellier, Théophile-Antoine-Pascal, 45, 46

Third Republic, 13, 66–67, 69

Thomas, Martin, 164–65

*tirailleurs sénégalais*, 7, 36, 78, 109, 143, 146, 150, 167; demobilization of, 10–11; political demands of, 50; remaining in France, 34; revolt and, 153–56

tourism, 11–12, 214n5

travel. *See* suspicion: and mobility

Tunisia, communism in, 32, 35

Union Intercoloniale (UIC), 8, 36

Union des Travailleurs Nègres (UTN), 151

unions. *See* syndicates (unions)

Universal Negro Improvement Association (UNIA), in Dakar, 63–64, 100–104, 201n49, 209n70, 209n71

Upper Volta, 145–47

urban areas, 3, 7, 9–10, 27, 54–55, 69, 182; and Great Depression, 41. *See also* Dakar

Van Vollenhoven, Joost, 39

Vichy regime, 177–78

Vietnam. *See* Indochina

Vietnamese. *See* Indochinese

violence: and Dahomey, 152; in Indochina, 35, 107; and Médina, 48

*La Voix du Dahomey* (newspaper), 78, 165, 166–69; articles of, 168; communism and, 167; political views of, 167–68; repression of, 168–69

Von Heinl, Paul, 1, 2, 18, 60

whites, 123; poor, 131–32, 215n37. *See also* Dakar: European community in; French metropolitans

Wilder, Gary, 69–70, 164

Williams, Winston (Bob), 63, 103, 173

Wilson, Wilfred, 64, 101

To order or obtain more information on these or other University
of Nebraska Press titles, visit nebraskapress.unl.edu.

CPSIA information can be obtained
at www.ICGtesting.com
Printed in the USA
LVOW11*0854260218
567707LV00023B/37/P